To Bruce Bennett—

Best Wishes,

[signature]

More Praise for *The Magic of Teamwork*

"A terrific read!"

> Dan Quayle
> Former Vice President of the United States

"Important lessons from someone willing to share a lifetime of valuable insight. Don't miss this book."

> H. Wayne Huizenga
> Owner, Miami Dolphins, Florida Marlins,
> and Florida Panthers

"Pat Williams has been a winner during his NBA career, and his book's a winner too."

> The Fabulous Sports Babe
> ESPN Radio

"Study the master of team leadership by reading this great book. I love it and learned from it."

> Mark Victor Hansen
> Co-Author of the #1 *New York Times*
> Bestseller, *Chicken Soup for the Soul*

"*The Magic of Teamwork* is about developing confidence in all team members so the unit can operate at peak efficiency."

> Arnold Palmer
> Golf Legend

"Pat Williams can bring the same magic to individuals, in sports or elsewhere, that he has brought to the Orlando Magic."

> Al Neuharth
> Founder, *USA Today*

"Pat Williams is a winner and so are his ideas on teamwork. Let him work his magic on you."

> Ken Blanchard
> Co-Author of *The One Minute Manager*

"This book covers teamwork and its entities particularly well."

> John Havlicek
> Former Boston Celtic Great

"Pat Williams writes from vast experience and with his usual insight and humor."

> Bob Costas
> NBC Sports

"Pat gives us his recipes for success not only on the hardwood, but in business, and in life."

Senator Bill Bradley
Former New York Knicks Star

"Pat Williams provides all the information you will need to become a top team player."

John C. Maxwell
Founder, INJOY, Inc., and Bestselling Author
of *Developing the Leader Within You*

"This book is long overdue and will be remembered as the ultimate text on teamwork."

Bowie Kuhn
Former Commissioner of Major League Baseball

"The main reason behind our success over the last six years is our ability to unite twenty-five guys and a coaching staff with one common goal: to win a world championship. *The Magic of Teamwork* tells you how to do the same thing."

Boby Cox
Manager, Atlanta Braves

"Every leader needs to read this book!"

Gary Smalley
Bestselling Author of *The Blessing*

"Few people know more about putting an effective team together than Pat Williams, whose head coach is Jesus Christ."

Cal Thomas
Syndicated Columnist

"Pat Williams captures the real essence of what teamwork is and how it leads to success."

Lenny Wilkens
Head Coach, Atlanta Hawks

"Pat's insight and understanding of what it takes to succeed has enabled him to write a very significant book on the value and importance of teamwork."

Mike Ditka
Head Coach, New Orleans Saints

"Individualism wins trophies, but teamwork wins championships. You can get a lot out of reading this book, and it can prepare you for any way of life."

Tom Lasorda
Former Manager, Los Angeles Dodgers

"Whether you're a team leader or a team member, the stories Pat shares will encourage you to be the very best you can be. It's terrific!

Dave Thomas
Founder, Wendy's Restaurants

"Pat Williams is one of the top team builders I know. I really have deep respect and admiration for him as a Christian sports executive and a father."

Joe Gibbs
NFL Analyst, NBC Sports and
Former Head Coach, Washington Redskins

"Pat Williams uses his unique style and draws from his extensive experience to give us the principles necessary to discover and unleash the power of teamwork."

Dr. Tony Evans
Pastor, Oak Cliff Bible Fellowship, Dallas, Texas
and Author of *The Victorious Christian Life*

"A must-read for everyone, not only in professional sports, but all of today's society."

Allan H. "Bud" Selig
President, Milwaukee Brewers and Chairman,
Executive Council of Major League Baseball

"Pat Williams illustrates Bible-based principles for successful living with real-life examples from sports, business, and other arenas. His book is enjoyable to read, as well as motivating and helpful."

Franklin Graham
President, Samaritan's Purse and World
Medical Mission and Bestselling Author of
Rebel with a Cause

"*The Magic of Teamwork* captures the essence of what teamwork truly is, and since everyone is a part of a team in one way or another, everyone should read it."

John Wooden
Former Head Basketball Coach, UCLA

The MAGIC of TEAM WORK

PAT WILLIAMS

A
JANET
THOMA
BOOK

THOMAS NELSON PUBLISHERS
Nashville • Atlanta • London • Vancouver

Published in Nashville, Tennessee, by Thomas Nelson, Inc.

Unless otherwise noted, Scripture used in this publication is from THE NEW KING JAMES VERSION. Copyright © 1979, 1980, 1982, 1990 Thomas Nelson, Inc.

Verses marked TLB are taken from *The Living Bible,* copyright 1971 by Tyndale House Publishers, Wheaton, IL. Used by permission.

Library of Congress Cataloging-in-Publication Data

Williams, Pat, 1940-
    The magic of teamwork : proven principles for building a winning team / Pat Williams with Jim Denney
        p.   cm.
    ISBN 0-7852-7584-3
    1. Teams in industry. 2. Teamwork (Sports) I. Denney, James D. II. Title.
HD66.W538 1997
658.4'02—dc21   97-1497
                                                                                    CIP

Printed in the United States of America.

4 5 6 BVG 02 01 00 99

To my mother, Ellen Williams, who at 83 is still going strong. She taught me very early in life the value of teamwork. I've never forgotten her lessons.

Contents

Acknowledgments

Every book is a team effort—and this book especially so!

It was my privilege to work closely on this book with two teammates who are passionate about excellence, who are committed to winning, who have pushed me to be the best I can be, and who have given everything they've got to make this book the best it can be: my editor, Janet Thoma, her assistant, Todd Ross, and my collaborator, Jim Denney.

I also want to thank the Magic owners, the DeVos family, our presdent, Bob Vander Weide, general manager John Gabriel, executive vice president Cari Coats, senior director of communications Alex Martins, and the entire Magic front office team.

In addition I'm grateful to some important people in my life who pored over this manuscript and made some key suggestions: Jay Strack, Ken Hussar, JimWhite, Jay Carty, Marlin Bushur, and my wife, Ruth.

The book you hold in your hands is proof of the theme of this book: When you put a great team together, you can achieve *anything*!

The Magic of Teamwork

In December 1995, I made a decision to run my first marathon, the Disney Marathon in Orlando. Before doing so, I consulted my podiatrist and my cardiologist—and my psychiatrist (he said I should have my head examined). To prepare myself for the 26.2-mile run, I began increasing my morning training runs, reaching for more distance and endurance, stretching my route farther and farther from home. One morning, at around 8:15, I was jogging along the road when, up ahead, I saw a group of junior-high-age kids waiting for a school bus. Something was wrong. As I jogged closer to the bus stop, I saw that there was a ruckus going on. Two boys were going at each other, really duking it out.

I ran as fast as I could and got right between these two boys immediately, with both my arms outstretched, trying to pull them apart from each other. Even with me in the middle they continued flailing away, trying to reach around me to get at each other. Somehow, I had to defuse the situation. I needed an attention getter. With scarcely a moment to think, I opened my mouth and shouted the first thing that came into my head: "Penny Hardaway wants you to know four things!"

They both stopped flailing and looked at me in puzzlement. "What do you mean?" asked one of the boys. "Do you know Penny?"

"Sure I do," I said.

"Well, what do you mean, Penny wants us to know four things?" asked the other boy.

I thought furiously. In the next few seconds, I had to think of four things Penny Hardaway wanted them to know. I quickly thought back to some of the breakfast table discussions we had had in the Williams household during times of conflict between kids. Then I said, "First of all, I think Penny wants you to know you've got to keep your mouth shut. Every problem starts with your mouth running. Second, he wants you to know you have to keep your eyes off each other. Quit staring each other down. Stop trying to intimidate each other. Third, keep your hands to yourself. Fights usually start with one kid touching or bumping or hitting another kid. Fourth, walk away from trouble. When you see trouble on the horizon, don't get as close to it as you dare; get as far away from it as you can."

I had their attention, and I thought I was in a position to reconcile the two boys. I was beginning to feel rather Spencer Tracyish—like his portrayal of Father Flannagan in *Boys Town*. I looked at the kid on my left, an African-American kid, and I said, "What's your name, Son?"

"Dwayne," he said.

Then I turned to the kid on my right. He was as white as could be—a blond-haired, blue-eyed Norwegian from all appearances. "And what's your name?" I asked.

"Wayne," he responded.

"Well, Dwayne and Wayne," I said, "I tell you what. I think you guys are ready to shake hands and become friends. What do you say?"

Dwayne, the black kid, immediately put his hand out.

Wayne, the white kid, was not quite getting into the spirit of things. Instead of putting his hand out, he growled something uncomplimentary about Dwayne's mother. Maybe I saw myself as Spencer Tracy, but this kid had apparently cast himself in the Mickey Rooney role—a real tough guy.

"Well, boys," I said, "we haven't made much progress here. So I'll tell you something else Penny wants you to know. He wants you to come to an Orlando Magic game one night—the two of you. And he wants you to sit together. And I'll tell you something. You're going to have to share the armrest. Our seats at the O-rena don't have two armrests on each side, so you guys are going to have to share an armrest. And chances are, you'll be eating out of the same box of popcorn. The thing is, you're going to have to be teammates that night—or you can't come to the game. So let me ask you one more time: are you both willing to shake hands?"

Both hands instantly went out, and they shook hands.

I said, "Tell you what, boys. Let me know when you're ready to come to the game, and Penny will set it up." And these two boys—once enemies, now teammates—went off to the Maitland Middle School to start their day.

My experience of turning Dwayne and Wayne into a team is really a metaphor of my life and my career. I've spent most of my life in team situations—either playing on a team or building a team. I played on my first sports team when I was twelve, and I've been involved with team sports almost every day of my life ever since. That's well over forty years of team experience, from junior high to high school to college to the pros.

And my team building chores don't stop when I leave the office, either. As a father, I'm raising nineteen children—and let me tell you, that's a job of trying to put a team together every single day.

Virtually every person on this planet either is or should be involved in team building, because we were designed to function in connected, interdependent relationships with other people. We were made to be team players. A family is a team. A ball club is a team. A business is a team. A church is a team. A hospital staff is a team. A government office is a team.

Even a military unit is a team. As Gen. George Patton said, "An army is a team. It eats, sleeps, lives, and fights as a team. Every man, every department, every unit is important to the vast scheme of things."

A business is also a team—and that's true whether we're talking Team IBM or Team Dave's Donut Shop. As I travel around the business community, not only giving speeches but listening and asking questions, I've become convinced that the number one issue on the minds of most owners, entrepreneurs, executives, managers, and even employees is "How do we make this company work better as a team?"

Whenever and wherever people come together (or are thrown together) to get a job done, that's a team. The first priority of any team should be to learn to function as effectively and as smoothly as possible so that, individually and corporately, the members of that team can achieve their goals. That's what this book is about.

COMMON PEOPLE, UNCOMMON RESULTS

Throughout the year, I get to do a lot of traveling and speaking to companies and groups. The number one question I am asked by the various executives, coaches, athletes, pastors, young people, and others I speak to goes something like this: "Pat, in a few short years, you've helped to take your organization from being a bottom-of-the-barrel expansion club to one of the best-run franchises in the NBA. How did you do it?"

First of all, *I* didn't do it. The *team* did it. And by that word *team,* I don't just mean the players. I mean the Orlando Magic organization *and* the entire Orlando community—the business community, the fans, the owners, the staff, the coaches, and the players. Walk through the offices and the locker rooms at the Orlando Arena and through the streets, malls, and neighborhoods of the city of Orlando. Virtually every person you meet is a member of the Magic team. Our team roster numbers in the hundreds of thousands. It only takes five guys on a basketball court to move the ball, but it takes an entire organization and an entire community to lift and motivate those five guys.

When my daughter Sarah (who is from South Korea) was twelve years old, she won her heat in the 200-yard individual medley in a swimming meet at the Aquatic Center in Orlando.

As she climbed out of the pool, she was awarded a T-shirt, which a couple of years later is still one of her proudest possessions. On the shirt is a silk-screened photo of eight men in a scull rowing in perfect unison. Beneath the picture is this statement, which is absolutely true:

> Teamwork is the ability to work together toward a common vision, the ability to direct individual accomplishments toward organizational objectives. It's the fuel that allows common people to attain uncommon results.

Common people, uncommon results—that's the power of teamwork.

The movie *Rocky* contains a memorable line that, in its understated simplicity, perfectly sums up the power of teamwork and synergy. In the movie, the boxer Rocky Balboa describes the relationship that exists between himself and his girlfriend, whose personality is so different from his. "I've got gaps, she's got gaps," says Rocky. "Together, we've got no gaps."

Working together as a team, individuals can perform extraordinary, unbelievable feats. In a team, we link arms, we link minds, we spark each other's imagination and creativity, we encourage and motivate one another, we magnify each other's efforts and abilities—and that is why a team is able to accomplish so much more than a loose collection of individuals. Working as a team, we can make the product better, deliver the service faster, move the ball closer to the basket, scale El Capitan's granite face in greater safety, end poverty and ignorance sooner, and explore the outer planets in our lifetime. TEAM is not just a word, it's an acronym for a powerful truth: Together Everyone Achieves More.

The TEAM concept is an expressed word you've certainly heard many times: *synergy.* Perhaps, however, you have never read a definition of the word. It's a powerful word, and I think it's important we understand what it means. It comes from the Greek *sunergos,* meaning "working together": from *sun* ("together") and *ergon* ("work"). *Synergy* means "the interaction of two or more individuals or forces which enables their combined power to exceed the sum of their individual power."

A perfect example of synergy took place some years ago when the Building Industry Association of San Diego County sponsored a competition among builders. The proposed home had three bedrooms, two bathrooms, and was made from standard materials.

The winning team: two hours and forty-five minutes. The winning team used 700 people, divided into subgroups of carpenters, plumbers, electricians, and other tradespeople. They spent weeks practicing, looking for ways to accelerate the process. During the competition, the winners completed the rough plumbing in eight minutes and set the main roof in just over nine minutes.

Another vivid demonstration of the principle of synergy was once demonstrated in a horse-pulling contest at a county fair. The first-place horse in this contest was able to move a sled weighing 4,500 pounds. The runner-up horse was able to pull 4,000 pounds. In theory, that meant that the two horses, hitched together, ought to be able to move a maximum of 8,500 pounds. To test the theory, the owners of the two horses hitched the animals together and loaded the sled. To the amazement of everyone who saw it, the two horses were able to pull 12,000 pounds—3,500 more pounds than the sum of their individual efforts. Synergy is the power of teamwork to combine individual strength, to compensate for individual shortcomings, to magnify individual efforts, so that more and greater feats can be accomplished.

Peggy Noonan is a friend of mine and a gifted speechwriter who has put brilliant words in the mouths of such people as broadcaster Dan Rather and Presidents Reagan and Bush. A number of years ago, she came up with a wonderful phrase for President George Bush—"a thousand points of light." The concept behind that phrase is a powerful one. As Americans, we are all part of a team, and our goal is to make America great. Working as a team, we can attack and solve the problems of our nation. In many cases, the best approach to a problem is *not* to generate another expensive federal bureau but to create teams of people who can apply their compassion, genius, talent, and time to the problems of their own communities. When the Thousand

Points of Light program was inaugurated, Orlando was the first city named as a City of Light. George Bush came and spoke to a crowd of volunteers and community leaders. "This is what I mean when I talk of a thousand points of light," he said. "It's that vast galaxy of people working together to solve problems in their own backyard."

A COLLECTION OF INDIVIDUALS— OR A TEAM?

Harry Artinian, formerly president of corporate quality for the Colgate-Palmolive Company, once said, "I like to tell the story about the entrepreneur who wanted to build the perfect car. He rented a warehouse and filled it with the 150 best cars ever built. Then he told his engineers to find the best part in each car he had bought. So they took the best engine from the Mercedes, the best door handle from the Buick, the best transmission from the Toyota, the best rack-and-pinion steering from the Ford, and so on and so on. When he was done, he had a car assembled out of the 15,000 best parts that human minds could engineer. Unfortunately, the car didn't function, because the parts didn't work together." Artinian's point is clear: In order for synergy and teamwork to take place, the people in the team have to function as a team, not just a collection of individuals.

My thirty-odd years in professional sports have brought me in contact with many of the most successful players and coaches in sports history. Every encounter with these fascinating individuals is an inspiration to me—and almost invariably, what these terrific athletes and coaches inspire in me is an even deeper belief and commitment to the concept of teamwork. Clearly, to win a football game, it takes not just the eleven guys on the field but a whole team working intricately together, a coordinated effort of the various squads: the offense, the defense, and the special teams. Here are some statements from three football standouts who know all about it:

"Quarterbacks don't win or lose football games. Teams do."
—Fran Tarkenton, the outstanding former Minnesota Vikings
quarterback

"When a team outgrows individual performance and learns
team confidence, excellence becomes a reality." —Joe Paterno,
Penn State football coach

"It doesn't matter what I do as an individual if the team does
not win. I never can put my ego ahead of the team."—Troy
Aikman, Dallas Cowboys quarterback

And then there's baseball—at its best, a beautiful ballet of
teamwork that reaches its pinnacle in the lightning grace of the
double play. Here's what two of the greatest figures of the diamond have said about teamwork:

"No pitcher would be worth a darn without a catcher who can
handle the hot fast balls." —Former Yankee manager Casey
Stengel

"You don't get the breaks unless you play with the team
instead of against it." —Legendary Yankee slugger Lou Gehrig.

Of course, I see the lessons of teamwork demonstrated on a
daily basis in the field of endeavor where I currently work: the
game of basketball. Sometimes those demonstrations of teamwork are very painful for me, as was the case in the 1995 NBA
championship play-offs when the Houston Rockets swept the
Orlando Magic four games to zip. It was a shattering loss for our
team, after we had come so close and battled so hard for our
first-ever NBA title. But I have to give credit where credit is due:
The Rockets truly earned that title, their second NBA championship in a row. When they won it in 1994, the Rockets' star
center, Hakeem Olajuwon, looked into the NBC cameras and
explained their win in a single word: "Teamwork!" When they
won again in '95, Hakeem used a few more words to make the
same statement: "If you play together as a team, you can do anything!" Hakeem's teammate, Clyde Drexler, put it this way: "We
think as a team."

Sounds simple, doesn't it? But it's really quite profound—and
practical. There are specific actions and attitudes each of us can

adopt that can enable us to create the kind of teamwork, team-play, and teamthink that Hakeem and Clyde are talking about and demonstrating on the court. Bill Bradley—the great Princeton all-American, former New York Knicks star forward, and former Democratic senator from New Jersey—once observed, "The point of the game is not how well the individual does, but whether the team wins. That's the beautiful heart of the game, the blending of personalities, the mutual sacrifices for group success."

Without question, the finest example of this principle in NBA history is the Boston Celtics under coach-general manager Red Auerbach. The Celtics of the '50s and early '60s were the great-est NBA dynasty ever assembled, and Red was the architect of that dynasty. Under his leadership, the Celtics brought fifteen NBA championships home to Boston. Red tells the story of for-mer Celtic Satch Sanders—a story that proves the crucial impor-tance of team accomplishment over individual glory.

"There was a time around his third or fourth year," Auerbach recalls, "when Satch Sanders got to thinking it might be nice to score a few points on his own. So without being too obvious about it, he began taking more shots. One night he scored fifteen points, the next night he managed to get eighteen. Meanwhile, no one said a word about it. Our policy was that the ball belonged to everyone; nobody had exclusive rights to it. If you thought you had a good shot, you were not only encouraged to take it, you were expected to take it.

"Then one night, Satch scored about twenty points and we lost. It bothered him all the way home. He thought about it long into the night, then came to the following conclusion: All it takes to upset the balance of this beautiful machine of ours is one man crossing over into another's specialty. So he decided that night it was a much bigger claim to say, 'I'm a member of the world championship Boston Celtics,' than it was to say, 'I averaged thirty-five points a game.'"

Chad Sheron was an outstanding basketball player at Vanderbilt University. He came up with a great metaphor describing the interaction of individuals and teams—but his metaphor comes not from the world of sports but from his premed studies at Vanderbilt. He observed that the various cells of the human body—muscle cells, blood cells, organ cells, bone cells, and all the other cells—are designed to work together to enhance the health and life of the entire body. Each cell is a part of the body's "team." But there is one kind of cell that can create enormous problems for the body—a cell called a *mutagen*. "A mutagen," Chad observes, "is a cell that has stopped acting like its peer cells and just grows for its own sake. Just as mutagens cause cancer in the human body, people who behave like mutagens can have a cancerous effect on a team."

What do you do when you have a "mutagen" player on your team? Ask former UCLA coach John Wooden. He has produced more NCAA basketball championship teams than any coach in history—ten championship titles in twelve years as head coach in the '60s and '70s. He was also the first to be inducted into the Basketball Hall of Fame as both a player and coach. Not long ago, Wooden looked back over some of the tough choices he had to make as a coach, dealing with an occasional player who would not get in sync with the team:

> I coached in an era when there were as many free spirits and individualists as there are today. You had players wanting to wear their hair long and dress in a very different way. And I never had any problems. I encouraged the young men to stand up for their rights. I think it's very important to stand up for what you believe in or else you don't believe in anything and people won't respect you.

> But I stood up for my rights, too. I just told them, if you want to wear your hair long and don't want to wear a coat and tie, that's certainly your right. It's just not your right to do it as a part of my basketball team. And if you want to go out and throw behind the back passes and break out of the pattern, to try a 360-degree reverse dunk, fine! You just won't do it here.

> Too many coaches are afraid to use the bench. It's the finest teaching tool there is. If somebody isn't going to play the game the way they've been taught to play it, you must put them on the bench. I've had coaches tell me, "But coach, I can't put that kid on the bench! He's my star player!" My answer to that is: If a player isn't doing what you tell him to do, he's not your

star player. He's a *potential* star, but he can't be a star until he does it as a part of the team.

Teamwork in basketball means going with the flow of the team, learning each other's style of play, reading each other's signals, feeding opportunities to your teammates, setting picks and screens for the other players so they can score, letting every individual on the team practice his specialty to the level of his ability, respecting and trusting each other's gifts and abilities. The great automobile magnate Henry Ford once said, "There are three keys to making a successful team: Number one, coming together is the beginning. Number two, working together is progress. Number three, staying together is success." Mr. Ford was right. He knew that many hands make light work.

Most important of all, what is true in the sports arena is equally true in the arena of life. It's true in the marketplace. (NBA coach Pat Riley said, "More than ever, it's clear that teamwork is the key to global competitiveness.") It's true on the battlefield. It's true in the field of religious endeavor and ministry. It's true within the four walls of your home. To achieve greatness, we must think and act not as a collection of individuals, but as a team.

LESSONS FROM NATURE

There is a beautiful paradox at work in a well-functioning team: Team effort does not overshadow individual strengths; it *enhances* them. At the same time, it is our individual strengths that bring greatness to the team. Every individual on the team must have the ability and confidence to make great individual contributions to the team effort—yet every individual must also have the humility and cooperative spirit to respect, encourage, and build upon the contributions of the rest of the team. It's a balancing act. Every individual member of the team must have supreme confidence in both his own abilities and in the team. That confidence enables a team member either to step up or to step back, to take a shot or to pass the ball off, as the situation requires.

Phil Jackson, head coach of the Chicago Bulls, understands this principle extraordinarily well—and because of the extraordinary treasure of talent Jackson has to work with in superstar Michael Jordan, he takes great pains to underscore to his players the need to rely on each other as a team, not on any one individual. Every year before the play-offs, Phil gathers his team together and reads them this passage from Rudyard Kipling's *Second Jungle Book*:

Now this is the Law of the Jungle—
as old and as true as the sky:
And the Wolf that shall keep it may prosper,
but the Wolf that shall break it must die.
As the creeper that girdles the tree trunk,
the Law runneth forward and back.
For the strength of the Pack is the Wolf,
and the strength of the Wolf is the Pack.

Nature is brimming with lessons about the importance of teamwork. Russian Prince Pyotr Kropotkin (1842-1921) once observed, "Mutual aid is as much a law of animal life as mutual struggle." At creation, God designed the animal kingdom to function on a teamwork model—and we would do well to copy His plan as we design and build our own kingdoms in the sports world, the business world, or the world of our own families.

In the summer of 1993, I was in Bogota, Colombia, for a week, and I went to a health club to work out. I didn't speak Spanish and hardly anyone there spoke much English. In the gym, I encountered a man who was working out, and I attempted to communicate with him in my badly fractured Spanish. I was surprised and abashed when he responded in perfect English and said, "Aren't you Pat Williams?" Apparently my reputation as a language-mangler had preceded me!

"Yes," I replied, "guilty as charged."

He introduced himself. Turns out he was a scientist named Greg Gangi from Bogota, and he had studied extensively in the United States. He was in the process of getting his doctorate at the University of North Carolina in Chapel Hill. "Oh, really!" I said. "A doctorate! What is your field?"

"I'm writing my thesis," he said, "on the New World tropics in the Amazon."

"Wow!" I said. "What a subject!"

"To be precise," he added, "I'm focusing on Amazonian leaf-cutter ants."

"Really? Tell me about them," I said.

"Well, it's a major problem here in South America," Greg replied. "These leaf-cutter ants can strip an area of all its vegetation overnight."

"How do they do that?"

"They break up into teams—" (there's that word again!) "—and these teams are specialized, with each team performing a different function. For example, some of the ants are the leaf-cutters. Others carry the leaves to the nest. Then there are teams of soldiers who defend against ant-eating insects. There are teams of tiny ants that ride on the leaves to protect against parasites. There's the queen ant who lays the eggs, and there are workers who tend to the queen and the larvae. Some of the ants are fungus guards, and they tend to the fungus that the leaves produce because the ants eat only the fungus, not the leaves themselves."

Then Greg explained to me the incredible power of a vast team of leaf-cutter ants. "One of the most awesome sights in nature," he said, "is to stand on a hillside and watch a marching army of green moving in perfect unison. You might see an area as large as two football fields just swarming with these creatures, carrying their little bits of leaf. They'll swarm over an area for a while, then—as if on a signal—they'll all disappear into a hole in the ground."

That's the awesome power of teamwork in nature—and it's a model we should all emulate in our own team experience. You combine all the amazing power of individual strengths, individual functions, individual abilities, and you harness them to operate in sync with each other, all moving toward a single goal. The team that can accomplish such complete synergy becomes an awesome, unstoppable force!

MAKING MAGIC HAPPEN

Bill Russell is one of the greatest basketball players in the history of the game. He played for the Boston Celtics during the great Red Auerbach-era and is remembered as a powerful, dominating center. Collecting more than 21,000 rebounds and 14,000 points in his career, he led the Celtics to eleven NBA championships in thirteen years, was a five-time league MVP, and served the game as a player, coach, general manager, and sportscaster. He once made this observation about his glory days with the Celts:

> By design and by talent, we were a team of specialists. And like a team of specialists in any field, our performance depended on individual excellence and how well we worked together. None of us had to strain to understand that we had to complement each other's specialties. It was simply a fact, and we all tried to figure out ways to make our combination more effective. Off the court, most of us were oddballs by society's standards—not the kind of people who blend in with others or who tailor their personalities to match what is expected of them. . . .
>
> Every so often, a Celtic game would heat up so that it would become more than a physical or mental game. It would be magical. The feeling is difficult to describe. And I certainly never talked about it when I was playing. When it happened, I could feel my play rise to a new level. It would surround not only me and the other Celtics, but also the players on the other team and even the referees.
>
> At that special level, all sorts of odd things happened. The game would be in the white heat of competition, and yet I wouldn't feel competitive—which is a miracle in itself. The game would move so fast that every fake, cut, and pass would be surprising—and yet nothing could surprise me. It was almost as if we were playing in slow motion. During those spells, I could almost sense how the next play would develop and where the next shot would be taken.

All sports fans are familiar with the phenomenon so aptly described by Bill Russell. We have all seen those magical moments when something seems to come over a team and every single member of the team is swept up in it. Almost every shot falls right in the bucket. Every move, every pass is executed with flawless precision. A team that moments before was thudding and squeaking on hardwood suddenly seems to float on air. Incredible three-point shots, laser-fired no-look passes, perfectly choreographed alley-oops just seem to happen, and the team can do no wrong.

We have also seen the antithesis of this kind of magic, where a team that is up by twenty points suddenly and mysteriously seems to fall apart. For no apparent reason, even great shooters have trouble making simple layups. Easy shots bang harmlessly off the iron. Open shooting opportunities are missed. Simple passes are bobbled and roll out-of-bounds. Confidence turns to desperation on the faces of the players as they press harder and harder to get something going, to recapture the miracle, all to no avail.

What we're talking about is the elusive mystery often referred to as "alignment"—that moment when the entire team comes together as a unit, functioning not merely as a machine but as a work of art. All the energies of the team pulsate in a unified, synchronized, harmonious flow toward the goal. When a team begins to slip out of alignment, there is usually no conscious awareness that it is happening. Two or three of your opponents' baskets go unanswered and you think, "That's okay. We still have a comfortable lead. We'll stay on top of it." But as the trend continues, you realize that you're out of step with your teammates—and they with you. Worst of all, you have no idea how to get the magic back.

If we could bottle the magical stuff called "alignment" or "synergy," you can bet we'd be sure and slip some into the Orlando Magic's cooler of Gatorade before every game. Fact is, you can't bottle it. You can't turn it on and off like a light switch. *But I believe there really are practical steps you can take that will enable you to tap into that magic!* I believe there are ways to *make miracles happen* in sports, in business, in the church, in the family, in any arena of endeavor that is important to you. Even if you can't summon that magic like the genie out of Aladdin's lamp, there are things you can do, steps you can take, skills and attitudes you can develop that can make the magic of teamwork happen more easily, more predictably, more frequently—and that can make the magic last longer. That's what this book is about: tapping into the magical synergy of teamwork so that the elusive miracle of team alignment can take place on an ever-increasing basis.

I don't believe that synergy is just a bolt of lightning that strikes a team out of the blue. It's a quality that can be encouraged, nurtured, and developed. Alignment is a quality that results when certain conditions fall into place like the tumblers of a combination lock—and we, as team leaders and team players, can consciously, deliberately help bring those conditions about through the application of certain practical, doable principles. While there is no guarantee that you can manufacture magic on demand, you *can* increase the chances of experiencing team magic by following the prescription outlined in the next eight chapters.

You may have paid only a few dollars for this book, but I believe the following pages contain truths that are actually worth zillions—not because I'm so brilliant, not because my words are inscribed in gold tablets. The fact is, this book isn't just about my thoughts and my experience. In the process of researching and writing this book, I have literally spoken to or corresponded with *every athletic leader* in the country I could reach, plus many leaders in the fields of entrepreneurship, management, government, medicine, religion, and psychology. The end result of all those conversations, all that research, all those observations are eight principles that are to be found at work in every great team, eight ingredients that provide the basis for team excellence and team success. Briefly stated, those principles are:

1. Acquire top talent.
2. Demonstrate and develop leadership.
3. Encourage team commitment.
4. Inspire team enthusiasm and passion.
5. Build a strong team attitude.
6. Empower individuals to excel in the team environment.

7. Create a team environment of mutual respect and trust.
8. Build on a foundation of team and individual character.

As you will see, I have built a chapter around each one of these powerful, transforming principles. So turn the page with me, Teammate! Walk through these stories with me. Live in these principles with me. I believe that even before you get to the end of this book you'll begin to see something wonderful start to happen. You'll sense it. You'll feel it. You'll see the results of it all around you.

So hold on tight! The magic is about to begin!

Principle I

Acquire Top Talent

W e called our team the Orlando Magic. But what happened to us in the early years of our franchise was more than magic. It was a *miracle*.

There's a verse in Proverbs in *The Living Bible*: "We toss the coin, but it is the Lord who controls its decision."[1] Boy, was He smiling on us in 1992 and '93! After we had painstakingly assembled our organization, we entered the NBA draft lottery— and with God's miraculous superblessing, we won two lotteries back-to-back!

The first year, 1992, was the year Shaquille O'Neal declared he'd come out early from Louisiana State University. It was the easiest draft choice anybody ever had. The minute the lottery was over, everyone knew that the first draft pick would be the Big Man himself. All eleven teams had Shaquille O'Neal jerseys made up, sitting under their chairs, ready to pull out. But only one team would have the honor of actually placing *its* Shaq jersey in Shaq's big hands.

We did no player interviews, no player workouts that year. Prior to the draft, both Shaq and his agent, Leonard Armato, kept the whole world guessing, never committing publicly to

Orlando. We finally got Shaq in for a visit right before the draft, and I think he was impressed by what he saw. Still, he never made any public statement about his plans—call it an excellent negotiating posture. Two days after the draft, we brought Orlando's community leaders to the Expo Center for a big celebration and luncheon, with more than three hundred of Orlando's leading citizens there.

At the appropriate time, Shaq got up to make his speech. It was the briefest speech I ever heard—and one of the most powerful. The big guy had the entire room in the palm of his hand. "I'm very excited about starting my NBA career . . . " He paused for what seemed like an eternity, maybe an eternity and a half. Then he concluded, ". . . right here in Orlando."

The crowd jumped to its collective feet and applauded uproariously.

That was the first time he had said he would come to Orlando. Man, we had a player!

PENNY POWER

If the '92 draft was a slam-dunk, the '93 draft was exactly the opposite. It was gut-wrenching and nerve-wracking. In the end, we were extremely fortunate again to bring some high-level talent to Orlando. But compared with the ease and good fortune we had acquiring Shaquille O'Neal, our acquisition of Penny Hardaway was a nail-biter and a hair-raiser all the way.

In the '93 draft, there were four top college players who had earned a very high place in the NBA draft. The most visible was Chris Webber, who had just finished two very successful years at Michigan. We had a great need for a power forward, and Chris was about as powerful as they get. From the time we won the '93 lottery, everyone—the fans, the press, and the Magic organization—just assumed that we would take Webber. In my own mind, we had a utopian dream of Shaq and Chris Webber playing together for the next ten years, becoming basketball's Dynamic Duo of the '90s.

Sure, we brought the other players in for interviews and workouts, including a pleasant young man from Memphis State named Anfernee Hardaway. But there was no question in anyone's mind: Chris Webber would have made an excellent pick. We were all agreed—all, that is, except John Gabriel, our basketball operations director. For some reason he could not get Anfernee "Penny" Hardaway off his mind. (He's been "Penny," by the way, ever since he was a baby and his grandmother said he was as pretty as a shiny new penny.)

Added to this, events were taking place in far-off Hollywood, U.S.A., that would also affect the shape of the Orlando Magic basketball team: Shaquille O'Neal and Penny Hardaway were making a movie together. Every day on the set of the hoops movie *Blue Chips,* Shaq and Penny were talking together, going before the cameras together, and playing basketball together. Even when John Gabriel asked Shaq for his opinion on Hardaway, he said, "Hey, Penny is our man! We can't pass this guy up! He's gonna be a superstar!"

At the same time, Penny and his agent kept calling and saying, "Penny wants to be in Orlando, and Orlando needs Penny Hardaway." Finally, one day before the draft, John Gabriel couldn't take it anymore and said, "All right, Penny, you're coming back for another workout." Now, you have to understand that this is practically unheard of! On the eve of the draft, NBA draft prospects don't fly off to franchise facilities for more tryouts. They don't want to see anybody. They go hide out somewhere and wait for their name to be called. But here was young Penny Hardaway, flying into Orlando for a full-scale workout. John told him, "Penny, just tell me what you need for this tryout, and I'll do it." Boy, that was a first.

And Penny said, "All I want is one hour of pickup ball. Everything you need to know about me, you'll see."

So for one hour in a church gym, in an old-fashioned shirts-and-skins game, up and down the floor they went. Let me tell you, Penny did everything on that court but change the lightbulbs and sweep the floor. I'll never forget how that scrimmage ended: Penny hit a three-pointer from long range to win that particular game—and I mean it must have been a thirty-five-footer.

Then he nonchalantly walked off the floor, looking up at us as if to say, "Anything else I can do for you? Seen enough?"

Well, we had seen enough. Penny walked out of that church gym, got in a cab, and took off for the airport to fly to Detroit, where the draft would be held. John Gabriel, team president Bob Vander Weide, and I just stood on the court, looking at each other and shaking our heads. "John," I said, "you have really messed things up now." We knew we had a very tough decision to make.

Another onion in this whole stew was coach Don Nelson of the Golden State Warriors. Don had been calling me almost daily since we won the lottery. We had first pick, while Don's Warriors had drawn third. His team desperately needed a big guy and he wanted Chris Webber. He kept saying he would give up a hefty package of draft picks if we would help him get Webber. "If you take Webber on your first pick and give him to us," he said, "we'll take Hardaway on our third pick and give him to you, plus three future draft picks." He had been offering variations on this deal for days, even before we decided to take a look at Hardaway, and for days I had been telling him, "No, no, no! Webber's the guy we want, not Hardaway." But suddenly, Penny Hardaway had captured our hearts—and Don Nelson's offer began to look very attractive.

One of the biggest headaches we faced was the enormous media and fan expectations surrounding Chris Webber. Everyone assumed Webber was Orlando-bound. Chris Webber, the number one college player in the country, was a highly visible player who had played a lot of games on national television and had become a household name among NCAA fans. Everyone knew we sorely needed to fill the position Webber played, and it would be insanity not to take the guy.

Penny, on the other hand, was not a marquee guy, he was just not all that visible—despite the fact that he was twice named Great Midwest Conference Player of the Year and was named to the all-American first team in 1993. The public and the press had not seen that shirts-and-skins game in the church gym, they had not been part of the discussions we had, the chemistry we saw, the interaction between Shaq and Penny out in California. If we took Penny instead of Chris Webber, we knew it would create such an explosion among our fans that the Big Bang would seem like a cap pistol in comparison.

Two hours before the draft, we were all still in mental agony about what to do. So I sat down with John Gabriel, looked right at him, and said, "John, forget the public, forget the media, forget your coaches, forget everybody. What does your heart tell you? Down inside your stomach, what do you want to do?"

"I want Hardaway. We have a better chance of winning championships with Shaq and Hardaway than with Shaq and Webber."

"John, let's do it."

We pulled the whole group together from the Magic front office, including Bob Vander Weide. At the meeting, John expressed his feelings. We all agreed. Penny was our man; we were dealing Webber to the Warriors. So I called Don Nelson and closed the deal for the three future firsts, and we had done it. Only one problem: We hadn't told the public.

The draft unfolded and, according to NBA rules, we took Webber. As you can imagine, our fans went wild—all ten thousand of them who were sitting at the draft party. Twenty minutes later, it was announced that we had traded Chris Webber. It was my job to walk out with Bob Vander Weide and explain our decision. As we walked out of our room, I saw a life-size cardboard cutout of Penny that he had sent us as a promotional aid. I picked that up and carried it out with me to the stage to help lead the cheers.

Except there were no cheers.

Instead, there were ten thousand extremely unhappy people who demanded to know which idiot was responsible for trading Chris Webber away. One look across that sea of hostility and I knew that this was the same mob that had chased Boris Karloff into the burning windmill in the old Universal movie, *Frankenstein* (the pitchforks and burning torches were a dead giveaway)! We realized we were in a no-win (and possibly a no-escape) situation. We couldn't outshout them. All I could do was raise that Penny Hardaway cutout (partly as a shield) and shout into the microphone, "You're booing tonight, folks, but Penny Hardaway will turn your jeers into cheers."

And we walked off the platform (actually, it was more of a dignified scramble). Those words were the only thing I could think to say in order to get out of there before the bottles started flying. But you know what? Those words were prophetic. Absolutely prophetic.

Sure, Penny had to earn the public's respect. His first few weeks with the Magic were not easy for him. Some of the early comments from the fans and the press were unkind not only to the Magic organization but to Penny himself. But as soon as he started showing his stuff on the court—his speed, his agility, his slammin' and jammin' and no-look wraparound passes—it became hard to find a single person in Orlando who would admit to ever having doubted us.

WHAT TO LOOK FOR IN A TEAM PLAYER

The acquisition of top talent like Shaq and Penny—as well as role players like Horace Grant, Nick Anderson, Dennis Scott, Brian Shaw, Jeff Turner, Donald Royal, Scott Skiles, and Anthony Bowie—contributed to the early emergence of the Magic from expansion-team obscurity to NBA powerhouse. "How you select people is more important than how you manage them once they're on the job," said Red Auerbach, a guy who really ought to know. As coach of the Boston Celtics, he held the record for most regular season wins in the NBA (938), a record that stood from 1966 until it was broken in '95 by Lenny Wilkens. Auerbach went on to say, "If you start with the right people, you won't have problems later on. If you hire the wrong people, for whatever reason, you're in serious trouble and all the management techniques in the world won't bail you out."

You want to build a winning team in sports, business, government, or ministry? You've gotta start with the right people. Not necessarily the most flashy people. Not necessarily the highest-priced people. I'm talking about the *right* people, the best mix, blend, and balance of people for the job you have to do. But how do you accomplish that? How do you know who the right people are as you assemble your team?

In a very real sense, I have been collecting the insights and principles that make up this book over a thirty-six-year career in sports management. During the past year as I approached the writing, I have also been intensely gathering the thoughts and experiences of team-building experts. Here are the steps to acquiring top talent, as I have learned them (often through painful trial and error) and as I have gleaned them from the top team-builders across the country:

Step 1: Assess Ability

Choose team players well, according to how well their strengths and skills fit the goals and tasks of your organization. This step seems obvious, yet it is an easy step to overlook. I know. I overlooked it.

As I was sharing an early outline of this book with various sports colleagues to get their feedback and advice, Dr. Jack Ramsay—a longtime NBA coach, a Hall of Famer, a broadcaster, and a man I greatly respect—called me and said, "Pat, you've forgotten the most important thing in building a team: How do you get the talent? You can have all these principles in place— the right leadership, the vision, the commitment, the passion, the team attitude, the character, and all the rest—but if you don't have the right people with the right skills to do the job, you're dead in the water. Assessing the talent of your players is the first step in building a sports organization, a business organization, or any other kind of team."

I said, "Good point, Dr. Jack. That's why you have a Ph.D."

When asked what he looked for in recruiting players, UCLA's legendary former basketball coach John Wooden used to say, "Talent, talent, talent."

Skill assessment in sports is a fairly simple matter, compared with other businesses and team enterprises. In the sports world, you have a record to look at, including stats, scouting reports, newspaper clippings, and video clips. And the job interview? Hey, the way you interview a ballplayer is the way we interviewed Penny—take the guy out on the court and have him show you his stuff.

But when you're interviewing a potential team player for your business, your organization, or your church—whether it's a kid to work in the mailroom or a corporate CEO or a church pastor—skill assessment becomes a little more complex. You have to ask yourself, "Why does this person want the job? Ambition, a love for this kind of work, a sense of calling, an eagerness to succeed in our organization? Or has this person simply failed in three or four previous jobs?"

Fact is, making a mistake in acquiring talent can be very costly for your team or organization. Hal Eskenazi, president of Profiles Worldwide, Inc., estimates the cost of hiring the wrong team player in a corporate environment at between $5,700 and $50,000—including wasted recruiting costs, the cost of the interview process, training costs, break-in time, wasted supervisor and coworker time, and lost productivity and business. Obviously, it's absolutely crucial, in dollars-and-cents terms, to assess accurately the ability and suitability of every person you put on your team.

In a real sense, the Orlando Magic "team" is much more than a bunch of guys who play basketball. It takes a lot of people to make our season happen—people the public never sees but who are just as much a part of the Orlando Magic as Penny Hardaway or Rony Seikaly. For the on-court part of our team, we use a number of evaluative tools, including the same kinds of psychological evaluation questionnaires used by many businesses, organizations, and churches. The particular tool we use—a highly regarded psychological profile—is a very helpful indicator of an individual's emotional stability and mental makeup, as well as that person's ability to function in a team environment. For the "front office" and "behind-the-scenes" parts of our team, we also rely on the usual assessment tools, such as résumés, references, and interviews.

Here's a different idea than the usual "human resources" approach to acquiring skilled talent. A "resource" is an asset, a supply of something, a thing that you utilize in order to produce a profit. I prefer to think of people as *partners,* as team members to build a relationship. I wonder if it wouldn't change our entire attitude and approach to employer-employee relationships if we viewed "human resources departments" as "team-building centers." This would open the door to a "team" approach to locating and acquiring top talent.

One of the most effective ways of locating new talent is by asking current team players personally to recommend people to fill the slots. People who are already on your team have an understanding of the team goals, the team chemistry, and the team needs—and they are much more likely to turn up the right people for the positions than any human resources director, employment agency, or newspaper "Help Wanted" ad.

Step 2: Choose Coachable People

One night, during the writing of this book, I was talking with my son Bobby, a baseball player at Rollins College in Winter Park, Florida. Bobby asked me about one of the guys who was on his high school team the previous year, now a high school senior and a very talented player. "I was talking to a scout the other day," I replied, "and I asked the scout where he's going to be drafted. The scout was very noncommittal, Bob. I'm not sure how high he's gonna go or even if he's going to be drafted at all."

"You're kidding!" Bobby said. "Why not?" He couldn't believe it, because the kid was definitely a college or pro prospect, judging by the level of his skills.

"Well, Bob," I said, "the word on him is that he isn't very coachable."

I've been around NBA coaches since 1968, and I have worked with some of the legends of the game—Jack Ramsay, Dick Motta, Cotton Fitzsimmons, Gene Shue, Billy Cunningham, Chuck Daly, Matt Guokas, Brian Hill, and more. Every one of these coaches is a unique individual with a unique style and personality—yet in one way or another, at one time or another, I have heard them make essentially the same statement. When it's time for the NBA draft in the spring, when the scouts have done their work, when all the information has been gathered about the players, their talent, their physical skills, their mental focus, their preparation, and their stats, every one of those coaches asks without fail: "Can I coach this kid? Will he listen? Does he have a teachable spirit?" And that's at the pro level, where a lot of guys come in thinking they've already learned it all. If coachability is so important at the highest level of the game, it is definitely important at every other level and in every other endeavor in life. You've got to have team players who keep learning and listening and growing in response to their coaches and leaders.

Johnny Oates, current manager of the Texas Rangers and the American League co-manager of the year for 1996, said, "Some players come up fast, but they waste their talents no matter what you do. They're just not coachable." And the late Jim Valvano, the flamboyant head basketball coach at North Carolina State, said, "The NBA is more complex than ever. They actually hire investigators to go into the player's hometown and find out what kind of kid he was. When the Utah Jazz coach, Frank Layden, was interested in Thurl Bailey, one of my players here at State, he wanted to know more than anything else, 'What type of young man was Thurl? Was he coachable?' The quality of the kid is just as important as talent."

Coaching keeps a team synchronized, harmonized, and growing together. A team without coachable players is not a team. It's just a collection of flying egos.

Step 3: Think "Chemistry"

Talent sticks out; chemistry is harder to see. We have scouts out around the country all year-round, going to games, looking at players firsthand, studying video, researching the talent level of a lot of players. You can build a wild, entertaining, rambunctious team with talent alone; but to build a *winning* team, a *championship* team, a team that works together and functions like a well-oiled machine to get the job done, you've got to have *chemistry*. That's the magic ingredient.

Back in July 1969, while Neil Armstrong was busy tracking up the moon, I was a twenty-nine-year-old business manager in Philadelphia. While working on preparations for the 76ers training camp, I got a call from my friend and mentor, Bill Veeck. He wanted me to talk to one of the owners of the Chicago Bulls, Phil Frye. So I called Mr. Frye, and he asked if I would be interested in becoming general manager of the Bulls. If you've followed the recent exploits of Jordan, Pippin, Rodman, and the rest of the 1996 NBA championship Chicago Bulls, you may have a hard time imagining the Bulls of '69—a rock-bottom team with hardly any fan following, making no money, winning few games. In Chicago, "sports" meant the Bears, the Black Hawks, the Cubbies, and the Sox, period. The Bulls were nowhere. Frye had seen how the 76ers had emerged as a moneymaking, fan-supported organization while I was the team's business manager, and he was interested in having me try some of my outrageous promotional ideas (such as having fans wrestle a real live bear at halftime!) in the City of the Big Shoulders. I was interested, to say the least.

So I went to the 76ers' owner, Irv Kosloff, and head coach Jack Ramsay, to discuss the offer and see if I could get a release from the last two years of my contract. Jack was intrigued to learn that the Bulls were interested in me, because the Bulls had something *he* wanted. For weeks, he had gotten nowhere in his negotiations with the Bulls to trade 76ers veteran star Chet Walker for Bulls forward Jimmy Washington (Jack believed Jimmy could become a superstar in the right team environment). Jack saw the possibility of sweetening the Walker-Washington trade by throwing Pat Williams into the deal.

So, with the blessing of Irv and Jack, I was permitted to continue talking to the Bulls about a future in Chicago. Ultimately, Bulls president Elmer Rich made a great offer to me, and I took the job—reluctantly in many ways, because Irv and Jack and the entire 76ers organization had been so good to me, but also expectantly, eager to begin a new adventure with a new ballclub.

Jack Ramsay had set a condition for okaying my departure: I had to deliver the Walker-Washington trade. That was fine with me. I knew that Chet Walker had been a tremendous player in Philly, and while Jimmy Washington showed enormous potential, there was no guarantee he would emerge as a superstar after leaving Chicago. I laid all my cards on the table with both teams, including the Bulls' head coach, Dick Motta—and it turned out that Motta was ecstatic at the prospect of getting Walker. For months, he had been begging Bulls management to try to get Walker, yet no one ever told him that a Walker-Washington deal had been offered by the 76ers! Dick knew that Walker's style of basketball would provide exactly the spark and the chemistry his team needed to get off the ground.

So my first official act as Bulls G.M. was to get the deal done—and acquire a great offensive player for Dick Motta. He had been burned on trades before when guys were brought in that he couldn't coach, or when some of his key players were traded out from under him. I couldn't believe an organization would leave the head coach out of the loop on such crucial matters as trades and talent acquisition. After all, it was Dick's job to build and motivate the team! Shouldn't he have a say in who he's supposed to coach? I promised Dick the final word on all future trades, and he was glad to hear it.

Jimmy Washington was happy to return to his hometown and play before the Philadelphia crowds—but Chet was another matter altogether. He didn't want to go to Chicago! He was used to playing before big, enthusiastic crowds in Philadelphia; the Chicago Bulls scarcely drew five thousand on a good night. Dick Motta and I flew to Philly together to talk to Chet, but when we got to his apartment door, he refused to answer our knock. "C'mon, Chet!" we called. "We know you're in there! We hear your stereo blaring!"

Finally, we went to a pay phone and called him, and he reluctantly agreed to let us in. We went back to Chet's place and talked to him. Actually, Dick did most of the talking. He spun a beautiful, glowing vision of building an entirely new team around Chet Walker. Dick talked about how Chet played Dick's brand of basketball—an aggressive, physical, end-to-end game. Most of all, he stressed the exciting chemistry he foresaw between Chet and the Bulls' staff of strong supporting players— a chemistry that was destined to energize and ignite the team and completely turn the Bulls franchise around. By the end of the conversation, Chet Walker was spellbound. So was I.

As it turned out, Dick's prediction came true. Chet Walker turned out to be the catalyst of an exciting new team chemistry and the centerpiece of the dramatic Bulls turnaround of the next few seasons. All the Bulls had needed to get them going was a strong, aggressive leader to rally around, draw energy from, and feed the ball to. Not that Chet carried the team, but boy, did he ever pump some life into that team. He was a motivator, an igniter, and when he stepped it up, he could bring all of his teammates up to the next level.

Of course, that whole deal made me look like a hero! To the people of Chicago, it looked like I had cut a major trade my first day on the job—and when Chet began propelling the Bulls upward in the ranks of the NBA, people remembered that Pat Williams brought him to town! Should I tell everyone the deal had been in the works long before I came on the scene? What—and disillusion all those fans?! No way!

The point is this: Chemistry—while harder to spot than talent—is even more important than talent. It's the magic ingredient of a winning team. What we call "chemistry" is really a combination of a lot of factors: ability and skill levels, drive and ambition, personality, emotional makeup, values, communication, and people skills. Chemistry is not easy to assess until you actually put the team together under real-world conditions and see how the individual members react to one another, play off one another, cooperate together, and synergize. Often, you have to experiment a few times, adding this, subtracting that, in order to get just the right chemistry going.

Joe Axelson, a longtime general manager in the NBA, said to me on more than one occasion, "Team chemistry is the most fragile of all chemical mixtures. You never know how you get it, and you never know why you lose it. But when you've got it, you know you've got it—and when you don't, you know that, too."

Red Auerbach knew. "Talent alone is not enough," he used to say. "They used to tell me you have to use your five best players, but I've found that you win with the five who fit together best." And Yankees slugger Babe Ruth put it this way: "The way a team plays as a whole determines its success. You may have the greatest bunch of individual stars in the world, but if they don't play together, the club won't be worth a dime." Actually, the Babe didn't use those exact words (I cleaned it up a little), but you get the idea.

All of what these sports greats say about chemistry is true—up to a point. Chemistry is mysterious, delicate, and elusive. You can't turn chemistry on and off at will. But does that mean there's *nothing* you can do to make good chemistry happen? Of course not! Chemistry may be as capricious as lightning—but you can put up a lightning rod or two or ten, so you'll be ready to grab a bolt the next time a lightning storm is in your area. The best way to create an environment where winning chemistry can strike your team is to seek a balance of personality types. You need some aggressive, high-energy types. You need some motivators and cheerleaders. You need some leaders; you need some followers. You need some people who are confident enough (and even egotistical and selfish enough) to be the risk-takers and slam-dunkers. You also need some people who are unselfish enough to be the hod-carriers, the ones who are content to forgo the glory, to move the ball around and feed it to the guy who gets the tomahawk jam and the instant replays.

When you've got a well-rounded, well-balanced blend of personalities who relate well to each other, mesh with each other, complement each other, and above all *trust* each other, you've really got a *team*. And if your team has great skills on top of that wonderful blend of personalities, then most likely you've got more than just a team, you've got *chemistry* and a chance to win championships.

Step 4: Strive for Balance

We just talked about balancing personalities in order to generate good chemistry. But it is equally important to balance skills in order to generate effective team play. The skills of each player have to balance and complement the skills of all the other players. If you had a team of five Dennis Rodmans, you'd have a colorful (!) team with a lot of rebounding, but not a lot of shooting. If you had a team of five Shaqs, you'd have a lot of jamming and stuffing, but no perimeter shooting and precious little success at the charity stripe. If you had a team of five Penny Hardaways or Michael Jordans, you'd have—

Now, wait a minute—that's not a bad idea! Just imagine a team of five Penny Hardaways or five Michael Jordans romping from bucket to bucket! The only problem is, where are you gonna find five all-around players like Penny or Michael?

Answer: You won't. So out here in the real world, you have to find specialists, and you have to match their specialized skills to the positions you have to fill, and you have to get your specialists to work and flow in sync. Diversity of skills, unity of purpose—that's how it's done. A balance of skills is an important key to effective teamwork.

I left the Bulls in 1973 to become G.M. of the Atlanta Hawks. Unlike the '69 Bulls, the '73 Hawks were an established NBA powerhouse. They had been annual play-off contenders for over a decade, and the year I came aboard as G.M. the team seemed poised for another great season. But after just a few games, the team began to unravel. It was a mystery, too, because it was an extremely talented team with a brilliant and able coach, Cotton Fitzsimmons. The team just wasn't cohesive; they couldn't get in sync to win the big games—or even the not-so-big games.

I had come up with the "brilliant" idea (in quotes, you'll notice) of televising all our away games in order to boost fan enthusiasm and attendance. I figured if enough people saw hot-shooting Lou Hudson and Pistol Pete Maravich in action on their TV screens, they'd come out to cheer them on the home court. Problem was, out of our first twenty-four televised games, we won four and lost twenty—not the kind of inspiring performance that gets the fans rushing to fill the Omni for a home game. It was a disaster!

Near the end of the '73-'74 season, I was talking to Fred Rosenfeld, an L.A. attorney who was one of the proud owners of the New Orleans Jazz, a brand-new expansion club just approved by the NBA. "You know," he said in the course of our conversation, "we need to talk about Pete Maravich. Pete went to Louisiana State University, and the people in New Orleans just love him. It would sure help us get this franchise off the ground to be able to put a hometown legend on the hometown court—you know, to pump up the gate during the growing years of the team."

I just laughed. "You don't have enough money to buy Pete Maravich." Fact is, we really did want to trade Maravich. He was a great player, but he had been suspended by the team for a couple of games during the season—something about a late-night ruckus at a Houston hotel, if memory serves correct —and with him or without him, the team wasn't winning enough games. The team chemistry just wasn't there. The losses of the season had shown us that we didn't have a synchronized, harmonized team—just one red-hot, run-and-gun performer and a bunch of other guys who ran up and down the court with him and watched him shoot. Even the great Pete Maravich couldn't win basketball games all by himself. If we could get a couple of more frontline ballplayers, we knew we could ignite the performance of the entire team—but no other teams in the NBA were willing to offer two starters in exchange for Pete.

Rosenfeld and the Jazz kept calling, wanting to do a deal, but as a brand-new expansion team they had no players to offer. Before the college draft, they would choose one player each from the rest of the teams in the league—but because each team had the right to protect its seven top players, the best New Orleans could do was field a team of "eighth" men—the kind of talent the rest of us in the NBA would consider substitute players. We weren't about to trade Pete for any amount of money and a couple of subs. But they kept calling and getting more creative, offering more and more stuff in exchange for Pete—players, draft picks, cash, a lifetime supply of crawdad gumbo and shrimp po' boys.

Finally, Rosenfeld called with a suggestion that was the perfect yes-yes solution to his problems and mine. As I listened, I realized that we were on the verge of making one of the greatest deals in the history of professional sports. I had Cotton sit in as I negotiated over the phone with Rosenfeld. I wanted our coach—our head team-builder—to have the final say on any talent we acquired or lost. So in one ear, I had Cotton telling me what he needed, and in the other ear, I had Rosenfeld telling me what he could offer. I ran Rosenfeld's offer by ownership and was told, "Don't take any more from them! If New Orleans gives you one more thing, their franchise will fold and those draft picks won't be worth a thing!"

By the time we were done, I felt we had committed highway robbery. It was a very sweet deal for our side. Yet, at the same time, I knew Rosenfeld could hardly believe his own good fortune. He had achieved the impossible: he had landed Pete Maravich. Even though the price tag had been steep, the deal would be a big moneymaker for New Orleans in the long run.

And what did we get out of the deal? We got the right to draft the first guard and forward in the expansion pool, which gave us Dean Meminger (from New York) and Bob Kauffman (from Buffalo). Plus we got New Orleans's first-round draft choices in '74 and '75, their second-round choices in '75 and '76, and in '76 and '77 we had the option of using their first choice or ours, whichever was most advantageous. In effect, we got eight top draftees, which could, over four or five years, be worth an entire franchise. And we had an added advantage: By taking so many top New Orleans draft picks, we made sure their club was bound to finish low in the standings for a few years, which meant their draft picks (which became ours) would be among the first and most valuable each year!

I drove over to Pete's apartment to give him the news. As I got out of the car and made my way up the walk, my knees turned to jelly. I knew that Pete was a guy who could get—well, let's just say he had been known to be physically demonstrative regarding his feelings from time to time. Having grown accustomed to having my facial features in a certain arrangement, I was not eager for Pete to start moving them around. He let me in, and I sat down and nervously laid out the deal we had made. Pete sat silently, just listening—and frowning. Finally he said, "What did you get for me?"

I listed all the concessions New Orleans had made—the players, the draft picks, the money, the gumbo, everything. It was the deal of the century, the most consideration ever offered for a single NBA player up to that time.

"That's it?" Pete sneered. "That's all you got?" The guy was actually insulted!

Well, he was a little reluctant to move to New Orleans at first. For one thing, he was annoyed because he felt he should have been informed during the negotiations. I understood his feelings, but it was really in everybody's best interests to keep the negotiations secret. If the deal had fallen through, the Hawks organization would have looked silly and Pete would have been offended for nothing. In the end, Pete was able to negotiate a new, more lucrative contract with New Orleans, and everyone was happy—and nobody was happier than me.

A final postscript to the Pete Maravich story: The Atlanta Hawks never realized the benefits of the incredible deal we made. I left the Hawks three months later to return to the 76ers, and my successors inexplicably failed to sign all the draft picks we had gotten from the Jazz. The Hawks could have become one of the dominant NBA teams of the late '70s. I've always wondered why they let the opportunity slip through their fingers.

Remember, to build a great team, you have to have a balance of skills.

Step 5: Recruit the Best

Build a quality team out of quality people who are always reaching for the next level of excellence, both individually and as a team. In the game of basketball, that means finding the best quality people in terms of game skills and athleticism. In our business, you've got to have great athletes, exceptional athletes. You can't just go out and create that. You can't hire a guy off the street and turn him into an NBA athlete. You have to find people who already have it, people who have spent their adolescence, their youth, their young adulthood preparing themselves for one thing: To play in the big leagues, to compete at the highest level, to make your team shine.

In the basketball business, we look for people who not only have great game skills on a given night but the athletic ability and endurance to take those skills to the court eighty-plus nights a year, to put those skills on the line, to perform on demand. In our business, a player has to want to play so badly he's even willing to perform in pain, with multiple injuries, with taped-up wrists and wrapped-up knees and a bit of tendinitis in the elbow, because he wants to make the play-offs, he wants to be a champion, he wants to be the best.

In August 1974, I moved back to Philadelphia for a second stint, this time as G.M. of the 76ers. It had been five years since I left the 76ers organization, and it was great to be back with Irv Kosloff's organization—but there was a lot of rebuilding to do.

The 1972-73 season had been an unmitigated disaster: the team had finished the season with 9 wins and 73 losses. The 1973-74 season had been a little better but still wretched—25 wins, 57 losses. It was hard to believe this was the same team that had won the NBA championship and set a regular season record of 68 wins and only 13 losses during the 1966-67 season.

We began rebuilding by re-signing a Sixers prodigal son, Billy Cunningham, who had left Philly in the early '70s to join not just another team but another league—the Carolina Cougars of the American Basketball Association (ABA). We tried to wrangle a couple of other deals: One was signing one of our draft choices, a tough, steel-hard, physical ABA player named George McGinnis. The other was a spectacular showman of a guard (and Philadelphia native son) named Earl Monroe, then with the Knicks. Both deals fell through. So we started the '74 season with essentially the same team that had won only 34 of its last 164 games, plus Billy Cunningham.

But as the season began, we got a very pleasant surprise. The name of that surprise: Doug Collins. Doug had been the Sixers number one draft choice in '73 but missed almost his entire rookie year with the Sixers because of a broken bone in his foot. The fracture was so severe that the surgeons had to transplant a piece of bone from his hip to his foot, which left him in a cast or on crutches throughout most of the season. He had been a great guard for Illinois State (in fact, I had previously seen him play and tried unsuccessfully to draft him when I was managing the Bulls). Since his surgery, however, nobody knew if he could play anymore. But when Doug came back into the game in '74, finally healthy and recovered, he really rocked! Furiously competitive, with a lot of sweet moves and a laser-guided shot, Doug began to demonstrate his star potential the same year I returned to Philly. He would go on to make the all-star team five times.

By the middle of the season, it was clear that we were improving, but we still had holes in the lineup—the biggest hole being that of the biggest man on the team, the center. There were a lot of promising big men in the college ranks, but they were all sophomores and juniors. The previous year, the best high school center in America, Moses Malone, had signed with Utah, an

ABA franchise, instead of showing up at the University of Maryland, where he was enrolled. That got us thinking in a new direction. If we couldn't trade for a top pro center, couldn't draft a top college center, why not just rob the cradle?

We got word of a monster six-foot-ten high school center in Orlando, Florida, by the name of Darryl Dawkins. Our two scouts, Jack McMahon and Jocko Collins, went to see him in action and were awed by his ability and potential. I went down to Florida in March 1975 to see him play—and I could scarcely believe what I saw. Darryl was all of eighteen years old, with his head shaved and polished, and he looked as menacing as the monster in the sci-fi movie *Alien*. I don't mean he was ugly; he was a handsome young man in a suit and tie. But put him in a jersey with a ball in his hand and watch him come bounding full-tilt in your direction and I guarantee your heart will be in your throat! He was a basketball exec's dream! It was love at first sight. I couldn't believe that this massive and massively talented *man* was actually a high school *kid*!

Our head coach, Gene Shue, went to Jacksonville and saw Darryl play in the state tournament finals. I called him at his motel to get his impressions of Darryl. Normally a very cautious, deliberative guy, Gene was unhesitating in his appraisal of this high school senior. "Let's go with him," he said. Our cautious and conservative owner, Irv Kosloff, listened to our report on Darryl and gave thumbs up to "the kid."

Landing "the kid," however, turned out to be a tricky and costly proposition. I started by calling Chicago attorney Herb Rudoy. I asked him to go to Orlando, present our offer, and make himself available to represent Dawkins in the negotiations. There was a long silence at the other end of the line when I told Herb that Dawkins was a senior in high school. But he went— and he called back from Orlando with Dawkins's reply. "Mr. Dawkins would be pleased and proud to suit up as a Philadelphia 76er," Herb said, pausing for dramatic effect and a deep intake of oxygen, "for $200,000 a year for seven years, plus a $100,000 signing bonus." While many high school kids put in their applications at the local car wash or McDonald's, big

Darryl was bucking for a six-figure income. It doesn't sound like a big deal now, but it was huge back then.

Well, we could afford his asking price—but the next trick was to keep him under wraps long enough to draft him. Let me tell you, it's not easy keeping a six-foot-ten, 250-pound high-octane hoop-smasher under wraps. We had to keep him out of the postseason high school tournaments so that other NBA scouts (not to mention about two hundred college scouts) wouldn't stumble onto him and try to steal him out from under us. That meant we had to hire his high school coach to "baby-sit" him, so to speak (the coach became our official Florida scout—at $5,000 a year for seven years).

When Herb Rudoy and I went down to Orlando to ink the deal between the Sixers and Darryl, up popped Darryl's "financial advisor," the Rev. Mr. William Judge, who was there to look out for Darryl's interests—and to take away a large piece of Herb's commission. The deal threatened to come unglued even before we got to the NBA draft. I managed to convince Herb to hold the deal together and take a smaller commission—half a loaf being better than no loaf at all. Barely mollified, Herb turned to the Rev. Mr. Judge and griped, "This isn't right. You're not a financial advisor. You're a preacher!" The Rev. Mr. Judge shrugged and said, "There are many kinds of reverends, Mr. Rudoy, and I am a financial reverend."

We had the fifth pick in the first round of the 1975 draft, and we held our collective breaths through the first four picks, hoping that no one had gotten wind of our big "kid." David Thompson was selected first, then David Meyers, Marvin Webster, and Alvan Adams. When we announced our pick, Darryl Dawkins, you could hear the murmurs go around the hall: "Darryl *Who*? What college does *he* play for?" When people found out that the Sixers had drafted a guy straight out of high school, the murmurs changed to snickers. Drafting guys out of high school wasn't *completely* unprecedented—Moses Malone had broken that barrier in the ABA—but it had never happened in the NBA before. People thought we had lost our minds.

But as soon as they saw Darryl Dawkins's potential, they thought we were a bunch of Einsteins.

We followed the Dawkins acquisition with players like hard-charging Lloyd Free, big-rebounding Caldwell Jones, and the mighty George McGinnis—a burly blacksmith of a basketball player, a guy with muscles in places most guys don't even have places, a guy who looked more like a football player or a decathlete than a basketball player. We opened the 1975-76 season with a pair of big wins—a road win in Chicago and a home win over the Lakers. Immediately, attendance at the Spectrum Arena jumped from around seven thousand to more than twelve thousand a game.

The summer of '76, the ABA folded and four ABA teams were adopted by the NBA—Denver, San Antonio, Indiana, and New Jersey. A lot of talent came into the NBA draft market from the other teams that were dissolved. We arranged to purchase Henry Bibby, a play-making guard from New Orleans, on top of rookie draftees Terry Furlow and Mike Dunleavy. Suddenly we were awash in talent. Yet, as crowded as the Sixers locker room had become, news reached my ears that made me want to make room for just one more: It seemed that a fella by the name of Julius Erving was about to become available. (Julius became available again in 1997 when we signed him to join our front office as an executive vice president of the Magic.)

Erving—the legendary Dr. J—was not happy with the owner of his team, the New York Nets. He felt he was not getting everything he was promised in his contract, so he was getting ready to take a hike. I quickly placed a call to Billy Melchionni, the Nets' G.M., and said, "If things deteriorate to the point that you have to trade Julius Erving, please let me know."

A few weeks later, Billy called. "Looks like Erving isn't coming back," he said. "If you want to buy out his contract, we're willing to listen. But the owner wants cash."

"How much cash?" I asked, feeling my windpipe constrict.

"Three million."

My windpipe sealed shut. Three million was only the beginning. That was just the money paid to the Nets to buy Dr. J's paper. How much would Erving himself want? In the end, the total package to both Erving and the Nets would total a cool six million. Again, small potatoes today, but in those days it was unbelievable money.

I went back and talked to the Sixers' new owner, Fitz Dixon. Incredibly, Fitz had never heard of Dr. J—but he understood the kind of talent Erving possessed when I described him as "the Babe Ruth of basketball." When I told Fitz what it was going to cost to get Julius, he smiled benignly and replied, "Fine and dandy." Imagine that! Making a decision to spend $6 million with three words: Fine and dandy.

Well, the story actually has a few more twists and turns to it, but the net-net of it all (pun intended) is that we opened the 1976-77 season with a home game against the San Antonio Spurs, and leading the charge was Julius Erving, closely followed by a whole roster of marquee names: George McGinnis, Doug Collins, Darryl Dawkins, Lloyd Free, Caldwell Jones, Joe Bryant—a team that the sports reporters instantly dubbed "The Best Team Money Can Buy." Amazingly, however, the best team money could buy went out and lost its first two games. I was convinced that our win column was empty because our roster was too full.

We didn't have a basketball team—we had a flying circus! The 76ers had become such a magnificent array of talent that we were actually overloaded. Everybody wanted twenty shots a night. We had *enormous* skills—but not a *balance* of skills.

We hurriedly began to make corrections. We traded a couple of players, put a couple more on the injured reserve list (medical reason: hangnail, athlete's foot, acute dandruff), and waived a couple of others. Once we pared the team back again, it was still a rambunctious collection of personalities—and I often pitied poor Gene Shue for having to coach this expensive collection of high-powered ball handlers.

After getting off to a rocky 0-2 start, we righted ourselves, eventually winning 50 out of 82 games, and taking the division title. We came close to taking it all, but lost the NBA championship series to the Portland Trailblazers, 4 games to 2.

This whole story—from the acquisition of Billy Cunningham and the emergence of Doug Collins to the surprise signings of

Darryl Dawkins and Dr. J—is all about one thing: Acquiring the best. In an astonishingly short time—from 1974 to 1976—we took the Philadelphia 76ers from the deepest cellar of the NBA to the top of the league. We did it by finding and acquiring the best talent in the game. We scoured every possible hiding place for top talent, from high schools to the top ranks of the NBA and ABA. We even found unexpected treasures of talent on our own bench, when Doug Collins burst off the disabled list and onto the court with incredible quickness and fury.

We also found out that it's possible to overshoot, to have too much of a good thing, to become top-heavy and overbalanced with too much talent. When that happens, you need to take a hard look at your team chemistry and how well your players' skills and personalities fit the slot you've assigned them to. And sometimes you have to prune the team like you would prune a tree. Pruning hurts, but pruning often helps a tree—or a team—to be more fruitful. To be successful, a team must have the highest caliber people, and they must be able to operate in sync, in harmony, and in balance.

For the past three-and-a-half decades, Caliper Human Strategies, Inc., has been using tests to hire prospects for corporations and professional sports franchises, including our own Orlando Magic. According to Caliper's president and CEO, Herb Greenberg, the company has tested around a million people and has made an in-depth study of the attributes that predict success in both business and sports. Not surprisingly, once you get past the obvious physical requirements of professional athletics, those attributes that produce success in one field are pretty much the same as those that produce success in any other:

- competitiveness—an unquenchable desire to win and succeed (a desirable quality in any player or employee);
- assertiveness—the ability to present oneself unabashedly and lead strongly without being pushy, inconsiderate, or bullying (an especially important asset in management and sales positions);
- aggressiveness—not the same as assertiveness, aggressiveness is the drive to push obstacles out of the way and cre-

ate opportunities, a trait with both positive and strongly negative potential, depending on whether or not the individual has his aggressiveness under control (an aggressive defensive lineman can win football games by running right over the other team to sack the quarterback, while an overly aggressive basketball player will foul out in the first half and a high-pressure salesman can drive away customers);

- ego-strength—in business or athletics, you want players who can take rejection with optimism and grace, and bounce back from failure; and
- self-discipline—you want players who are self-starting, self-motivated individuals who will start early, stay late, practice, improve their skills, plan, and organize themselves without the boss or the coach standing over them with a stick.

According to Herb Greenberg, if you're waiting for the perfect applicant or the perfect team player, you're going to have a long wait ahead of you. But if you focus on people who provide a good balance of these traits for the particular position you seek to fill, then you will likely be assured of team success.

TEAM DEVELOPMENT

To sum up, the five steps to acquiring top talent and building a winning team are:

Step 1: Assess ability
Step 2: Choose coachable people
Step 3: Think "chemistry"
Step 4: Strive for balance
Step 5: Recruit the best

Then, once you have acquired the quality and balance of talent to make a winning team, you need to *develop* your team in order to keep winning over the long haul. In the various sports organizations I've worked for, we have attempted to develop our talent in four essential areas:

- The physical dimension
- The skill dimension
- The emotional dimension
- The spiritual dimension

Let's take a closer look at each of these dimensions.

Developing the Physical Dimension

In the field of athletics, the need to develop and maintain a player's physical being is obvious. Physical development has become a huge industry-within-an-industry in the sports world today. All pro teams now have coaches, trainers, therapists, and specialists who are accountable to develop and maintain specific aspects of the players' physical health: weight training, flexibility, nutrition—a myriad of disciplines devoted to the physical side of ballplayers. In past years, when I first got into the sports business, these things were not only never done, they were never even imagined. Today, it is commonplace. The goal is to get every last ounce of advantage out of an athlete's physical being, to stretch that athlete's skills to just a little higher level, so that we can get just that much closer to an NBA championship, a World Series, or a Super Bowl.

The physical dimension of a player is, perhaps, a little less important if we take it out of the sports realm and begin talking about a business team or a ministry team or a family team. Notice, I say "a little less important"—but *not* unimportant. The physical dimension of your players is still important no matter what kind of team you are fielding, no matter what arena you play in.

I'm not saying you should avoid hiring people with physical handicaps—people with physical impairments, matched to the right job, are often the most productive employees you can find. I'm saying that when you as an employer or team-builder make it easier for your employees to stay in good physical shape, the money you spend on HMOs, fitness club memberships, on-site gym equipment, health-related incentives and awards, and work time reserved for fitness and exercise activities can often pay tangible dividends to you and your bottom line.

Not long ago, the L.A. Clippers were in town for an exhibition game. The Clippers' head coach, Bill Fitch, is a good friend. Now in his sixties, he has coached in the NBA for almost thirty years—in Cleveland, Boston, Houston, New Jersey, and now in L.A. About two months before training camp, he was going through an airport and started having trouble breathing. He was rushed to the hospital for an examination, and the doctors instantly took him in for triple bypass surgery. Just a couple of months later, he was back coaching again.

Bill and I talked about it, and he said, "Pat, I did it to myself. We can talk about genes and heredity and all that, but the fact is that for thirty years or more, that's the lifestyle I've been in: eating improperly, not taking care of myself, not getting proper exercise—it was just a matter of time. There were just some things I thought I couldn't change about my lifestyle—but I have now. When I used to eat, I'd eat in the film room—always fast food, always ordering the fried food. I needed a hand free to run the remote control to the VCR, so if I couldn't eat it one-handed, I didn't eat it. Well, no more remote-control eating for me. I can't eat those french fries anymore."

The point is clear: Whether you're a leader or a player, you've got to look after the physical dimension. Whatever your team, whatever your game, make sure you and your players keep in great shape. It makes the team run a whole lot smoother.

Developing the Skill Dimension

The greatest players of any game don't feel that they have arrived once they get to the pros—they know that they have only stepped up to the next level of play and that even higher levels await them. They listen to coaches and veteran players, and they continue to learn, grow, and sharpen their skills. Winning teams provide personnel and programs to help those players in their effort to step up to the next level, and the level after that, and the level after that. Winning coaches and players spend hours and hours drilling, studying game film, and strengthening their passing, shooting, rebounding, and defending skills.

The same should be true of any team, any player, any endeavor. Whatever team you're on, keep growing, keep reaching for the next level. And if you are in the role of "team owner" or "team coach"—that is, if you are a manager, executive, business owner, pastor, or parent—keep looking for ways to help your team stay on the growing edge. Employees need to be continually exposed to skill-sharpening experiences—on-the-job training, seminars, in-services, and so forth. Your family team needs continual experiences and challenges in such areas as athletics, music, dance, scouting, camping, 4-H, continuing education, and on and on.

One of the most important skills any team needs to work on is the skill of communicating. Staying connected with your other team members is crucial to the team's success. Bert Decker is founder and president of Decker Communications, Inc., a training firm that has trained thousands of people—from leading politicians to corporate heads to middle managers to salespeople—in the skills of effective communication. In his book *You've Got to Be Believed to Be Heard,* Decker observes,

> To be effective communicators we must be able not only to talk, but to listen. At first glance, communication appears to be 50 percent speaking and 50 percent listening. You talk, I listen. I talk, you listen. Fifty-fifty. But communication doesn't work that way in the real world.
>
> In a study conducted by Decker Communications, we found that top-level business executives spend about 80 percent of their time communicating, and their time spent in different types of communicating activities is:
>
> Listening 45 percent
> Speaking 30 percent
> Reading 16 percent
> Writing 9 percent

If businesspeople spend about 80 percent of their day communicating, and the bulk of that communicating time is spent speaking or listening, then it becomes clear that speaking and listening are team skills we would do well to sharpen and strengthen. To do so, we may need to take a course or two in speech communication at the local junior college, or take a course from Mr. Decker himself, or—if there are communication needs within a family—talk to a counselor and sharpen our relational skills.

Developing the Emotional Dimension

Developing the emotional side of a ballplayer or any team player is harder than developing the physical and skill dimensions. An individual's emotional development is closely related to his or her overall maturation. I don't mean *chronological* maturation; I've known people in their sixties and seventies who were completely immature in their approach to life, and I've known people in their twenties and even their teens who were wise far beyond their years. Emotional strength and maturity are demonstrated in such qualities as:

- The ability to remain cool and poised under pressure;
- A willingness to shoulder personal responsibility;
- A tendency to solve problems rather than gripe about them;
- A strong work ethic;
- The ability to self-start and self-motivate;
- Respect for self and others;
- The ability to focus and stay on task;
- The ability to celebrate—not be threatened by—others' achievements;
- A willingness to sacrifice for the team effort.

Developing the Spiritual Dimension

In April 1996, *Sports Illustrated* devoted a cover story to the spiritual dimension of one of the greatest players in the game of basketball, David Robinson. I immediately made that article required reading for all of my kids. Though raised in a Christian home and "forced" to attend church and Sunday school in early life by his devout mother, the San Antonio Spurs' seven-foot-one star center dates his spiritual rebirth as having occurred on June 8, 1991, several years after his emergence as one of the mighty men of the NBA. Before committing his life to Christ, David was strongly encouraged to read the Bible by Greg Ball, a "locker-room evangelist" with Champions for Christ. Once David started reading the Bible, he couldn't put it down. Realizing he had discovered the "owner's manual" for the human soul, he became absorbed in the practical, applicable life truths he found in the pages of the Bible.

David Robinson credits his relationship with Jesus Christ as the single factor that has enabled him to keep his bearings in the world of professional sports—a world that has consumed many unwary young athletes. Robinson has seen more than a few promising young lives destroyed by success. Money, sex, and drugs are readily available to the gifted young men of professional sports who pull down salaries of six or seven figures a year. David doesn't want his marriage to be destroyed by his success. A Goliath in stature, this David is a tower of moral and spiritual strength.

"I made a rule when I got married," he told *S.I.* "I decided that if anyone's feelings are going to be hurt, they're not going to be my wife's." Sexual temptation, he says, is "the oldest trick in the book, the naked lady offering an apple," and he is so serious about avoiding sexual temptation that he even avoids watching the Spurs' cheerleaders performing on-court during breaks in the game. He asks close friends to hold him accountable. "Tell me if I ever change," he says. Even after winning the NBA Rookie of the Year award in 1990, after being named league MVP in 1995, and after landing a six-year, $66 million contract, David Robinson keeps his feet on the ground, and his hat size is the same as it ever was.

In addition to the money he receives from the Spurs, he earns endorsement cash from companies like Nike, Arrow shirts, Casio, Franklin sporting goods, and Frito-Lay—all brands he likes, and which do not raise any conflict with his position as a Christian role model. Much of that money goes to Christian and social charities, including his own David Robinson Foundation, which serves the needs of young people in South Texas.

He signs autographs for free—an increasingly rare grace among sports figures nowadays—and adds a reference to a Bible passage after his signature and jersey number, 50.

Alongside fellow evangelical Christian Avery Johnson, the Spurs' tough point guard, Robinson often leads pregame prayer for the team. Players like Johnson and Robinson exemplify a principle I have seen at work again and again in the arena of sports competition: A competitor with a well-developed spiritual dimension tends to be more intense, more tenacious, more committed to excellence in his game. Like many intensely spiritual athletes, Robinson sees his basketball ability as a gift from God, and he believes that the best way he can serve God is by using his God-given ability to the max.

"I'm not playing for the fans or the money, but to honor God," he told *Sports Illustrated*. "I know my motivation. I know where I'm headed. Every night I try to go out there to honor Him and play great. . . . I found the Lord, and since then everything has been like a magic walk."[2]

One of the most exciting things I have seen in college and pro sports over the last few decades has been the increase in spirituality among athletes. God has raised up some very special people of faith in the sports world: from '50s baseball stars like Bobby Richardson of the Yankees, American League outfielder Albie Pearson, Randy Hundley of the Cubs, and Jim Kaat of the Twins, all of whom used their public platform to share their faith; to NFL defensive end Bill Glass, who practically invented team chapel services back in the '60s; to my friend John Tolson, who started chapel services for the Houston Rockets in the mid-'70s, and Bobby Jones who began the Philadelphia 76ers chapels in 1979. Today, Pro Basketball Fellowship is one of the strongest fellowship groups in pro sports, quietly impacting the sport and changing lives.

The spiritual dimension is crucial to any team in any arena of endeavor. Players who stay in sync with God tend to stay in sync with each other, too.

TURNOVER—A TEAM KILLER

Once you've acquired top talent for your team, you have to find a way to hang onto them. Low turnover of key people is crucial to the success of a great team. You hire the right people to run your office and to run your basketball team—and then you stay with them. You can't field a successful team if people are continually moving in and out of team positions as if your team was a revolving door. Through thick and thin, you have to stay with them and give them reasons to stay with you.

And that's not easy, is it? Today's workforce is the most mobile workforce in American history. A 1993 Small Business Administration study found that companies with fewer than 100 employees suffered 15.2 percent annual turnover, compared with 9 percent for larger firms. Many experts believe that, in view of widespread corporate cost-cutting and downsizing, those numbers are probably much higher today. And when it costs between $5,700 and $50,000 to replace a lost worker with a new worker, it becomes easy to see that the cost of high turnover can be a killer for both large and small companies.

So, what's the solution? More money? Better benefits? Obviously, it never hurts to sweeten the pot. Money—from salary to health benefits to paid vacation to paid retirement programs—is certainly an important consideration to every employee. It can often be a false economy to underpay workers, then have to deal with the high (and often hidden) costs of high employee turnover.

But quite often, the key to lower team turnover has more to do with emotional satisfaction than with money alone. You can reduce turnover by making sure players feel valued and affirmed, that their jobs are meaningful and exciting, that there is room for growth and advancement, that the team recognizes their contributions, that they are listened to, that the team has a strong vision or goal, and that they work in a happy, positive, family-like environment. A recent study of 110 entrepreneurial companies by the Center for Creative Leadership in San Diego showed that companies whose leadership was rated high in ethics, employee motivation, employee development, and communication enjoyed lower turnover and 20 percent higher profits.[3]

At the Magic, many of our key administrative people have been here right from the beginning. They've learned to mesh together and be successful together. We try to live by the dictum of Dallas businessman John Stemmons, who said, "Find some people who are comers, who are going to be achievers in their own field, and people you can trust—then grow old together."

MAKE TODAY PAY OFF TOMORROW

The final—and perhaps most important—thing I have to say about acquiring top talent to build a successful team is this:

Invest for the long range. Make today pay off tomorrow.

So many teams make the mistake of living only for today. In order to be successful and maintain your success as a team, you have to do the things today that will pay off tomorrow. You have to plow some ground, plant some seeds, and do some watering if you're ever going to reap a harvest. A woman named Anne Scheiber understood this principle.

After a twenty-three-year career, Anne Scheiber retired from her job with the IRS in 1944. During all those years, she never earned more than $4,000 a year and never received a promotion despite having a law degree and leading her office in turning up underpayments and underreporting. Upon her retirement, she took her $5,000 in savings and invested it in the stock market. Some fifty years later, in January 1995, Anne died at age 101. By that time, her $5,000 investment had grown to $22 million in stocks. She made all of her own investment decisions, scouring the *Wall Street Journal* every day, and her portfolio included such companies as Paramount and Coca-Cola. She willed all of her stock holdings to Yeshiva University in New York—a university that had never even heard of her. Here was a lady who invested for the future—big-time.

Building a team requires a different kind of investment—an investment in human lives. The Magic organization has been very good at that, and one of the reasons is that our owner, Rich DeVos and the entire DeVos Family are so incredibly people-oriented. They really believe in making an investment in the lives of everyone in our organization, from the players who run the floor to the guy who sweeps the floors. Rich personally gives time to the team, taking a genuine interest in their lives, imparting his life values to them, showing them that they are more than just athletes, that they really can impact society.

In late March of '96, out of a clear blue sky, I received living proof of the importance of investing in the future. A fax arrived on my desk in Orlando. It read,

Dear Mr. Williams,

On March 20th, my wife, three children, and I had the opportunity to attend the Celtics-Magic game at the Fleet Center in Boston. We had the good fortune of sitting on courtside seats, directly across from the Magic bench. This was particularly fortunate because my nine-year-old daughter, Kelly, lives and dies with Shaq, Penny, Horace Grant, Dennis "3D" Scott, and the rest of the Magic. Kelly, attired in her Magic sweatshirt, her Magic hat, and her official Magic game jersey, was not to be denied!

Front row seats watching the Celtics versus the Magic with my family—what a thrill! And it only gets better!

During pre-game warmups, my little Kelly was getting a piece of gum for herself. Just then, Horace Grant looked over to her. Kelly then held up a piece of gum for Horace. He came over, said he would love a piece of gum. That was the beginning of a two-hour friendship between Mr. Grant and Kelly—it was noticed by a lot of fans seated around us and will never be forgotten by this family!

During the game, Horace would turn and give Kelly a wink and a smile, or he would give the ball to Kelly and Kelly would toss it to the ref to put it back in play. He made Kelly feel like she was the sixth Magic on the court!

The crowning glory came with about two minutes left in the game. A time-out was called. Horace left the bench, walked over to Kelly, and presented her with an autographed towel—a souvenir for life!

Mr. Williams, you should be very proud of your team and especially Horace Grant. We sure are!

Sincerely,
Tom Monahan and family
Nashua, New Hampshire

I don't know if Horace knew it or not, but he was making an incredible investment in the life of that nine-year-old girl, Kelly Monahan. Her life has been impacted forever because of what he did that night. And there's more to this story—a lot more! About a week after I got the fax, a package arrived for Horace via FedEx, and in the package were three items—a pack of Big Red cinnamon gum, a photograph of Horace handing Kelly the towel, and a handwritten letter from Kelly to Horace. The letter read:

Dear Horace,
I'm the girl in the front row in Boston, with the gum. Thank you so much for your towel. It really means a lot to me. My whole family thought you were nice. Please say "hi" to everyone on your team for me. Write back when you can.

Love,
Kelly Monahan
P.S. You played awesome on Wednesday!

Now, here's the exciting footnote to this story:

A couple of weeks later, on April 15, I ran in the 100th running of the Boston Marathon. I'll never forget what it felt like, lining up in Hopkinton, Massachusetts, 26.2 miles from downtown Boston, with more than forty thousand runners. As the race began and the throngs of runners moved out to the cheers of thousands of spectators along the street, the excitement I felt was beyond anything I can describe. Mile by mile, however, the excitement gave way to pain and fatigue. My feet, calves, and hamstrings got sore, my lungs began to strain, my heart began to hammer against my ribcage.

Around the twentieth mile of the race, you're faced with a huge, daunting challenge: Heartbreak Hill. That hill has doomed many a runner over the past hundred years. Somehow or other, I managed to get to the top of Heartbreak Hill. At that point, I knew I had about six miles to go, but my body was screaming.

Just as I was coming down on the other side of the hill, I heard my name being called from the crowd: "Pat Williams!"

I was kind of spaced out at that point, and I thought someone must have been calling some *other* Pat Williams, so I didn't respond.

Then I heard it again, from a short distance behind me: "Pat! Pat Williams!" I looked over my shoulder, and there was a man on the sidewalk, waving and yelling at me: "Pat! Tom Monahan from Nashua, New Hampshire!" I turned around and jogged toward him.

Tom waved me back, and said, "No, I didn't want you to stop! You need to keep going!"

"Tom," I wheezed, "I'm coming to shake your hand!" Just knowing I had someone there on the downside of Heartbreak Hill, pulling for me and cheering for me, put new spring into my step and new strength into my muscles. I reached out and grabbed his hand and thanked him for coming; then I said, "Where's Kelly?"

A pretty nine-year-old girl stepped forward. She held up a handmade sign. My mind was a little fuzzy from exhaustion at that point, but I think it said something like, "GO MAGIC! HANG IN THERE, PAT!" "Hi, Mr. Williams!" she said, beaming.

"Call me Pat," I said—and in my sweaty T-shirt, I leaned over and gave her a big hug. Then Kelly and her dad waved me off, and I rejoined my fellow runners, refreshed and re-energized for the last few miles of my run.

Something very special happened at that moment. I realized as I was running that a past investment had paid off in a number of lives, including mine. Rich DeVos has always stressed to our players the importance of making a positive difference in the lives of others. A few weeks earlier, at the Fleet Center in Boston, one of those players, Horace Grant, had done just that, making an investment in the life of a nine-year-old girl he didn't even know. Three weeks later, that same girl and her father returned to Boston and stood along the marathon route, waiting to make an investment of encouragement in my life, as I took on the biggest athletic challenge of my entire career.

Thanks, Kelly. Thanks, Tom. I'm so glad you're on my team!

Principle 2

Be a
Great Leader

I had a speaking engagement over the Fourth of July, 1996, in Kansas City, Missouri. Wherever I am, even away from home, I try to get a good run in every day. So I came out of my hotel and turned left on Main Street, Kansas City. When I got to the corner of 40th and Main, I noticed, off to my left, a little park area. In the park area was a memorial— not a statue, just a rather large, simple, dignified marker. I'm always curious about such things, so I veered over toward it and looked it over as I jogged in place.

Reading the inscription on it, I saw that the memorial was dedicated to a K.C. native, Major Murray Davis, who was killed at Exermont, France, on September 28, 1918, during World War I. On one side of the monument, chiseled into the stone, were these words:

A KINDLY, JUST, AND BELOVED
OFFICER, WISE IN COUNSEL,
RESOLUTE IN ACTION,
COURAGEOUS UNTO DEATH.

Intrigued to learn more of this man, I jogged around to the other side of the monument and read further:

SERIOUSLY WOUNDED, HE
REFUSED TO RELINQUISH HIS
COMMAND UNTIL, MORTALLY
WOUNDED, HE FELL, LEADING
HIS COMRADES TO VICTORY.
HIS LAST WORDS WERE,
"TAKE CARE OF MY MEN."

As I read those words, I thought, *Murray Davis must have been some awesome leader!* In fact, he may have exemplified everything I want to share in this chapter. Leadership often entails incredible courage and sacrifice, as the spirit of Major Murray Davis testifies.

Leadership is not for wimps.

NBA Hall of Fame coach Chuck Daly, now the coach of the Magic, is a man I really admire and respect as a team leader and as a person. He led the Detroit Pistons to a couple of championships and coached the 1992 Dream Team in the Olympics, so he really knows what he's talking about. Reflecting on his coaching days, he said, "I was like a pilot in a storm. My job was to get the plane through the storm and land it safely."

Anyone who is a leader—a team leader, a business leader, a political leader, a church leader, a family leader—has the same task before him or her. There are storms along the way—always have been, always will be. In fact, if there weren't any storms, you wouldn't need leaders. Leadership must be exercised in the midst of lightning, thunder, crosswinds, headwinds, updrafts, downdrafts, windshear—and while the people in the plane along with you are screaming in terror, while your own heart is pounding out the macarena, you've got to keep a cool, calm smile on your face and show 'em there's nothing to be concerned about.

Yessir, leadership is definitely not for wimps. And without leadership, there is no teamwork.

Having interviewed coaches, sports executives, and business executives across the country, I've identified six qualities that all effective team leaders must possess. In the rest of this chapter, we'll take a good, hard look at each of these qualities:

1. Vision
2. Communication Skills
3. People Skills
4. Character
5. Competence
6. Boldness

These six qualities are not in order of importance or priority. If I could, I'd make them *all* Number 1—but you have to start somewhere. So let's start with . . .

LEADERSHIP QUALITY NUMBER 1: VISION

When you walk into our office here at the Orlando Magic, the first thing you see is our vision statement, molded in metal relief, hanging in our lobby. It reads:

The vision of the Orlando Magic is to be recognized as the professional sports model of the 21st Century by exemplifying the principles and practices of a championship organization in both the sport and business of basketball. We intend to achieve world-class status as a franchise through unwavering commitment to integrity, service, quality, and consumer value, while emphasizing the partnership among our community, our fans, our coaches, our players, our staff, and our owners.

That is our vision. All of us in the Magic organization have this vision before us every hour of every day as we carry out our tasks and fill our roles. Explicitly stated in this vision are our dreams and values as a team, as a model sports organization for the next century. Our dream is to "be recognized as the professional sports model of the 21st Century." Our values are "integrity, service, quality, and consumer value" and we are committed unswervingly, daily, moment by moment, to living our lives and conducting our business according to those values.

Every winning team has a vision. Without it, a team will never succeed. In fact, without a vision, a team can't even know what success is and won't even know how to get there. Your vision is your definition of what success is to you as a team. It is what pulls you along. It is what you struggle for, compete for, fight for, sacrifice for.

A vision is more than a set of goals. Often, a boss or a coach sets up a list of quotas or standards he wants the team to meet. He says, "These are our goals," and he thinks he has articulated a team vision. But a vision is far more than a set of quotas. A true vision gives the team more than just a target to shoot for; it gives the team a *mission,* a sense of purpose to get excited about. It gives the team a reason for being charged up, enthused, and motivated.

The people in our Magic organization believe they are involved in a very special enterprise. From top to bottom, from the front office to the locker rooms, our players are excited about the vision of becoming *the* professional sports model of the twenty-first century. Our vision is not winning an NBA championship. That's certainly one of our goals, and it's a goal that would go a long way toward achieving our vision of becoming the professional sports model of the twenty-first century. But we don't confuse goals and vision. Our vision is larger, grander, even more exciting than our goals. Our vision inspires us and empowers us to reach for our goals and to make our dreams come true. All leaders and teams have the ability to set goals. But great leaders and great teams are driven by a *vision*—a true sense of mission and purpose.

Once the team has a clear sense of mission and purpose to get charged up about, you are ready to roll, you are ready to sound the charge to battle. "Vision is the essence of leadership," said Notre Dame University president Father Theodore Hesburgh. "Knowing where you want to go requires three things: Having a clear vision, articulating it well, and getting your team enthusiastic about sharing it. Above all, any leader must be consistent. As the Bible says, no one follows an uncertain trumpet."

LEADERSHIP QUALITY NUMBER 2: COMMUNICATION SKILLS

So you have formulated your vision—now what do you do? Well, your grand team vision is worthless if you, as a leader, cannot sell that vision to your team! Whether you know it or not, if you are a leader, you are a salesman. You've got to sell your vision to your players—not as "*my* vision for this team," but as "*our* vision for success." This is true whether you are selling a basketball team on a new strategy or your kids on a new set of family rules.

What about you? How are you doing at communicating your team vision to your players? Here are some ideas I've gathered that can make you a better leader-communicator in your team environment:

Communicate Optimism

Be upbeat and enthusiastic. Communicate enthusiasm, encouragement, and praise. When you speak, put your shoulders back, smile, and project supreme confidence. When problems arise, let your players see you approaching those problems with assurance, cheerfulness, and a can-do attitude. Put energy and enthusiasm in your voice when you communicate with the troops. Optimism is contagious—and *optimism wins*.

Jim Frey, former manager of the Chicago Cubs, put it this way: Leadership, he said, "is where you lose four straight games in August and you lie awake all night trying to think what to do and you get up not knowing the answer. Then you come into the clubhouse the next day, smiling and clapping your hands, and you say, 'All right, everybody relax. We've got 'em now!'"

Former Los Angeles Dodger manager Tommy Lasorda once said to me that the key to his success was his attitude. "As a leader, the most important thing I did took place at the clubhouse door every day. Whether I was tired or discouraged or upset, I'd always put on a different face at the door. It was my upbeat, competitive, confident, enthusiastic face. If my players saw me down and depressed that would have spread all over the clubhouse. In the same way, if my players saw their manager excited and optimistic, that would infect them and help them play better."

Those are the words and actions of two men who know how to communicate optimism.

Become a Storyteller

Stories are the best way to make your point forcefully and memorably. When people hear you tell a story, their imaginations are engaged, forming pictures in their minds, triggering emotions that cause your message to be imprinted on their minds. All the great communicators of history, from Jesus Christ to Abraham Lincoln to Winston Churchill to Walt Disney to JFK to Ronald Reagan, communicated largely through the medium of stories.

One of the greatest American storytellers was Herman Melville, author of *Moby Dick*. One evening, Melville visited with his friend and fellow storyteller Nathaniel Hawthorne. During the visit, Melville told Hawthorne and his wife a story about an adventure he had on a South Sea island. As he told the story, he strode around the room, acting out a battle he witnessed between two groups of island warriors. The Hawthornes were enthralled by Melville's swashbuckling story, told with wild gestures and vivid word pictures.

The next day, Hawthorne stopped by Melville's house and said, "I'd like to take another look at that club."

"What club?" asked Melville.

"The one you were swinging about your head while you were telling us about your adventures in the South Seas," said Hawthorne.

"But I had no club!" said Melville. In fact, it took Melville several minutes to convince his friend that there had never been any club. His storytelling had been so vivid and convincing, that both Hawthorne and his wife were *certain* Melville had been swinging an authentic Polynesian war club as he told his story!

That's the power of good storytelling. When you communicate with stories, believing is seeing!

Check the Perceptions of Your Players

Make sure they understand and can articulate the team vision and goals. Remember that communication is not a matter of what you say, but of *what they hear you say.* Communication often gets distorted somewhere between the speaker and the hearer. If you find your message has not gotten through the first time, patiently restate and re-restate it until you know you have been heard and understood, and that the team has captured and internalized the team vision and goals.

Fred Smith, the great motivational speaker and founder of Federal Express, proudly tells a story that illustrates how his company has communicated its vision to every player on the Federal Express team:

> Lucy Nygen is a Federal Express service agent who works in a drive-through center in the middle of a parking lot in Wauwatosa, Wisconsin. One day last fall, one of her regular customers asked her to tell him something about Federal Express, specifically what P-S-P meant. "Why, that's People-Service-Profit, sir . . . that's our corporate philosophy statement." And she went on to explain what it meant.
>
> About two weeks later, the gentleman showed up again. This time he wanted to know how Federal Express measured service. She told him that we measure every shipment that goes through our system, that we count every failure and weigh it by how much trouble that failure causes our customers, and itemize it into one of eleven possible categories. "It's called our SQI—Service Quality Indicator," she told him.
>
> That gentleman appeared a third time and asked her what the Malcolm Baldrige National Quality Award was. She explained that the Department of Commerce sponsored it and that it was the highest award given for quality in the United States. He continued to stop by the drive-through, but he had stopped asking questions. About a month later, it was announced that Federal Express won the Malcolm Baldrige Award. Federal Express was elated, and so was Lucy.
>
> What Lucy didn't know was that the gentleman who had questioned her time and again was the man assigned to be a judge in the final round of the Malcolm Baldrige competition. At the award ceremony in Washington, D.C., he approached several of us and said, "I want to tell you why I argued so strongly for Federal Express to win the Baldrige Award." And he proceeded to tell us about his conversations with Lucy

Nygren. He said, "I figured if one person, working alone in the middle of a parking lot in Wauwatosa, Wisconsin, knew that much about service and quality, Federal Express deserved to win!"

FedEx has obviously learned the secret of communicating its vision of customer service to its team—and there is no doubt that the shared team vision of FedEx has a lot to do with the company's phenomenal success.

Be a Good Listener

One of the leading complaints about leaders is that they often don't listen well. They don't have the patience to listen. Fact is, the best leaders are good listeners. They know that listening is silent flattery. Good listeners are not only well-liked and popular, but they tend to learn a lot more than poor listeners!

I will confess to you that listening does not come easy to me. I'm naturally more of a talker than a listener—but I'm working on it. And it's a good thing I'm working on it, because every day there's a child in the Williams family who wants and needs to be listened to. Many times the child can't even express it. It's a daily discipline for me, trying to read the moods and body language of my kids. The need to be heard may only be demonstrated by a downturned face or a little rebellious behavior or a bit of sulkiness—but my challenge is to look beyond the outward appearance and see a child who feels neglected and misunderstood, a child who wants to be listened to. That's one of my key jobs as a father.

A lot of leaders claim to have an open-door policy, but they don't really listen to people who come in the door. They allow all kinds of distractions and interruptions (such as phone calls) to get in the way of really listening to people. These leaders give little or no eye contact, and often try to get other work done while supposedly "listening." They interrupt and finish sentences for other people. Instead of really hearing what the other person says, they think they already know what the person is going to say—and they have already stopped listening. Instead, they are formulating an answer or argument to what they think the other person is saying.

Listening intently shows you take a player seriously, that you care. Good listeners give focused, undivided attention and continuous eye contact. They listen completely before speaking and then rephrase the speaker's points to show they hear and understand. They set aside plenty of uninterrupted time to hear the matter out. They don't roll their eyes or shake their heads when they hear a point they disagree with. They are not interested in having their own way, but in finding the best way.

Communication is not a one-way street. Whenever we communicate—whether we are talking to God in prayer, talking with the team, or sharing with the family—we must not only talk, we must *listen*. And as you listen, never underestimate the power of silence. Merv Griffin, the businessman-entertainer, used listening and silence effectively to buy Resorts International from Donald Trump. "My ability to listen helped enormously," he said. "When Trump and I sat down, he talked and I listened. He almost collapsed because I just sat there staring at him. He didn't know what to do. He talked for thirty minutes and I never said a word."

IF YOU ARE NOT A NATURAL PUBLIC SPEAKER, GET TRAINING AND PRACTICE

CBS News correspondent Charles Osgood once said, "There are leaders in this world and there are followers. Leaders do better than followers, for the most part. They live in nicer homes, drive better cars, and make more money. Imagine a leader in your mind. Imagine a follower. What is the leader doing? The leader is up there speaking to a group of people. The follower is out there listening." Osgood's point is clear: The defining difference between the greatest leaders and their followers is public speaking—the ability to communicate ideas and beliefs to large numbers of people. If a leader ignores or neglects his or her speaking skills, it is no different from neglecting his or her career.

Former president Gerald Ford is not exactly the most exciting speaker in the world—and that may have been one of the reasons he was not rehired by the American people for a full term in office. With some obvious regret, Ford once reflected, "If I went back to college again, I'd concentrate on two areas: learning to write and learning to speak before an audience. Nothing in life is more important than the ability to communicate effectively." Ford learned the hard way: In order to be an effective, successful leader in any team environment, you've got to be able to communicate with your players.

LEADERSHIP QUALITY NUMBER 3: PEOPLE SKILLS

"I will pay more for the ability to deal with people than any other ability under the sun," said John D. Rockefeller. And J. Paul Getty, when asked what was the most important ingredient in a successful business leader, said, "It doesn't make much difference how much knowledge and experience an executive possesses—if he is unable to achieve results through people, he's worthless as an executive."

We can all improve our people skills—I know I can, and I'm betting you can, too. Here are some skills and attitudes I'm working on in my team environments in the Magic organization, in my community, and in my family:

Be Visible and Available

Let people see that you are involved, accessible, and close to the action. Talk to the team. Visit the locker room or the work site. Ask questions and build relationships.

Let me tell you who's got the art of being visible and available down pat: Tommy Lasorda. The Dodgers conduct spring training near Orlando, in Vero Beach, Florida. In the spring of 1995, the year before he retired as manager of the Dodgers, Tommy called and said he wanted to come to a Magic game that night. So we got some tickets for Tommy and a couple of his coaches. A few hours later, there was a commotion outside the arena. It seems that Tommy had gotten there early and his tickets weren't ready yet. So Tommy was outside "barbering" with a bunch of our fans—no, he wasn't cutting their hair, he was entertaining and chatting with the people.

I went down and personally ushered Tommy into the arena. He had two big packages with him—a Dodger blue jacket for our owner, Rich DeVos, and a nice, blue Dodger sweater for me. He came into the locker room and talked to all the players. Then he went out into the hallway outside the locker room, where a bunch of kids were waiting to meet Shaq and Penny—and did their eyes pop out! They obviously never expected to see an L.A. baseball legend in the hallway of an Orlando basketball arena. Well, Tommy jumped right in and gave them a big motivational speech.

During the game, Tommy was in the stands all night, talking to fans, signing autographs, and whooping and cheering for the Magic like a big kid. At halftime he took part in a three-point shooting contest with pitcher Frank Viola. After the game, he came back in the locker room to continue visiting with the players. There, I introduced him to my son Bobby, who at that time was a ball boy and planning to go to Rollins College to be a catcher. Tommy pulled him aside, talked to him for ten minutes, and told him everything he expected from a future Dodger catcher from Rollins.

About five hours after he arrived, Tommy departed—and I couldn't stop thinking of all the dozens and dozens of people he had talked to, encouraged, challenged, excited, instructed, and impacted that night. Tommy Lasorda is a leader who is available, accessible, and visible among the people. Maybe that's the reason he is so universally loved and respected by both players and fans.

I've seen too many team leaders who—either because they felt too pressured or became too comfortable or felt pulled and tugged in every direction—reacted by isolating themselves. They shut themselves up behind closed doors. They retreated even from their own people, their own players. A leader is really in trouble when he isolates himself and loses touch with people. At that point, the leader has usually had it, he's in trouble, he's lost the team.

I think the leader who taught me the most about being available to people was Bill Veeck, when he was the president of his various baseball teams such as the Cleveland Indians, St. Louis Browns, and Chicago White Sox. He mixed and mingled, was always out front, never had a door on his office, answered his own mail, and never screened his phone calls. He was a marvelous man, and he left a big impact on me that way, to the point that over these past thirty-six years that I've been in sports management, I've tried to run my office the same way.

Praise in Public, Criticize in Private

Public praise inspires and boosts morale. Public criticism destroys team spirit and generates resentment. Always ask questions before reprimanding; make sure you've got your facts straight. Notice the good performance your players do and let them know you appreciate it. "Most of us can run pretty well all day long on one compliment," said Mark Twain. I am convinced encouragement is as vital to the soul as oxygen is to the body.

At the start of my son Bobby's senior year of high school baseball, he had a particularly good game. He was seventeen years old, playing catcher, got two hits, blocked the plate well, threw out a runner, and made a great tag play at the plate. After the game I asked him, "Bobby, what are you going to remember most about this game?"

"Coach Barton shook my hand," he said, "and told me what a great job I did." The words of a leader are never forgotten. *A leader's praise is often remembered more warmly and vividly than the achievement itself!*

On June 2, 1949, Philadelphia Phillies catcher Andy Seminick had a day for the record books. Playing in Philly, Andy hit three home runs in a night game against Cincinnati—including two homers in one inning! Over the years, I got to know Andy and he has become a good friend. In fact, in the two years I played professional baseball in Miami, Andy managed the club. So I ended up playing for my boyhood idol. Every June 2, in little agate type in newspapers across the country, the syndicated column "This Day in Baseball" mentions the feat performed by Andy Seminick on June 2, 1949—a nice little plug.

A couple of years ago, I saw that plug in my local paper, and I thought, *I'm gonna give Andy a call.* So I reached him at his home in Melbourne, Florida. "Hey, Andy," I said, "I just called to tell you that you were in the news again. It was really fun to read about you again. Say, tell me something. What do you remember most about that night?" I thought he would say he remembered the drama, the particular pitch, or that the count was such-and-such. But that's not what he said.

"The thing I most remember," said Andy, "was the next day. I went to my locker and there was a note from the owner, R.R.M. Carpenter Sr., congratulating me and telling me how proud he was of me for hitting those three homers." Imagine that! Here we were, forty-five years later, and the thing he remembered most was a note of praise from the top man in the organization. And there was more. "You know what?" Andy concluded. "Nine days later, Mr. Carpenter was dead. But that kind note of his will never be forgotten."

So knowing how to praise your players is a crucial part of leadership. But praise is only half the story. Sometimes you have to confront a player and hold him accountable. Sometimes you have to be tough. That's a leader's job. That's understood. But a leader should never destroy a player's self-esteem in the process. When you criticize a player, try to do it in private, without shaming him. Let the player know you are confronting him for his own good, because you care, you believe he is capable of more, and you want to see him playing to his full potential.

Chuck Daly tells a wonderful story. He says, "I'm teaching a philosophy class at Duke, some years ago. We meet in a room between two handball courts, and I'm in there one day telling everyone, 'You can get on the players. That's okay, because once they leave the court it's all over, it's forgotten.' No sooner had I said that when this football player gets up and says, 'That's not right! It's *not* forgotten! Whatever you say *is* remembered! You can't get on a player one minute and expect him to forget it the next minute!' The guy caught me by surprise, but that statement has meant as much to me as anything I've ever heard in my coaching career. I learned more in those few minutes than at any other time in my life."

A story illustrating former Pittsburgh Steelers owner Art Rooney's kind spirit concerns Johnny Unitas, the Pittsburgh native whom the Steelers cut from their roster. Rooney's son kept telling him that the team should keep Unitas, but Rooney did not want to interfere with his coach, Walter Kiesling.

As chance would have it, shortly after the quarterback had been let go, Rooney's car—with Kiesling and Rooney in the back seat—happened to pull alongside Unitas's car. Rooney leaned across Kiesling and yelled over to Unitas, "Johnny, I hope you become the greatest quarterback in football."

Bob Brunet, one of the best running backs of the Lombardi-era Washington Redskins, suffered a painful shoulder separation. He walked out of the training camp and retired from football for good. When coach Vince Lombardi was asked why Brunet left, he shrugged. "Maybe he had enough of football—or Lombardi." As it turned out, Brunet had had enough of Lombardi. Though Lombardi was a winning legend among coaches, Brunet told reporters that he didn't respond to the often harsh and verbally insulting Lombardi method. "Things that are said stay with me all day and all night," Brunet said. "Coach Lombardi says he forgets what he says right away, but twenty years from now I will remember *exactly* what he said."

Terry Bradshaw, the great Steelers quarterback, once reflected on the waning days of his incredible career. "When my elbow was hurting near the end of my career," he said, "coach Chuck Noll announced, 'Maybe it's time Mr. Bradshaw got on with his life's work.' To this day, that remark galls me. I thought, 'Why am I being treated like this?' All I wanted at the end of my career was a kind word." Fact is, Terry Bradshaw had earned a kind word at the end of his career. Chuck Noll owed it to him. Leaders owe it to their players to praise in public, criticize in private.

Use Authority Sparingly

One thing I've seen all too often over the years is the leader who is elevated into a leadership position and the power overcomes him. He is not capable of handling power wisely. Some people are just born bossy, that's all. In other cases, power seems to go to a guy's head. Often, you have an individual who has been ordered around all his life; suddenly he rises to a level where he can order other people around—and he uses his little bit of authority with a vengeance. In other cases, people who are otherwise very nice individuals are suddenly thrust into leadership and they feel they have to live up to the image of a powerful leader. In most cases, however, bossiness is nothing more than a sign of insecurity: The leader is scared to death of failing, of being thought of as weak or incompetent—so he overcompensates.

I saw this happen early in my baseball career with the Phillies. A young exec in the major-league office was promoted to a major leadership role with the club. He had been very effective in his secondary role, and everybody had really liked him because he was one of the guys. Once he was promoted, however, he took his leadership role and absolutely abused it. He needed to dominate, intimidate, have everybody under his thumb, impress everybody with what a big shot he was. He was a classic example of not using power wisely—and he didn't last very long in that job.

I believe all team leaders should set a goal of never interfering with the freedom, initiative, and aspirations of their players unless it is absolutely necessary for the success of the team. To me, a leader who wields his authority as a club or continually forces players to choke down their pride as individuals is not a true leader. He's just a boss.

Cultivate a Healthy Sense of Humor

Nothing is more unpleasant to be around than a leader who is a grim, gray, humorless stiff. Herm Albright said, "Laughing a hundred times a day yields the same cardiovascular workout as ten minutes of rowing. During a good belly-laugh, your heart rate can top 120 beats a minute. So laugh it up! It's good for you."

And sports entrepreneur Mark McCormack said, "Common sense aside, the most important asset in business is a sense of humor—an ability to laugh at yourself or the situation. Laughter is the most potent constructive force for defusing business tension—and you want to be the one who controls it. If you can point out what is humorous or absurd about a situation or confrontation, then defuse the tension by getting the other party to share your feeling, you'll be guaranteed the upper hand. . . . I've never seen it fail."

Never Allow Murmuring

There is nothing more disruptive to a team than murmuring and complaining. In every sports team, every family, every company, every church, murmuring can run rampant—and when it does, it can destroy you. Matty Guokas, our first coach with the Magic and now a sports broadcaster, referred to murmuring players as "chirpers." After his first year here, he said, "We've got a problem in our locker room. We've got too many chirpers— and we're going to start weeding them out." So, little by little, we began to deal off the chirpers to other teams, and the Magic became a stronger team as a result.

It cuts both ways—a leader can be a murmurer as well. If he complains to his staff or others in the organization, murmuring about players or the officiating or the ownership, he sets a horrible example to the team—and he creates dissension, unhappiness, and negativity. Any little bit of murmuring, from the top down or the bottom up, can soon become a dangerous epidemic. FedEx founder Fred Smith gives us the simple antidote: Say nice things. "One of my bosses," he recalls, "had a way of saying nice things about his workers that got back to them. They were true things but nice things. We appreciated it. And we couldn't keep from trying to do more things that he could tell others about. People will work hard to uphold a good reputation." If you've got to have murmuring in your organization, make sure it's only the good kind, the positive kind. Make sure when you and others in your organization talk behind others' backs, you only say nice things.

Cultivate a Healthy Respect for Your Leadership

Not fear. Not love. Not hate. *Respect.*

Having people skills and being a people person doesn't necessarily mean you have to be a "buddy" to your team. Obviously, friendship and love should be a part of many team environments, such as a family or a church. But in some team environments, it may actually work against you to "buddy up" to your players too much. The great NFL coach Don Shula puts it this way: "Lots of leaders want to be popular. I never cared about that. I want to be respected." And Stormin' Norman Schwarzkopf agrees: "I've met a lot of leaders who were never loved. I have never met a great leader who was not respected."

When John Wooden coached at UCLA, he said to his players, "I like some of you more than others, but I promise you I'll treat you all the same on the court."

I recently read an article about Dean Smith, basketball coach at North Carolina, describing how he maintains discipline and respect for his authority. He makes sure his players know that being on the court is a privilege, not a right, and he demands that they respect his authority by training hard, playing hard, attending all team activities, standing from the bench to applaud and encourage teammates on the floor, attend classes, and follow directions. "I think as a coach, I can manage discipline and command respect because I have in my hands the one thing players must have," he said, "and that's playing time." You cut a player's playing time and other privileges, and he may not like you—but he'll soon learn to respect you and to follow your directions as leader of the team.

LEADERSHIP QUALITY NUMBER 4: CHARACTER

I once heard General Schwarzkopf when he came to speak in Orlando. "People choose their leaders based on character," he said. "I admire men of character. I judge character not by how men deal with their superiors, but by how they deal with their subordinates. That's how you find out what the character of a man is. Leaders have to lead by example."

A leader must have character. As John Maxwell observed, "People buy into the leader before they buy into the leader's vision." The stress of competition and combat is the refining fire of leadership, proving the mettle of a leader's character, testing whether or not he has what it takes to lead the team. A leader who has little character soon has few followers—and little success. Authentic character is made up of a number of crucial qualities:

Be Humble

One of the perils of leadership is that it so often leads to arrogance. Because we lead, because we are visible, because we have power and authority, we get the idea that we are more important than other people. I truly believe that personal ruin almost always begins with the little thought, *Ain't I great!*

One of the true leaders in the sports world is my friend Reggie White, defensive end for the Super Bowl XXXI Champion Green Bay Packers. As the NFL all-time sack leader and as a Christian pastor, "the Minister of Defense" is a role model to athletes and young people, a motivational inspiration to all, and a leader in the fight for racial justice in America. In his book *In the Trenches,* he makes this powerful, humble observation:

> A lot of people look at athletes as role models. I try to live in constant awareness of that responsibility. I try to live a certain way, in the hope that my life might have some effect on other lives. But I also try to keep it all in perspective. Football has made me a celebrity, and I accept that—but I don't glory in that for my own ego-enlargement. I understand and continually remind myself of something that I think a lot of celebrities forget: Celebrities don't deserve to be celebrities. Celebrities have not acquired godhood simply because they are idolized by the public. The fact is, celebrities—athletes, actors, authors, entertainers—are the most overrated people in America. People make heroes out of us and say that we are great. Most of us in the entertainment business (and let's face it, professional sports is nothing more or less than entertainment) do not use our celebrity status wisely or well. We do not use it for the benefit of others. In fact, many of us end up being killed by our celebrity status—by the money, power, sex, and drugs it can bring our way.
>
> As celebrities, we have achieved a level we don't deserve—but since God has allowed me to share in it, I will use that platform to tell people that God isn't going to let Reggie White into

heaven because of who he is but because of the change in Reggie White's heart; to tell people that God has a plan for lifting up people and for healing the division between the races. Every person in the world, every homeless derelict on every sewer grate and park bench in America, every criminal on death row, every person working to feed a family on minimum wage, is as important in God's eyes as the football stars and talk show hosts and movie stars that the public praises and follows. When I face the final judgment, God isn't going to ask me how many Pro Bowls I played in or ask me to recite my stats. He's going to ask me if I knew Jesus, and if I helped to bind up the wounds of people.[1]

Don Keough, the former president of Coca-Cola, is a very humble man. One day, he and the CEO of McDonald's were part of a grand opening and were in a McDonald's restaurant, actually waiting on customers. Don's job was to dispense Coke. After spending an hour or so filling cups with ice and Coke, he turned to the young lady next to him who was filling hamburger orders and said, "How am I doing?"

"Well, Mr. Keough," she said, "you're a very nice man, but you're kind of slow filling those cups."

Humility is probably the last quality most people think of when they consider what it takes to be a leader—but humility is an indispensable quality for all those who aspire to be *great* leaders.

Maintain Absolute Integrity

Billy Graham, at age seventy-seven, was asked how he'd like to be remembered. He replied, "That I was faithful to what God wanted me to do, that I maintained integrity in every area of my life, and that I lived what I preached."

According to thirteen hundred senior executives who responded to a recent survey, integrity is the human quality most necessary to business and team success. Seventy-one percent put it at the top of a list of sixteen traits responsible for enhancing a leader's effectiveness.

The dictionary defines integrity as the state of being complete and unified. When people have integrity, their words and deeds match up, no matter where they are or who they are with. People with integrity are not divided (that's duplicity) or merely pretending (that's hypocrisy). They are whole, and their lives are put together so tightly you can't find the seam. People with integrity have nothing to hide and nothing to fear. Their lives are open books.

Integrity means doing what is right, even when no one else can see you. Integrity means doing what is right, even when it costs you, even when it hurts, even when it's unpopular. Integrity means you don't fudge on ethics, you don't shade the facts a little on your income taxes, you don't slip a few office supplies in your briefcase to take home at the end of the day, you don't compromise the truth. Your integrity and the example of your life shape not only your own decisions and leadership style, but also the team atmosphere.

The Richard DeVos Sports organization, which owns the Orlando Magic, emphasizes integrity as a key ingredient of our winning formula. One of our organizational values statements puts it plainly in black and white:

> In the spirit of good sportsmanship, RDV Sports will do whatever is right and honest while treating all individuals with respect. We acknowledge that we make a living by what we get, but we make a life by what we give.

John Feinstein tells the story about golfer Davis Love III. In 1994, Love was having a great game in the second round of the Western Open. On one hole, he moved his marker on the green to get it out of the way of another player's putting line. A couple of holes later, he wondered if he had put the marker back in its original position—and he couldn't remember. So he called a one-stroke penalty on himself. He didn't have to do it. No one would have known—and as it turned out, that one stroke caused him to miss the cut and get knocked out of the tournament. That penalty he took on himself was expensive—even a dead-last finish in the tournament would have earned him $2,000.

And it gets worse. By year's end, Love was $590 short of automatically qualifying for next year's Masters Tournament. He could still get into the event—but he would have to win a tournament to make it. A reporter asked him how much it would bother him if he missed the Masters because he had called a one-stroke penalty on himself. "That's not the question to ask," Love replied. "The real question is: How would I feel if I won the Masters—then wondered for the rest of my life if I cheated to get in?"

The story has a happy ending, however, because Love went on to win a tournament in New Orleans just one week before the Masters—and he finished second in the Masters, earning $237,000. Best of all, as long as he lives, Davis Love will always know he did it fair and square.

Be Flexible and Adaptable

More team efforts have been stifled and killed by the statement, "It's always been done that way." A team, the team leader, and all the individual players have to be flexible and adaptable to change. There is nothing so certain in this world as change—and with each passing year, the changes become more rapid and more radical. If you can't adapt as a leader and as a team, you can't survive and succeed.

Former Princeton basketball coach Pete Carril said, "Two words to avoid are *always* and *never*. There is nothing that happens a certain way 100 percent of the time. Another way of saying that is a coach does not want to be right more than 85 percent of the time. Flexibility is the key. Coaches and players who recognize that will not make the mistake of doing something the same way all the time. If you always do something one way, it will kill you."

As this book was being written, the Orlando Magic were forced to adjust to change—big-time! We finished the 1995-96 season looking like a team poised for a championship. Characterized no longer as a team of fresh, new talent but as battle-seasoned veterans, we were prepared to go head-to-head with the Bulls in 1996-97, competing on equal terms for NBA supremacy. Then a massive hole opened up literally in the "center" of our on-court formation: Shaquille O'Neal opted for free agency, departing for the L.A. Lakers.

We were stunned. We were reeling. Shaq's agent, Leonard Armato, never even gave us the opportunity to make a final offer. After weeks of Shaq's public wobbling and repeated attempts by G. M. John Gabriel and Magic president Bob Vander Weide to negotiate a contract, there was an abrupt announcement that Shaq was signing with the Lakers. He didn't leave for more money—we offered more money than the Lakers. He didn't leave for family reasons—his family was settled in Florida. He didn't leave for a championship ring—he clearly had a better shot at an NBA championship in O-town than in La-La-Land. He didn't leave so he could make more movies—he could only make movies in the off-season anyway, and it only takes a few hours to get to L.A. from here.

So why did he go? In hindsight, it was probably in the cards all along. In chapter three of Shaq's 1993 autobiography, *Shaq Attaq,* he talks about his own long-standing desire to play for the Lakers and agent Armato's dislike of Orlando and Armato's attempts to orchestrate a deal in which we would trade the Big Guy to the Lakers. Shaq loves the L.A. celebrity lifestyle, no doubt about it. And that's okay. We tried very hard to keep him, but in the end, Shaq made a choice that he had every right in the world to make—and I wish him well. (I would question, however, whether Leonard Armato did a better job of representing the interests of Shaquille O'Neal or the interests of Leonard Armato.)

Shaq's departure created a major change in the Magic lineup—and it was only going to get worse. A few weeks after Shaq announced his decision to sign with the Lakers, Jon Koncak—our backup center and Shaq's replacement—was running downcourt during practice when he suddenly went down to the floor, clutching his knee. As it turns out, it was a career-ending injury for big Jon.

We had taken two big hits at center. Suddenly, the team of the twenty-first century was reeling. No franchise had ever been forced to face such dramatic change as we did for the 1996-1997 season. We have to change direction completely and overhaul our strategy—a strategy that has largely been built around a high-altitude tower of power at the rim. We will be a totally different-looking team, and our new coaching staff will have to build an entirely new game around the speed and skill of Penny Hardaway.

Who knows? It may work out for the best, and the Magic may emerge from this crisis even stronger than before. Only time will tell. The most important thing is that we *can* adapt to change, and we are committed not merely to surviving, but to succeeding.

Dave Odom, the basketball coach at my alma mater, Wake Forest, put it all in perspective for me when he wrote, "Things do change, and when they do, we are left with two options: fight the changes or understand them. Just as we know that the treadmill always wins, so does change."

Be Transparent

A true leader is not afraid to be vulnerable, to admit flaws and mistakes, to share both triumphs and failures, to forgive himself and others, and to let his emotions show through. If your players suspect you cover up your mistakes, they'll cover up theirs. Leadership requires that we examine our own lives, that we reflect on who we are and why we are here and why we do what we do. Those who live examined, transparent lives have something of value to pass on to their players: an example of emotional and moral wholeness.

In July 1996, I spoke at the National Speakers Association convention in Orlando. There, I met the great motivational author Og Mandino. Just before I spoke, I told him how much I enjoyed his new book, *Secrets for Success and Happiness,* a book in which he reflected on his life. "Thank you," he said. "You know, I haven't seen my daughter in forty-two years, but she picked that book up in a bookstore and wrote me a letter after all these years. In her early years, I was a drunken bum, but I loved her and tried to be a good father. Her mother divorced me, took my daughter away, and I can't imagine what she must have told her about me that kept her away all these years. In 1988, my ex-wife died. Six months ago, I received a letter from my daughter, seeking reconciliation. We haven't seen each other yet, but we're exchanging letters. We both want to let go of the past, overcome its pain, and build a new life for the future."

Two nights later, at the formal NSA banquet, singer Gladys Knight was the evening's entertainment for the five hundred people in attendance. At one point, motivational speaker Les Brown, Gladys Knight's former husband, escorted Og Mandino up onto the stage and said, "I don't usually allow my wife to sing to other men, but tonight I'm making an exception. I just learned that one of Og's lifetime wishes is to be serenaded by Gladys Knight singing 'You're the Best Thing that Ever Happened to Me.' Tonight he's going to get his wish." So Gladys began singing to Og, who blushed and was very enchanted by it all.

When the song was finished, Og—a man in his seventies—said, "If I died now, I'd die a very happy man." The crowd gave Og and Gladys a standing ovation—not knowing how prophetic his words would turn out to be. As I watched all this, I thought, *If his daughter could only see this! She has no idea how many people have been touched by this man.*

Six weeks after that evening, Og Mandino was at his home in New Hampshire when he fell and hit his head. That evening he went to bed, slept through the night, and woke up the next morning with a headache. He asked his wife to get him some aspirin, and when she came back with the aspirin, she found him dead.

I don't know if Og and his daughter ever got together for a reunion. I certainly hope so. At least they were communicating, and they were letting go of the past and looking forward to the future. But one thing I do know for sure: Og Mandino was a leader. He impacted so many lives—and one of the reasons he had such a powerful, positive impact was his transparency, his vulnerability, his honest sharing of himself both in his books and one-on-one, as when he told me of this area of deep hurt and amazing healing with his daughter. A genuine leader is like that: real, vulnerable, and completely transparent.

Be Confident

This is one of those catch-22 situations: To succeed, you have to have confidence. And where does confidence come from?

From success! So how do you gain the confidence you need in order to take on a challenge in which you've never succeeded? You face your terrifying challenge, you play through your fear, you win a few, you lose a few, and you gradually gain confidence so that you can take on *new,* even *more* terrifying challenges! As Muhammad Ali used to say, "To be a great champion, you must believe you're the best. If you're not, *pretend* you are."

I constantly stress this principle with my children, whether they face a challenge in school, in sports, at church, or wherever: You've got to approach life with confidence, and confidence comes from doing the thing you fear. Whether kids or adults, people naturally tend to be afraid of new things. They tend to think, "I can't do this. I don't even want to try." They figure, "If I don't try, I won't fail—and I won't be embarrassed in front of everyone else. So I'll just play it safe." Problem is, if you don't try, you never gain confidence. A leader is a person who has tried many things, who has failed many times, but who has succeeded enough times to have gained a measure of confidence.

My son Bobby went into the baseball program at Rollins College as a freshman, feeling very nervous and unsure of himself, not knowing if he could play at that level. They started their practices last fall, and I went over to watch a scrimmage. Bobby was catching, and he happened to be catching a very wild left-handed pitcher. The kid on the mound was throwing curveball after curveball, all of them ending up in the dirt.

Afterwards, I took Bobby out to eat, and I said, "Bobby, you must have had a tough time out there, catching for that kid who was pitching all those curveballs in the dirt."

"Oh, no," he said. "I kept calling for more curveballs. I did that hoping he'd throw 'em in the dirt, and I'd get to show off my blocking ability to the coaches."

I grinned and said, "Bob, I love it!" It warmed me up inside to see how much confidence my son had gained after just a few weeks in college.

"Confidence is contagious," said Vince Lombardi. "So is lack of confidence." So a leader *must* exude confidence.

In 1944, during one of the most intense battles of World War II, the famous Battle of the Bulge, U.S. Army General

Anthony McAuliffe found his forces completely surrounded at Bastogne, Belgium. It was December, in the depths of a bitter winter, and McAuliffe's forces were running low on everything—including morale. Finally, the Germans sent General McAuliffe a message demanding his surrender.

The general assembled his soldiers and said to them, "Men, we are surrounded by the enemy. We have the greatest opportunity ever presented an army. We can attack in *any* direction." He then delivered his famous, terse reply to the German demand for surrender: "Nuts!" (Some historians say his reply was actually unprintable.) Bolstered by their commander's supreme confidence, the Americans fought with renewed spirit and stopped the German drive in its tracks. The American stand at Bastogne is credited as one of the major turning points in the European war.

When the leader demonstrates confidence, the players will soak it up—and the team usually *wins*.

LEADERSHIP QUALITY NUMBER 5: COMPETENCE

If the team is going to follow you, the players have to have complete confidence in your competence to lead them. Notice that the first seven letters of the word "competence" are C-O-M-P-E-T-E. Your players want to know that you are a competitive and competent leader—that you are going to fight hard to make winners out of them, and that you have the savvy, the skill, and the experience to mold them into a competitive and competent team. Some of the ingredients that make a competent leader are:

A Strong Track Record

A competent leader is not only experienced but has experienced *success*. A leader with a strong track record inspires confidence. A team will follow such a leader anywhere he wants to take them, because he has proven he is a *winner*.

In early September 1996, as this book was being written, I decided to try something really off-the-wall. I had already run two marathons during the year, so I thought, *What next?* I decided to climb a mountain. I'm told that one of the biggest, toughest mountains in the United States is Mt. Ranier—so that's the one I picked.

Now, I'm a guy who's terribly afraid of heights. I'm so scared of heights, the treehouse I built as a boy was built on a stump. I'm so scared of heights that when someone sneezes, I only say, "Gesund!" But there I was, preparing to climb a mountain and taking on the tallest glacier peak in the forty-eight contiguous states. There were five of us who took a day of training, and then we started the ascent together, about a forty-eight-hour endeavor. I have many memories of the experience, and someday I'd love to write a book about the life lessons I learned on Mount Ranier.

First, an unseasonal storm hit, so we had to fight our way through the blizzard, the deep snow drifts, and the high winds. It prevented us from getting to the summit, though we came pretty close. The most vivid memory I have is of our team leader, a professional guide named George Dunn—the ultimate image of a mountain man. He looks like a six-foot-three Bill Walton—with good knees. George has lived in the mountains his whole life; he's been to the summit of Mt. Ranier 365 times and has even made four attempts on Mt. Everest, reaching the summit in 1991.

Are those pretty good credentials? Do you get a sense of competence from this man? You bet! When George Dunn spoke, Pat Williams listened. He was so competent, so experienced, I was ready to plug in to this venture without any hesitation. Competent leadership is essential to any successful team effort.

The Ability to Delegate

One of the toughest lessons I've had to learn as a leader is delegating. I think most leaders struggle with it. We think the best way to ensure that a project goes well is by leaving our own fingerprints on everything. Friend, that's a prescription for disaster in any team situation.

When I worked with the 76ers, we lived in Moorestown, New Jersey, across from Philadelphia. One of the highlights for me each year was watching the Canada geese winging their way over our wooded section of South Jersey every spring and fall. Naturalists love to study these birds, and they have made some fascinating discoveries. For example, they have learned that Canada geese rotate the leadership of the V formation they fly in. Every twenty minutes or so, the leader drops back and lets a new bird take the lead position. These birds instinctively know that the leadership position in the V is the toughest spot to be in, because you're heading right into the wind. They understand that no one bird should have to bear all the duties and responsibilities for the flock. What's true of Canada geese is true of people. The burdens of the flock or the team must be shared and spread around—or the leader will wear out, burn out, and fall from the sky.

I truly became aware of the importance of delegating when I was running a minor-league baseball team for the Phillies in Spartanburg, South Carolina, in the mid-1960s. I was just a young guy in my mid-twenties, starting my career, aching for success, really wanting to make that thing work. Obviously, in minor-league baseball, you don't have a very big staff because you just can't afford it. But as I look back on that time, some thirty years ago, it amazes me that I tried to do *everything*. I had the keys on my belt, so I had to unlock all the doors. I did all the selling, I did all the game-night promoting, I did all the publicity work, I even got the brooms out after the game to get the cleanup crew ready for the next morning. I took the gate receipts in my car to the night deposit at the bank. I was afraid to delegate anything.

And I was killing myself, running myself right into the ground. Sure, I slept soundly at night—who wouldn't, being so exhausted?—but I paid a high price in stomach lining. I knew I should be delegating—but I couldn't bring myself to hand off responsibility. I had a lot to learn.

Soon after my Spartanburg days, I got into the NBA. Understand, the NBA in the late '60s and early '70s wasn't the huge mega-showbiz enterprise it is today—but it wasn't minor-league baseball in Spartanburg, either. I had graduated to the big leagues, yet I was still doing everything and delegating nothing and running myself into the ground. I mean, as recently as my 76ers years in the early '80s, I was still banging out the press releases and writing the promotional materials myself—stuff that easily could have been handed off or farmed out.

There was no great kazaam of insight: "Wow! Delegating is the answer I've been searching for!" No, I had to learn the hard way, the gradual way—but I got it. It just slowly dawned on me, as the basketball business kept getting bigger and bigger, that I was going to have to spin off pieces of my job description to other people. I learned I had to push as many tasks as possible down the chain of command—even decision making! I learned I had to trust the people I had hired to work with me and for me.

The more I began to delegate, the more I discovered I had hired some pretty doggone competent people—people who, in many cases, were doing a better job at those tasks and making better decisions than I would have done. Even more surprising, the people who worked around me were happier because they finally felt they were making a contribution, they were doing something meaningful, they were trusted with responsibility.

Soon, I made another big discovery: As I delegated less important stuff, more important stuff began to come my way. Since I was no longer bogged down in the details and the minutiae, I was able to handle more important issues—the kind of stuff only I could handle, the big decisions and big tasks I was hired to handle in the first place.

You still have to be aware of the details, you have to get reports, you have to stay on top of things, you have to hold people accountable—but you don't have to do it all yourself. Those (like the old me) who have trouble delegating are usually people who feel insecure and even fearful. I truly believe my problem was that I needed to feel irreplaceable so that the competence of others in the organization didn't make me feel threatened.

The leader who runs the team like a one-man (or one-woman) show is really practicing a selfish form of management. If you're having trouble trusting your people and delegating tasks and decisions, then you need to realize that it's to your credit that you have the best possible people around you, working to their full potential. If they succeed, it's not a threat. Their success is your success.

A Passion for Excellence

A competent leader sets high but realistic standards for himself and the team and maintains those standards by holding himself and the players accountable. A competent leader understands his product—whether that product is a fun basketball game, a gold-plated steel-reinforced widget, a church ministry, or family relationships—and he or she constantly strives to improve that product.

Oscar Hammerstein II once remarked about a picture he saw of the Statue of Liberty, taken from a helicopter. This aerial photo showed the amazing detail that the sculptor, Frédéric-Auguste Bartholdi, had designed into the top of the statue's head—even though, at the time he was designing the statue in the 1870s, there was no way anyone could have possibly seen that detail. The age of aviation was still decades away, and the only eyewitnesses to Bartholdi's passion for detail and excellence would have been a few high-flying seagulls—yet the sculptor refused to skimp or cut corners. He was committed to excellence.

"When you are creating a work of art or any other kind of work," Hammerstein concludes, "finish the job off perfectly. You may think no one will ever know the difference if you cut corners—but you never know when someone will fly over your work and find you out."

A Commitment to Continual Personal Growth

A competent leader is focused on constantly increasing the level of his or her competence. He or she is a sponge for information and ideas. As Mark Twain said, "The person who *doesn't* read books has no advantage over the person who *can't* read them." NFL great Bill Glass once told me, "If you read five books on any one subject, you'll be considered a world-leading authority on that subject." And the great philosopher, Erasmus, said, "When I get a little money, I buy books. If there is any left over, I buy food." A man after my own heart.

I strongly encourage leaders to read outside of the area of their particular interests and expertise. Microsoft founder Bill Gates, the acknowledged leader of the world of information technology, has said,

> People cannot become truly knowledgeable without being excellent readers. While multimedia systems can use video and sound to deliver information in compelling ways, text is still one of the best ways to convey details.
>
> I try to make time for reading each night. In addition to the usual newspapers and magazines, I make it a priority to read at least one newsweekly from cover to cover. If I were to read only what intrigues me, say the Science and Business sections, then I would finish the magazine the same person I was when I started. So I read it all.

You've got to have your antennae out for new thoughts and new trends. That means being well-read, attending seminars and training sessions, taking organized notes, tapping electronic information sources such as America OnLine and the Internet, and learning from people at every opportunity—and you can learn from anybody, whether that person is a sports star, a corporate CEO, or the guy who empties the wastebaskets and sweeps the floor.

A Commitment to Hard Work

A leader has to work harder than anyone else. A competent leader continually pushes himself or herself to the next level of his or her potential.

I'm a huge Ted Williams fan, and one of the qualities I most admire in the man is his dedication to hard work and to being the best. At the peak of his career, Ted said, "It's practice that makes the hitter—conscientious practice. I'd say that Ted Williams has hit more balls than any guy living except maybe Ty Cobb. I don't say that to brag. I just state it as a fact. From the time I was eleven years old, I've taken every possible opportunity to swing at a ball. I've swung and I've swung and I've swung."

Some years ago, when I was with the 76ers, Neil Diamond came to the Spectrum to put on a concert. We got tickets and as we went to the Spectrum that night, I noticed a sign that said no one was allowed on the lower level, the locker-room level. I wondered why, since this was not normally the case. We attended the concert, and Neil Diamond did three hours nonstop, all his great hits, no intermission.

As the evening ended, I decided to see if I could get backstage, signs or no signs. So I walked down the stairwell to the lower level and was met by a Spectrum Arena security guard—but he was a good friend and he didn't stop me. He just gave me a little wink and turned his back like I wasn't there. As I walked down the stairwell to the door to the lower concourse, I saw a golf cart coming around the corner from behind the stage area. A man was stretched out prone on the back of the cart, covered with towels, being driven back to his locker.

"Who's that?" I asked the guard. "What's going on?"

"That's Neil Diamond," the man said.

I thought, *Holy cow, this man has given everything he had! Every ounce of strength he possessed went into this concert, and now his limp body is being driven back to the dressing room!*

"Usually they walk," added the guard, "but this guy had nothing left to walk with."

The sight of Neil Diamond, collapsed under all those towels, left a lasting impact on me. That's what leaders have to do in order truly to lead.

A number of years ago, I spoke at a Martin Luther King Day luncheon here in Orlando. One of the people who shared the podium with me was an African-American woman named Clara Walters, who worked for the Orange County School Board in Orlando. During her remarks, she talked about her life.

"I grew up in DeLand, Florida," she said, "and in the summers I was a cabbage cutter. They would put you out in the field on a cart between the rows of cabbages. You have a machete in one hand, and you lean out of the cart and whack the cabbages at ground level, and other people come along after you and pick them up. But I learned a little secret. I put a machete in both hands, and I'd lean out of the right side of the cart, then the left side, and I was whacking cabbages on both sides. So when the day was over, I had cut twice as many cabbages as everybody else. Now, all my life, ever since, I've been a cabbage cutter. So whenever they make cuts in the Orange County School system, they'll never be able to get rid of me, because it'll take two people to replace me—because I am a cabbage cutter."

That's what this world truly needs—more cabbage cutters, more people who are so committed to hard work that they are irreplaceable, more leaders who are willing to do the work of two, without sacrificing their families, in order to inspire a winning, hardworking performance from the team.

LEADERSHIP QUALITY NUMBER 6: BOLDNESS

Even though I've listed it last, *boldness* is a leadership quality that—like all the other qualities we've just explored—deserves to be listed Number 1. If a leader isn't bold, he isn't a leader. Another word for boldness is *courage*. Walt Disney once said, "Courage is the main quality of leadership—courage to initiate something and keep it going, a pioneering spirit, an adventurous spirit, the courage to blaze new ways in our land of opportunity." To demonstrate boldness, you as a leader must be willing to:

Take Risks and Encourage Risk-Taking Among Your Players

"Wherever you see a successful business," said management guru Peter Drucker, "someone once made a courageous decision." No team ever rocked the world on its ear by punting on every fourth-and-one situation. Sometimes you have to suck up your courage and run it straight up the middle. You'll pick up a few turnovers that way—but also some first downs and touchdowns. You've got to take risks every now and then to be a leader of a successful team. Without risk, there is no adventure.

As this book was being written, I took part in the twenty-seventh running of the Marine Corps Marathon in Washington, D.C., October 27, 1996. We started by the statue of the flag raising on Iwo Jima in Virginia, and wound our way through the nation's capital, past all the great monuments—Washington,

Lincoln, and Jefferson. It was awesome! The lady who started next to me was from Baltimore and was running her first marathon. She wore a T-shirt with a great message about taking risks and living the adventure: WHEN WAS THE LAST TIME YOU DID SOMETHING FOR THE FIRST TIME? I loved it! What a great spirit was expressed in that question!

We started the race, and before long I noticed a little gray-haired lady trotting along. "How are you doing?" I asked her. "Fine, just fine," she replied. I asked where she was from, and she said she was from College Park, Maryland. She added that she was eighty-two, and this was her eighth marathon—she had run her first when she was seventy-three. I wished her well and continued past her and thought to myself of the adventurous, risk-taking spirit of this amazing octogenarian marathoner. I could just imagine the discussions that must have taken place between this woman and her kids—and probably her grandkids as well—before she laced up to run her first marathon: "Grandma, this is crazy! Why do you want to take such chances? You'll have a heart attack out there! You'll fall and break your hip!" But there she was, putting in her 26.2 miles, living life to the fullest, an expression of joy on her face as she ran. It was inspiring.

That evening I had a delightful dinner with George McGovern, the former senator from South Dakota and presidential candidate who lost in a landslide to Richard Nixon in 1972. He is a marvelous conversationalist with a very humble touch. He shared stories about his famous friends and opponents—JFK, RFK, LBJ, Hubert Humphrey, Nixon. He told me about the young man he hired as his campaign director for the state of Texas in 1972, a twenty-six-year-old go-getter by the name of Bill Clinton who brought his girlfriend, Hillary Rodham along with him to help. When we talked about the '72 election, in which he received such a humiliating whipping that he only carried one out of all fifty states, I asked him how that felt.

"Well," he said, "I knew it was going to be a steep uphill fight from the start. To begin with, I had to emerge from an unprecedented field of seventeen candidates for the Democratic nomination. Then I had to go up against an enormously popular president—and a lot of people, who only remember Nixon for Watergate, forget how popular he was in 1972. It hurt to lose in such a big landslide, of course, but it was the chance of a lifetime and I have no regrets. I like to quote Marv Levy. You know, he coached the Buffalo Bills to four Super Bowls in a row, from 1991 to '94, and the Bills lost all four games. The reporters asked Levy how he dealt with four consecutive Super Bowl losses, and he said, 'I'd rather get to this final level and lose than be sitting home watching.' That's how I look at it. I'd rather take the risk and live the adventure than be a spectator to what's going on in the world."

We need to be risk-takers and adventurers as team leaders, and we have to encourage boldness in our players. One way we do that is by standing by our players when they take a risk and fail. When players know that you're on their side even in times of downfall and spectacular defeat, they will feel empowered to innovate and experiment with boldness in the future. The next bold experiment may be a spectacular success—but they have to know that you will back their big play, win, lose, or draw. If they see you as someone who punishes failure without mercy, they'll turn into a collection of play-it-safe performers.

Mistakes are a valuable learning tool. When your team feels free to risk, experiment, fail (occasionally), and admit human flaws, you and your team will gain valuable information that can be used to refine and strengthen the entire team effort. Celebrate success—but be honest about failures. When people risk and fail, help them to feel proud of having made the effort.

Learn to Take Conflict, Controversy, and Criticism in Stride

To be in leadership is to be in the eye of the storm. All the conflicts that arise on your team seem to swirl around you—and many of them are directed at you. A leader must have the ability to accept and work through that and to help the players adjust to one another and accept one another. If a leader can't work with the team and get the players to work with each other, either resolving or setting aside their differences for the good of the team, then the team will cease to be a team and the leader will cease to lead.

Coach Chuck Daly once said to me, "I could have conflict in this job every minute of every day. There's a conflict waiting to happen with every one of these players, with my assistant coaches, with the front office, with the media, with the owners. So the key, from the start of training camp through the playoffs, is to get my team through the minefield of conflict as safely as possible. It's not that I'm afraid of confrontation or that I shy away from it when push comes to shove. But I'm realistic enough to know that conflict is always there. If I want it, I can find it. So my job is to avoid or resolve conflict if possible, because our mission is to win basketball games, not resolve conflicts every day." Chuck's advice is very sound, and I've never forgotten it.

It's the same with a family. In our large family with nineteen children of many different ages, from many different backgrounds, there's potential for conflict every day. (That's right! Nineteen children—five birth kids, fourteen adopted from four foreign countries.) My job as the father of all these kids is to do all I can to make the relationships function smoothly. I don't believe in papering over or repressing conflict; when fights and arguments rear their ugly heads, we have to resolve issues and forgive wrongs. But many needless conflicts can actually be avoided. I try to give my kids the tools to avoid conflicts before they ever get started. "Look," I'll say, "you two never agree on this, so just don't talk to each other about it. Stay off this subject and you'll be okay." Or "These are the rules we agreed to, these are the chores each of you has been assigned, and we're not going to go switching things around. If everyone stays within their assigned roles, then nobody has to argue over renegotiating those roles." My job is to create an atmosphere where conflicts are resolved in a healthy way, at the lowest possible level of intensity and anger.

A leader is constantly coming in contact with personalities, practices, values, viewpoints, and beliefs that clash with his own. In order to maintain effectiveness, a leader must develop a thick hide—and a lot of tolerance. I encountered an object lesson in this principle while this book was being written. My daughter Karyn is a senior in high school and captain of her cheerleading team. She was coming home night after night feeling absolutely crushed. My kids are good about coming to me with their problems when they are ready, but Karyn was carrying this problem around by herself. Finally, I figured I'd better find out what was bothering her, so I said, "Karyn, you just seem to be so depressed. Is there something I can help you with?"

"Well, Dad," she said, "I don't like being a leader on the cheerleading team."

"Why not, Karyn?"

"Because none of these kids want to be led. All twelve of them want to be the captain, and each of them has her own idea about the way things ought to be done. They won't listen to me. I want to quit."

"Karyn," I said, "you're going to have to be tolerant of their beliefs. You need to sit them down and say, 'I'm the captain and this is the way it's going to be. I want to hear your ideas and I will consider them, but ultimately the decision is mine.' Now, Karyn, understand that they all come from different backgrounds and philosophies. Every leader who ever led a team, whether in the military or in business or in sports or wherever, has had that same challenge in front of them: How do I lead while still being accepting of the differences among the players on my team? It takes enormous patience and tolerance. You've got a long way to go, because after football, you've got the entire basketball season to go. When football and basketball are over, you'll determine how you did."

Karyn wanted to quit—but she stuck it out. It was tough sledding for her, but by sticking it out she grew in her leadership role.

Being a leader means walking around with a bull's-eye on your chest. People are going to take their shots at you. It goes with the territory. A true leader doesn't cave in to pressure, doesn't fold under adversity, doesn't hide from controversy. Sure, listen to your critics, see if they have something constructive to say—but then, if you are still convinced that you are right and the critics are wrong, stay the course and keep moving forward.

Just remember there are two steps difference between a leader and a target. If you get too far ahead, they'll shoot you.

TO BE A LEADER, BE A SERVANT

If there is one theme that weaves its way through all seven of these principles of leadership, it is this: Authentic leadership is not about being "the boss." Paradoxically, it's about being a servant. One of the greatest team leaders in human history, Jesus Christ, knew what it was all about. He sat His twelve-man team down on the grass and gave it to them straight:

> You know that those who are considered rulers over the Gentiles lord it over them, and their great ones exercise authority over them. Yet it shall not be so among you; but whoever desires to become great among you shall be your servant. And whoever of you desires to be first shall be slave of all. For even the Son of Man [that is, Jesus Himself] did not come to be served, but to serve, and to give His life a ransom for many.[2]

Later, when He was just hours away from being crucified, He and His team were in an upstairs room, about to have a meal together, when an argument broke out among the twelve players. It seems each of them wanted to be the boss. Seeing what was going on, Jesus got up, filled a basin with water, wrapped a towel around his waist, and went from player to player, quietly kneeling down and washing each man's feet. That shut them up. Here was the one true Leader of the team—and He was being a servant to them! "The guy who governs and leads," He said, "should be like a servant. I've shown you fellas the way to be a real leader. Now go do it." (That's the Pat Williams Loose Translation—you can check out the original in Luke 22:24-27 and John 13:3-17.)

Dr. Martin Luther King Jr. once said, "Everybody can be great, because anybody can serve. You don't have to have a college degree to serve. You don't have to make your subject and verb agree to serve. You only need a heart full of grace. A soul generated by love."

If you want to lead, you gotta serve. If you don't get this concept of servanthood, you don't get leadership. Period. A story from the American Revolution makes the point more eloquently than any admonition of mine.

On a bitterly cold day in Pennsylvania, a group of American soldiers, commanded by a corporal, were building a log fortification alongside a road. The corporal strutted proudly up and down the side of the road, shouting orders to his men. "Get that log up there!" he bellowed. "Put your shoulder into it! Push harder! Harder! Up with that log!"

The men managed to muscle the huge log to the top of the fortification. But before they could settle the log into its resting place, the men's strength would give out or their feet would slip in the ice and snow, and the log would come crashing back down to the ground. It was obvious that the strength of just one more soldier would have made the difference—but the only other available soldier was the corporal himself, and he was too busy giving orders to put his own shoulder to the task.

The corporal gave the soldiers a tongue-lashing and ordered them to try again. As the soldiers prepared to give it another try, a man came down out of the woods. Unbeknownst to the corporal and his men, this stranger had been watching from the woods for several minutes. He was tall and his features were hidden in a heavy cloak and muffler. "Let me help you, men," he said. With the added muscle-power of the stranger—and the usual shouts and threats of the corporal—the soldiers managed to force the log to the top of the fortification and settle it in place. When the job was done, the stranger went to the corporal.

"Why didn't you help your own men put that log into place?" he said. "As you can see, all they needed was the strength of one more man to get the job done. You should have been that man."

"Me?! Lift logs?!" ranted the corporal. "That's footsoldiers' work! Can't you see I'm a corporal?!"

"Oh, pardon me, sir!" said the stranger, throwing open his coat and removing his muffler to reveal his face. "I wasn't aware that you were such an important man! Me, I am a mere commander-in-chief. George Washington, at your service, corporal.

The next time you have a log too heavy for your men to lift, and you don't want to dirty your own hands, send for me and I will come do the job myself."

All too often, people look at leadership in terms of status, prestige, and worth. The leader is viewed as the most important person. That's a totally false view of leadership. Does being an executive of the Orlando Magic organization make me more important than Penny Hardaway or Horace Grant? No way! I can't do their job. I can't do the job of our front office receptionist—I wouldn't know where to begin! Clearly, leadership is not about being important or indispensable or more knowledgeable than anybody else on the team. Leadership is just one role among many.

A team is not just a collection of individuals. When everything clicks into place, a team is truly a community, a tightly knit fellowship. It's much easier to get a fellowship or community to focus on a single vision than it is to get a mere collection of individuals to do so. If you want to build an atmosphere in which everybody pulls together in order to win, then you, as a leader, have to recognize that it all starts with *you*. It starts with your attitude, your commitment, your caring, your passion for excellence, your dedication to winning. It starts with the example you set. It starts with the way you treat and relate to your players.

Before the Florida Marlins became National League Champions, I was watching a Marlins-Dodgers game in Miami with Frank Wren, Florida's assistant general manager. I asked Frank, "What makes your manager, Jim Leyland, so unique? His background is similar to hundreds of other managers. Why is he considered the top manager in baseball today?"

"I think the quality that distinguishes Jim is that he takes the time every day to talk with each player on the roster," Frank said. "Before the game begins he walks around the field or locker area and has a brief dialogue with everyone. He will check on a player's family or kid with them in order to get a reading on where their mind is that day and how they are doing. Not many leaders care that much or will take the time to do this on a consistent basis."

Teamwork begins with the person in charge. If that person is a servant rather than a boss, then the team has a real leader. That's the team I'm betting on to win.

Principle 3

Be Committed!

In August 1982, I joined Julius Erving and half a dozen other NBA players for a two-week, once-in-a-lifetime trip through mainland China. It was a fabulous vacation, a totally carefree adventure through an exotic land. Our wonderful vacation came to a sudden, jarring halt when we got back to Hong Kong and I phoned the 76ers office in Philadelphia and asked, "Any news from Philly?"

Oh, there was news, all right. Big news. One of our stars, a big Philly fan favorite named Darryl Dawkins, had been sent to the New Jersey Nets in exchange for $600,000 cash and a first-round draft pick in '83. There I was, twelve time zones away, and I had to learn that a huge talent trade had been conducted in my absence. I knew this was not going to sit well with the fans, especially coming on the heels of a hefty hike in ticket prices. Darryl busted a lot of backboards in Philadelphia, and the fans loved him—and I was sure they'd be storming the ramparts when the news of the trade hit the papers.

Arriving stateside, I discovered that there was a ray of hope, a scant possibility that I and all the other 76ers execs could placate the fans and save ourselves from a public lynching in front of Independence Hall. Like the children of Israel in Bible times, we turned to the one man who could rescue us—a man named Moses.

Moses Malone was a two-time league MVP, the NBA's leading scorer and rebounder, and unquestionably among the best centers in the game of basketball at that time. He had spent the past few seasons in a Houston Rockets uniform. In fact, Moses Malone practically *was* the Houston Rockets. Suddenly, he had become available as a free agent, and 76ers' owner Harold Katz became obsessed with putting him in a Sixers uniform. After a marathon, all-night meeting in New York City, Harold finally signed Moses to a six-year, $13.2 million deal.

That may not sound like a lot of money for a star center these days, but it was a heck of a lot of money in 1982 dollars. Of course, the Houston Rockets had the option to match the deal, and they wanted to put the matter in arbitration. So we arbitrated. And we arbitrated. And we arbitrated some more. And by the time we were just about arbitrated right into the ground, we reached an agreement that left the Rockets feeling barely mollified and left us feeling stung. In addition to the $13.2 mill we put in Moses Malone's pocket, we had to cough up a player and a draft pick to the Rockets. They took Caldwell Jones, a reliable, durable, productive player—plus they took a first-round pick we had gotten from Cleveland and had been guarding for the past five years.

Still, we had Moses Malone! We felt sure we had finally put together everything we needed for an NBA championship. We made the announcement at a press conference in a room at Veterans Stadium. There was a Phillies baseball game at the Vet that night, so a lot of sports fans were lining the stadium concourse as Moses and a group of Sixers execs were on their way to the press conference. Suddenly a spontaneous cheer went up all along the concourse, followed by an exuberant chant of "Mo-ses! Mo-ses! Mo-ses!" Malone looked around and smiled a somewhat bewildered smile at the fans. He later remarked that in all his seasons in Houston, he had *never* received the kind of fan response he got that night from a spontaneous and unrehearsed bunch of Philadelphia fans who had come to watch a baseball game.

Moses completed the picture, and man, did we ever have a team that season! We had The Doctor himself, Julius Erving. We had Moses. We had Bobby Jones and Andrew Toney and Maurice Cheeks. We had talent that just wouldn't stop. The one-two punch of Moses and The Doctor led the Sixers to a regular season record of 65 wins and 17 losses. Moses confidently promised the sports reporters and the fans that it would be "Fo'—fo'—fo'!" in the playoffs—three four-game sweeps in a row. We started the playoffs by handing the Knicks a 112-102 pounding, a 98-91 come-from-behind thrashing, a 107-105 squeaker, and a 105-102 heart-stopper. Moses got his first predicted fo'-game sweep, scoring 125 points and inhaling 62 rebounds in those four games.

Next, the Sixers took on the Milwaukee Bucks (who had shocked everybody by knocking the Boston Celtics out of the playoffs) in the NBA Semifinals. We took the first three games, failed to hang on to a fourth-quarter lead in the fourth, then came back to win the fifth game. "Okay," said Moses, "so it'll be fo'-*five*-fo'."

We went on to face down the L.A. Lakers for the best-of-seven final series—and it was a clash of the titans. The defending champion Lakers were led by such legendary names as Kareem, Magic, and Silk, not to mention Bob McAdoo, Norm Nixon, and Michael Cooper. Yet the Sixers downed these legends in four games. In all, both regular season and play-off games, the Sixers had won 77 games and lost 18. Lakers coach Pat Riley paid us the ultimate compliment: "The Sixers just never let up. They were always able to take their aggressiveness up to another level. Their disposition to dominate was better than ours."

The Sixers locker room was awash in spewing champagne after the championship-clinching game. Doctor J, who had been battling to bring an NBA championship home to Philly since 1977, was elated. Holding the trophy, he said, "Seven years is a long time—but it was worth the wait." And Moses (who bucketed 24 points and snatched 23 rebounds in the final game) wrapped his arms around Sixers head coach Billy Cunningham. Billy had been rumored to be thinking of quitting after that season, so Moses yelled in his ear, "Hey, Billy C! You gotta come back, man, 'cause we're gonna repeat, and 'peat, and 'peat, and 'peat!" I heard that and thought, Hmm, catchy. Almost as catchy as "Fo'—fo'—fo'!"

What was the extra horsepower that enabled the Philadelphia 76ers to go all the way to an NBA championship that year? Certainly, it was a combination of many factors. But the number one factor, I am convinced, was a man named Moses—a man who prophesied three sweeps in a row, then parted the waters and led us to the Promised Land of an NBA championship. And what was it about Moses Malone that gave the Sixers that championship edge? I believe it is the man's extra measure of *commitment*.

A GUY WHO JUST WON'T QUIT

Physically, Moses Malone didn't give the appearance of a great basketball player. At six-foot-ten and 255 pounds, he was an imposing physical presence—but in the NBA, he was actually a shorter-than-average center. He wasn't that fast. He didn't have the large hands of a great ball-handler. He was not the most accurate shooter. He was not a high jumper. The power of Moses Malone was not in his physique or his skills. It was in his heart. It was his total dedication and commitment to the game, to the team, and to winning.

When Sixers owner Harold Katz first met with Moses Malone, they talked for hours and hours—and never once in that entire conversation did Moses mention money. All he talked about was competing, winning, and taking a championship. Harold, who is very good at sizing up the character of people, saw that Moses was the genuine article—genuinely committed to winning, genuinely committed to teamwork.

One way you can tell that an athlete is totally committed is when you see that he never quits. That's Moses. The guy just would not quit. Take rebounding. He operated on the assumption that every shot taken in a game will be a miss. As a result, every time someone made a shot, whether at our basket or theirs, he positioned himself to go for the rebound. A lot of players will make a grab for six or seven of every ten rebounds—but Moses went after ten of ten, and a hundred of a hundred.

And making shots? Hey, Moses was never finished with the ball until it dropped through the hoop, or he got fouled, or he made an outlet pass to someone else who could put it down. Sometimes, you'd swear Moses was playing volleyball against the backboard, just tip-tip-tip-tip-tipping the ball until it finally went in. He never said to himself, "That's enough trying. I guess it just won't go." He just kept trying until he got the job done.

The concentration and focus of Moses Malone was nothing short of awesome. He was never out of the game. Even if he was off the floor, resting, in foul trouble, or whatever, his head was in the game. His eyes were roving, watching the action, sizing up the different players, studying their moves, looking for weak spots and opportunities to exploit. Then, when he would go back into the game, it was as if he'd never left. He had a look on his face that was mean and intimidating—but it wasn't a mask or a put-on game face. It was merely a reflection of his absolute commitment and concentration on the game.

That kind of absolute commitment wins games. It wins championships. It's the stuff great players and great teams are made of. As I see it, there are at least seven facets or components to a committed team attitude. They are:

1. Loyalty: commitment to each other on the team;
2. Sense of mission: commitment to the team vision or cause;
3. Class: commitment to quality and excellence;
4. Competitiveness: commitment to winning;
5. Accountability: commitment to continual improvement;
6. Mental toughness: commitment to hustling and finishing;
7. Self-discipline: commitment to control and self-mastery.

Let's take a closer look at each of these forms of commitment.

I. Loyalty: Commitment to Each Other on the Team

Back when Bill Bradley was an all-American basketball player at Princeton, I heard him give a talk at a Fellowship of Christian Athletes summer conference about the five qualities of a champion. I don't even remember the first four. But I'll always remember the fifth. He said, "A champion is somebody who does it for somebody else." These are the words of a man who is committed to his teammates. These are the words of a champion.

I once heard a speech in Atlanta by Ralph David Abernathy, Dr. Martin Luther King's successor as head of the Southern Christian Leadership Council. It was a mixed audience of blacks and whites, and one thing he said stands out vividly in my mind. "Some of your relatives may have come over on the Mayflower," he said. "Some of your relatives may have come over on slave ships. But if we do not all get together in the same ship, we're all going to drown!"

Regardless of what kind of team you are on or what goal your team is aiming for, those words are so true, and they have been said in so many ways, in so many situations before. Benjamin Franklin, on signing the Declaration of Independence, put it this way: "We must all hang together or we will all hang separately." And Abraham Lincoln (echoing the words of Jesus in Mark 3:25) said, "A house divided against itself cannot stand."

Coach John Wooden put this concept in basketball terms after watching a UCLA player make an outstanding shot. "It took ten hands to make that basket," he said. And that's absolutely true. No player can play the game of basketball by himself. Every individual success is truly the result of a massive team effort.

Publishing executive John Roach applies this concept to teams in the business world, using a seafaring word picture. "My ideal business organization," he said, "is modeled on a pirate ship. If everyone works together, they all share in the booty. If not, they all walk the plank."

We *must* be loyal to one another on the team. We must be committed to each other. We cannot let anything divide us—least of all such superficial differences as skin color or ethnicity, political affiliations, or generational differences. Teamwork transcends all those things. After all, snowflakes are among the smallest, most fragile things in nature—but just look at what they can do when they stick together!

Moses Malone understood this truth. When the 76ers introduced him at a press conference in September 1982, Malone didn't come out and say, "This is my team now. I'm going to lead it, and everyone's going to support me." No way! His first act as a 76er was to demonstrate his commitment to his fellow players and to the team mission. Totally impromptu, he said, "This is Doc's show. I've got a chance to play with Doctor J, and now it's gonna be a better show than ever. But it's his show, and my job is to support what he does." It was an attitude he maintained straight through the regular season, through the play-offs, and all the way to the NBA championship. The night of the Sixers' defeat of the Lakers for the NBA title, Tuesday, May 31, 1983, Moses gave credit to the team, and especially to Julius Erving. "This is Doc's team," he said, "not Moses' team. Moses is just here to help him win. Moses is just a player, that's all Moses is."

That's loyalty. That's total commitment to one another on the team. That's Moses Malone. That's a winning attitude.

2. Sense of Mission: Commitment to the Team Vision or Cause

The leader "envisions a vision" and communicates it to the team. But that vision will never become reality until the players rally around it, commit to it, and bend their backs to make that vision a tangible reality.

We see a powerful demonstration of this principle in the Old Testament book of Nehemiah. When the book of Nehemiah opens, the city of Jerusalem is in ruins. The city walls were laid waste when Jerusalem was sacked by the Babylonians forty years earlier. Many of the people of the city were carried off into captivity by the Babylonians—but there were some who stayed behind. For forty years, people huddled fearfully among the piles of rubble that had once been a beautiful city.

Finally, a man named Nehemiah came back to Jerusalem from the Babylonian captivity. He was a man with a vision—and he enthusiastically began to sell his vision to the people. It was a vision of a restored city of Jerusalem with rebuilt walls—a place of beauty, commerce, civic activity, and safety once more. If the people had listened to Nehemiah's vision, shrugged their shoulders, and said, "So what?" then where would Nehemiah have been? Where would Jerusalem have been? Square one. No progress. No rebuilding. No city walls, no safety, no hope.

Fortunately, the people didn't say, "So what?" They said, "Let's do it!" Charged up and excited by Nehemiah's grand vision, the people committed themselves to it. They immediately set to work and began rebuilding the city walls. In only forty days, the walls were rebuilt. A task that could not even be started in forty years became a finished reality in only forty days—in part because of one man's vision, but also because the entire team captured that vision and committed themselves to it.

"Each individual player has much greater ability than he thinks he has," said former Ohio State football coach Woody Hayes, "particularly when he uses that ability in a committed team effort."

3. Class: Commitment to Quality and Excellence

Class. We hear that word thrown around a lot these days, especially in the world of sports: "There's an athlete with a lot of class," or "That team showed a lot of class today." Different people mean different things when they use that word. They may mean style. Or appearance. Or a quality attitude. But I think you can boil it all down to a passion for excellence in everything you do, both as an individual and as a team. Coach John Wooden describes class as "an intangible quality which commands, rather than demands, the respect of others."

Charles Plumb was a fighter pilot in Vietnam. After seventy-five combat missions, he was shot down over the North by a surface-to-air missile. Ejecting, he parachuted into enemy hands and spent six years as a POW. Today, he lectures about the lessons he learned during his ordeal. He tells of sitting in a restaurant, years after his return to the States, when a man came up to him and said, "You're Charles Plumb, aren't you?"

"Yes," he replied.

"You flew a fighter over 'Nam, right?" asked the stranger. "From the deck of the *Kitty Hawk*?"

"That's right," Plumb responded. "How did you know?"

"I was on the *Kitty Hawk* myself," said the man. "You didn't know me, but I knew who all the pilots were. I was a parachute packer. Fact is, I packed the silk you were wearing the day you were shot down. I guess it deployed okay."

"Well, if it hadn't," said Plumb, reaching out and shaking the man's hand, "you and I wouldn't be having this conversation. You did a good job, Buddy. Thanks!"

On every team, there are sky jockeys like Charles Plumb—and there are also chute packers, guys who spend their days in the belly of the ship, patiently folding silk and shrouds, earning no wings or medals but making sure that the job gets done thoroughly, carefully, and with excellence. Chute packers get no praise or reward except the satisfaction of knowing that if the chute is ever needed, it will do its job and save a pilot's life. Every team needs dedicated chute packers. Everyone on the team, from the head coach and top scorer all the way to the subs, assistants, and ball boys, must be committed to carrying out his or her assigned role with consummate skill, dedication, and excellence.

As Martin Luther King once said, "If a man is called to be a street sweeper, he should sweep streets even as Michelangelo painted, or Beethoven composed music, or Shakespeare wrote poetry. He should sweep streets so well that all the hosts of heaven and earth will pause to say, 'Here lived a great street sweeper who did his job well.'" That's class. That's a passion for excellence. The great Packers coach, Vince Lombardi, said it this way: "The quality of a person's life is in direct proportion to their commitment to excellence, regardless of their chosen field of endeavor."

4. Competitiveness: Commitment to Winning

When I went to Tower Hill School in Wilmington, Delaware, there was a sign on the wall of the gym quoting these lines by the legendary sportswriter Grantland Rice:

> When the one Great Scorer comes
> To write against your name,
> He writes not whether you won or lost,
> But how you played the game.

Now I hate to disagree with the great Grantland Rice, and I'm certainly all for good sportsmanship. I don't approve of trash-talking, dirty play, breaking the rules, bench-clearing incidents, and the like. Good sportsmanship is absolutely crucial to any game.

But I believe it matters *a lot* whether you win or lose. I think winning is overwhelmingly important. I think it's important on the basketball court. I think it's important in the workplace, in the marketplace, in the classroom, on the battlefield, in the political arena, on the mission field, in the operating room, in every place where people gather together as a team. I think it *all* matters: whether you win or lose *and* how you play the game.

At the beginning of the 1996-97 season, Anfernee Hardaway went into the operating room for surgery on his knee. It was a crucially important surgical procedure for the future of Penny Hardaway—and of the Orlando Magic. Let me tell you something: We devoutly prayed that Penny's surgeon, Dr. Jim Barnett, was committed to winning. Just suppose, as Penny was being wheeled into the operating room he saw a sign on the wall that read:

> On the judgment day, when your life is weighed
> On the scales of the Great Physician,
> He cares not if your patients lived or died,
> But how you made the incision.

I don't think Penny would stay on that operating table another second. Regardless of how much his knee was hurting, he'd be out of that hospital like a shot—and he'd be looking for a surgeon who is uncompromisingly committed to winning. I don't care what endeavor you engage in, you'd better be intensely, passionately committed to winning. You should eat, sleep, live, and breathe winning—and never apologize for it. One of the most important commitments we make in any team environment is the commitment to winning and to welcoming competition. Single-minded, passionate, dedicated competitiveness is an absolute must in building successful teams. You must be willing to go all out to win, to do whatever it takes within the bounds of good sportsmanship to achieve victory.

My son David was fifteen years old in 1995 when he played with the Winter Park Little League team. That summer, David and his teammates earned the great honor of playing in the Little League World Series in Kissimmee, Florida. Some six thousand Little League teams worldwide were whittled down to just eight teams that came from all over—even Asia and South America. This was truly a once-in-a-lifetime experience.

The Winter Park team had a lot of talent and a great chance to win the entire series. I was surprised as I watched the early games, however, to see the coaches make continual substitutions and at times put kids on the field who were clearly not the best nine on the team. Soon, the team was out of contention in double eliminations. The kids were extremely disappointed.

Now, I'm not the kind of parent to second-guess my kids' coaches. Fact is, I have some inkling how tough it is to be a coach at this level. I've only coached one time, when the regular coach couldn't make it to a YMCA basketball game that two of my sons were in. I jumped in to coach the game, and it was like I suddenly got a personality transplant: I was yelling, carrying on, and screaming at the refs, and I quickly knew what coaches go through. So I don't like to look over the shoulder of any of my kids' coaches. Seeing the way these Little League coaches rotated their lineup, I figured, "Well, that's their call. They wanted to give every kid on the team a chance to play—and at least they won't be hearing 'Why didn't you play my kid?' from any parents." Still, knowing that the Little League World Series is for all the marbles, I knew I wouldn't have made the same call.

After the series ended, the mayor of Winter Park held a ceremony to honor the kids for just being in the competition. The ceremony was at city hall after school one day. I wasn't able to be there, so at dinner that night I asked David how it went. He hung his head. "I didn't go," he muttered.

"You what?!" For a moment, I thought he had simply forgotten or something, and I was all ready to jump on him—then I saw that he was really hurting.

"Dad," he said, "I just couldn't go. We could have won the Series, but we didn't put our best team on the field. We didn't do everything we could have done to win. I just couldn't face it, Dad."

You can argue about whether it would have been better for the second-string kids to have played in a losing game or sat out most of a game their team won. There are legitimate pros and cons to that question. But one thing you can't argue with is the hurt I saw on my son David's face. I wish he'd been given a chance to win. It's not easy to get to that level, and I wish David and his teammates had been given a realistic chance to prove themselves at that level. Fact is, when they got there, winning was not the team's number one priority.

I was once at an Amway convention, and one of the speakers, Les Brown, told a story about a board game he played with his eleven-year-old son. They played and they played—ten games straight—and the dad won every game. Finally, he said, "You know, Son, it's getting late. Time for bed."

"Aw, Dad!" the boy pleaded. "Just one more game!"

Les kept insisting it was time for bed. Finally the boy countered with this argument: "But Dad, you don't understand! It ain't over till I win!"

Well, they played one more game and the kid won. (Do you suppose Les "took a dive"?) The important thing is that this kid really understood competition. He had a refuse-to-lose attitude.

Magic Johnson was asked to describe his longtime opponent, Larry Bird. Magic said, "He just knows how to win, and he will do anything to win. That's Larry Bird in a nutshell."

General Norman Schwarzkopf once spoke at a Magic charity benefit I attended. At the cocktail reception prior to the dinner, I noticed that "Stormin' Norman" was standing alone, no one near him, so I went over and enjoyed twenty uninterrupted minutes with him. I'm not bashful about asking questions, so I asked, "General, have you ever thought about the fact that because of the actions of one madman in the Middle East, you have become a celebrity to the world?"

"I've thought about it many times," he replied. "No one ever would have heard of me if not for Saddam Hussein. What's more, no one would have had any use for me if we hadn't won."

The general was right. Winning makes all the difference. As General Schwarzkopf's colleague, General Colin Powell, once said, "Americans love to win. Whenever you make a decision, you don't do it to fool around. You do it to *win*. That's a pretty good rule for life, as well as for military operations."

Bill Russell, former star center and later coach of the Boston Celtics, explained his theory on winning when he said, "Winning is the only thing I really cared about because I found that when I left the cocoon of my childhood I came into the world and found that individual awards were mostly political. But with winning and losing there are no politics, only numbers. It's the most democratic thing in the world. You either win or lose. So I decided early in my career that the only really important thing was to try and win every game. There is nothing subjective about that."

Our immediate reaction, when we encounter competition, is to shy from it, walk away from it, or be overwhelmed by it. But a committed player loves competition, because competition pulls out the best in people. It forces us to achieve at a level that we should be achieving at anyway but don't until our competition forces us to do so.

When Roosevelt Grier was in the NFL, he used to say, "When my competition is fair, I'm fair. When my competition is good, I'm great." Coach Joe Paterno of Penn State said, "I love my competition. If it weren't for them, I wouldn't be as good as I am." And the successful gymnastics coach Bela Karoly said, "No competition, no progress."

Let me tell you a story about competition. In February of 1996, I went to the NBA All-Star weekend in San Antonio, along with two of my kids, Jimmy and Karyn. We were sitting and watching the game, and I noticed that two young business-women from Dallas were sitting next to us. During the game, one of them, Sanka Saviddes, ordered a soft drink.

I have never seen a soft drink consumed the way Sanka consumed hers. Usually a woman will leave lipstick marks on one part of the cup, but Sanka left lipstick marks all around the cup. She sipped from every angle of that cup—and then put a straw in the drink, imbibed a little of the liquid through the straw, held it in her mouth, swished it around, and practically gargled with it. Finally, I couldn't take it anymore. I said, "What in the world are you doing with that drink?"

She said, "I'm making sure it's not a Pepsi!"

"What's the big deal?" I asked.

"Well, it *is* a big deal!" Sanka responded, practically indignant. "I work for Coca-Cola!"

And she's right. It is a big deal. The point is that Pepsi continually forces Coke to be the best-tasting, best-fizzing, best-packaged, best-advertised product it can possibly be. That's the value and the power of competition. That conversation with "the Coca-Cola lady" got me to wondering how this whole Coke-and-Pepsi battle got started. Here's what I found out:

Coke and Pepsi have been competitors practically from day one. In fact, the famous "Cola Wars" actually go back over a hundred years! Coca-Cola had its start as a nonalcoholic "nerve medicine," cooked up by Atlanta pharmacist John Pemberton in 1886. He brewed up a batch of syrup from water, sugar, cola nuts, herbs, and coca leaves—then he mixed the stuff with tap water (that's right, the original Coca-Cola was so flat there wasn't one burp in a barrelful). Pemberton got the idea of selling it as a carbonated beverage only after a drugstore patron with an upset stomach asked him to mix up some Coca-Cola with club soda to settle his stomach.

Seeing the success of Pemberton's product, North Carolina pharmacist Caleb Bradham came up with his own cola drink formula in 1893. Naming it after pepsin, a popular stomach remedy, Bradham sold his Pepsi as a soft drink syrup. By the turn of the century, both Coca-Cola and Pepsi were selling around

100,000 gallons of cola syrup a year. In 1915, Coca-Cola began bottling its drinks in the now-famous bottles with the hourglass figure, which—together with the famous Coca-Cola script-design logo—made the product uniquely recognizable.

In 1917, Pepsi made an unwise investment in sugar futures and went bankrupt. From 1920 to 1931, several attempts were made to revive the Pepsi label and product, each ending in bankruptcy. Pepsi was resurrected once more when Charles Guth of the 115-store Loft Candy Store chain got mad at Coca-Cola for not giving him a quantity discount, even though he sold four million servings of Coke every year. Guth bought the Pepsi name and formula and began bottling syrup and soda to sell in the Loft stores. Coke responded by filing a trademark infringement suit against Pepsi that lingered in the courts for the next ten years.

In the mid-1930s, Guth cut Pepsi's price from a dime to a nickel and bottled Pepsi in 12-ounce bottles (larger than Coke's), enabling Pepsi to grab a big share of Coke's market. Then at the end of World War II, as prosperity returned to America, Pepsi's share plummeted as people saw Pepsi as a "cheap" cola. Coke soon gobbled up over 80 percent of the soft drink market and Pepsi slid once again toward bankruptcy. Then Coke made a big mistake, allowing disgruntled vice president Alfred Steele to jump ship and join Pepsi. Taking a slew of Coca-Cola's top marketing talent with him, Steele retooled Pepsi's image with a new logo, fancy swirl bottles, and a bold new ad campaign. Steele even had his wife—actress and former Coke endorser Joan Crawford—appear in Pepsi ads. By 1960, Pepsi cut Coke's lead in half.

Another interesting sidebar in the Cola Wars is the part that presidential politics has played. In the 1950s, Pepsi was active in conservative politics, supporting the candidacies of Vice President Richard Nixon and Senator Joe McCarthy. In 1959, Nixon traveled to the Soviet Union for a trade show. At one point during the show, Nixon and Soviet premier Nikita Khrushchev got into a heated capitalism vs. communism exchange. At one point, Nixon handed the Soviet strongman a chilled bottle of Pepsi. Soon, newswires hummed with the famous picture of the Soviet premier chugging from an ice-cold bottle of Pepsi—a public relations triumph. Later, as president, Nixon maintained a close relationship with Pepsi, pulling diplomatic strings in Pepsi's overseas markets and making Pepsi the only soft drink served at the White House.

Atlanta-based Coca-Cola allied itself with Democrats, including a young Georgia politician named Jimmy Carter. By the time Carter ran for president, he was well-supplied with image-makers, admen, and international experts from Coca-Cola. The same people who had skillfully opened overseas markets for Coke also shaped Carter's understanding of foreign affairs. Carter kicked Pepsi out of the White House, replaced it with Coke, and helped Coke get its product into China and Portugal.

Today, Coke and Pepsi continue to be extremely intense rivals. All of this is just to say that when Sanka, the young soft-drink-gargling Coca-Cola executive told me, "It is a big deal," hey, it's a big deal! It always has been. It always will be. And consumers of both Coke and Pepsi should be glad that such fierce competition goes on.

Not long ago, I was in the office of an Orlando businessman and I noticed a plaque on the wall that read:

> My competitors do more for me than my friends do. My friends are too polite to point out my weaknesses, but my competitors go to great expense to advertise them. My competitors are efficient, diligent, and attentive. They make me search for ways to improve my products and service. My competitors would take my business away from me if they could. This keeps me alert to hold onto what I have. If I had no competitors, I would be lazy, incompetent, and inattentive. I need the discipline they force upon me. I salute my competitors. They've been good to me. God bless them all.

That's a great attitude. That's the attitude every team leader and every team player ought to have. It ties in with having a class attitude, with having a commitment to excellence. When you are committed to being the best, you don't shy away from competition—you welcome it, because you know competition will keep you on your toes and make you the best you can be at whatever you do.

On a radio show I host here in Orlando, I once had as my guest longtime Detroit News sports columnist Joe Falls. During the show, he told me this story: "Years ago, I called Joe DiMaggio on his seventieth birthday to get a column and wish him well. We ended up talking for half an hour. The next spring I was at the Red Sox spring training camp in Winter Haven, Florida, and I saw Ted Williams behind the batting cage. I told Ted about my talk that winter with Joe DiMaggio.

"As we finished our conversation, I started to walk away from Ted. He yelled back at me, 'Hey, Bush!' Ted calls everybody 'Bush.' He said, 'When I'm seventy, you call that day and I'll give you an *hour*.' I thought, *Man, after all these years, DiMaggio and Ted Williams are still competing! They competed in the 1930s, the 1940s, the 1950s, and here they are at age seventy, a couple of old men, and they're still competing with each other!*"

Whatever arena you compete in, competition is the great teacher, the great motivator, the great energizer. Welcome it, tackle it, give it all you've got. If you can't win, then at least make the fella ahead of you break the record. If he beats you, and you've absolutely done the best you can do, you've still won. You've become more than you were before. Competition did it.

5. Accountability: Commitment to Continual Improvement

Accountability is absolutely essential to the health and success of any team. A team without accountability is not truly a team; it's just a collection of individuals pursuing their own goals. Accountability is a commitment to:

- do whatever it takes to improve;
- take full responsibility for your own actions;
- accept the consequences of your behavior and choices;
- admit your failures and flaws to your teammates;
- allow your teammates to critique your performance and point out your mistakes and weaknesses;
- be coachable and teachable.

Accountability is the glue that holds a team together. It's the mechanism that produces team synergy and alignment so that all members of the team are working in sync toward a unified goal, with all their energies in harmony. Accountability provides the tempered strength of the steel chain, because each link in the chain is reinforced and locked in place by the surrounding links. Genuine accountability is always mutual: You are accountable to me and I am accountable to you for the good of everyone on the team.

Accountability takes many forms, both formal and informal. On many sports teams, coaches will choose a few players—frequently those who have a demonstrated leadership role on the team—to serve either formally or informally as a kind of peer review committee. These players will hold the entire team accountable on matters of various infractions, such as missed practices or a negative attitude. This takes a load off the coach—but it also does something even more profound: It underscores the fact that each player is responsible to the entire team. If one player slacks off or screws up, the entire team suffers. Players who don't understand this truth tend to become prima donnas and lone rangers.

Team accountability is no less important in business, in churches, in government, and in families than it is in sports. Many businesses have found it advantageous to divide the company into task groups or teams and to practice mutual accountability within each team. Team members even evaluate each others' performance. Sound intimidating? Sure it does, at first—but there are many advantages to team accountability and team performance reviews. For example:

- The players interact with each other closely and daily, so they often have a better feel for other players' performance than do leaders, coaches, or managers, which means their evaluations are frequently more accurate.
- Knowing that a player will have to face peer review can be a powerful motivator for better performance, increased productivity, and heightened commitment to the team vision.

- Team reviews involve the input of the entire team, and the larger pool of observations and reviews tends to be more complete and more objective than a single review by a manager or coach.
- Players who are accountable for maintaining performance and behavior standards tend to be more aware of those standards and tend to be more diligent about meeting them.

Healthy mutual accountability is fostered in a team when there is agreement and complete "buying in" on the vision, expectations, and procedures of the team; when there is an atmosphere of respect and trust between the leaders and the team and among all players; when team goals and performance objectives are clearly defined and achievable; when there is good communication, feedback, and coaching on a continual basis.

6. Mental Toughness: Commitment to Hustling and Finishing

Napoleon Hill said, "The moment you commit and quit holding back, all sorts of unforeseen incidents, meetings, and material assistance will rise up to help you. The simple act of commitment is a powerful magnet for help."

One of my favorite guests on my Orlando radio show was Bill Russell. We talked about his coaching years, and I reminded him of a statement he once made to the press: "Hustle is a talent." I asked Bill what he meant.

"Hustle," he replied, "is drive, commitment, persistence, fire in the belly. The guy I think of when I think of hustle is John Havlicek, who played for me in Boston. We called him 'Mr. Perpetual Motion.' He played sixteen seasons and never gave an ounce less than 100 percent. He was there to play basketball. Man, did that guy have hustle! A Boston sportswriter once said to me, 'Well, all John Havlicek has is hustle.' I mean, he just tossed him off like that. I was blown away. I said, 'All he has is hustle! All he has?! Listen, *hustle is a talent,* because not everybody does it! The guy with hustle is the guy who's left standing when it's over.'"

Remembering what Bill Russell said about John Havlicek, I decided to send a copy of my outline for this book to John. And John responded with a wonderful statement of what mental toughness and hustle are all about:

"When two people are playing against each other," John Havlicek said, "the question is who will give up first. It becomes a mental game of one-on-one to see who is the toughest mentally. Not just in the game, but on every single move, every individual shot. The guy who wins is the guy who works a little harder, who goes a little longer. I believe you will pass out before you are overworked, but most people don't know that. They *think* they are overworked, so they stop. They could have kept going, but they didn't. They weren't beat physically. They were beat mentally."

Sixty years ago, St. Louis Cardinals Hall of Famer Enos Slaughter learned a lifelong lesson. He recalled trotting in from the outfield one day, discouraged about a hitting slump. Manager Eddie Dyer said to Enos sarcastically, "Tired, Kid? If so, I'll get some help for you."

Slaughter lay awake that night in his rooming house thinking over Dyer's words. As he later told writer Bob Broeg, "I realized that here it was, the depths of the Depression, and I was cheating the people who were paying their quarters, dimes, and nickels to see me play. They had problems of their own, and I vowed never to walk onto a ballfield again."

Thus was born Slaughter's determination to hustle out *every play*, which helps account for the number of triples in his career: 44 in three minor league seasons and 148 more in the big leagues.

I have to keep going back to Moses Malone. He personified everything Bill Russell, John Havlicek, and Enos Slaughter said about mental toughness and hustle. I mean, the man was mental toughness personified. Dr. Michael Clancy, the Sixers team physician in the 1980s, called Moses a "freak of nature." He explained, "He can't jump. He doesn't run well. Bad hands. But he doesn't ever run down. He doesn't ever quit trying. And the rougher the competition gets, the better he plays. It's like he thrives on the banging and the contact. He plays his best when there are three people hanging all over him. I swear there are times when he goes out of his way to get bumped."

Bill Parcells, coach of the 1996 AFC Champion New England Patriots, said this about mental toughness: "As I tell my players, 'This game can make you wealthy; it can make you famous. It can give you a lot of things, but it can't give you a championship. You've got to earn that. And unless you're willing to pay the collective price—to play as a *team*—you will not get it. Because the competition is too great, and someone else will have that little edge.'" That little edge is mental toughness—a willingness to pay the price, *any* price, in order to win.

7. Self-Discipline: Commitment to Control and Self-Mastery

This is probably the toughest facet of commitment to master. It means being committed to conquering our own flaws, weaknesses, procrastination, appetites, and laziness. It means being tough on ourselves, denying ourselves some things we want for the moment in order to win what we want for all time. A self-disciplined player will work hard not only during the regular season, when the coach is screaming at him and the players are watching him, but during the off-season, when it's easy to slack off. A self-disciplined player doesn't need the inducements of external punishments or rewards to make him work harder. He works all out and goes full tilt because he has made it his nature and habit to do so. Former NFL coach Bum Phillips once said, "The only kind of discipline that lasts is self-discipline"

The greatest definition of self-discipline I've ever heard comes from Bobby Knight, the great basketball coach at Indiana University. "Self-discipline," he said, "is (1) doing what needs to be done; (2) doing it when it needs to be done; (3) doing it the best it can be done; (4) doing it that way every time you do it." Let me tell you: My kids can recite that statement backwards and forwards, because they've heard it a hundred times.

Football coach George Allen once said, "The secret to success, whether in athletics, business, or school, is self-discipline. Those that have it will make it, and the reason why is the competition will say, 'Oh, it's not worth it,' and they'll let you beat them out. If you want it badly enough, you'll work for it." The man knew whereof he spoke. The tougher we are on ourselves, the easier life becomes. Those who want to succeed as individuals and as part of a winning team must first learn to be disciplined from within.

Sometime in 1995, I received an invitation to play in a celebrity golf tournament in Orlando. It was months away, so I accepted. The day of the tournament eventually arrived—sneaked up on me, in fact. One of our secretaries, Barbara Jones, came in and reminded me that I had a golf tournament that day. I had completely forgotten.

"What kind of tournament is it?" I asked.

"It's a celebrity pro-am," she said.

"What?!" My blood turned to Jell-O in my veins. "I can't play in a celebrity pro-am! These are top celebrity golfers! I mean, these are the Johnny Benches, the Joe Namaths, the Mike Schmidts of the world!"

"Well," Barbara said sweetly, "it sounds like it should be a lot of fun."

"Fun!" I exclaimed. "What's fun about going out in front of a lot of famous people and TV cameras and crowds, and hearing them all laughing at my golf swing?"

"Okay," said Barbara, "maybe it won't be fun. But you promised to be there, so I guess you'll just have to play golf."

"Oh-ho-ho-no I'm not! I've done for golf what the *Titanic* did for the winter cruise business!"

"Oh, Pat, you have to," said Barbara. "Besides, you're not out there to play golf anyway!"

"I'm not?"

"No," she said. "You're out there to collect stories."

Well, Barbara really had my number. I thought to myself, *Wow, I never thought of that! She's right. I may make a complete fool of myself—but I'm bound to get some good stories.*

So I went. And wouldn'tcha know it, the celebrity golfer in our group was Ken "Hawk" Harrelson, the longtime American League home-run hitter, now the radio voice of the Chicago White Sox. Worst of all, he happens to be one of the best golfers of any ex-athlete in the nation, good enough to go on the Senior

Tour—and one of the most wicked kidders you'll ever meet. Hawk was my partner, and he didn't let me get away with a thing.

Well, on one hole, I managed to get on the green, but it was a long putt. I mean, I sighted to the hole and thought I was looking across a football field—there should've been hash marks on the green and goal posts over the hole. I stepped up to the ball, carefully measured my stroke—

And practically putted the darn ball onto the *next* green. It was embarrassing. But I knew I could count on my partner to say just the right word to lift my spirits. Looking back at Ken Harrelson, I saw him shaking his head. "Williams," he said, "that was the worst putt I have ever seen. And I've seen a lot of them."

"Thanks, Hawk," I said. "I needed that."

Well, I endured the rest of the game—and so did Ken Harrelson. And sure enough, just as Barbara Jones had predicted, I got a story from my golf partner. Here's the story Hawk told me (which was told to him by longtime Chicago White Sox trainer Herm Schneider):

When Michael Jordan left basketball for a time and attempted to build a new career as a baseball player, Herm Schneider watched him train. "Michael Jordan," Schneider told Hawk Harrelson, "was the hardest-working baseball player I ever met in all my years of baseball. Man, that guy was committed. He was so dedicated to the game he spent hours and hours at batting practice—so many hours swinging the bat that he developed blisters on his hands and blisters on the blisters. We would tape up his hands, and he would go right back to swinging that bat. He'd practice until the blood from his blisters came right through the tape, and still he'd keep swinging that bat. The man was incredibly committed, and that really made an impression on me. And as a basketball player, Michael would say, 'I practice harder than anyone. I deserve what I get.'"

And that story made a big impression on me. To succeed as a player, as a leader, as a team, you've got to be committed.

You've got to be intensely focused. You've got to be willing to pay the price of success. That's a great big chunk of what teamwork is all about: commitment. Being committed to each other. Being committed to winning. Being committed to a dream.

Commitment makes it happen.

Principle 4

Be Passionate!

Let's talk a little more about M.J.

Go back to October 6, 1993. On that day, Michael Jordan—probably the greatest basketball player of all time—sat down at a table before the nation's sports media and stunned the world, announcing his retirement from the game. At age thirty, he was at the top of his game, having led the Chicago Bulls to three NBA championships in a row. One of the few players in the game who was actually greater than his hype, M.J. always played the game with intensity and passion. And it has to be stated, he played the game with outright, exuberant *joy*! The man just loved to play basketball. You could see it in his face, in his moves, in his soaring trajectory while racking up frequent flyer miles between the hardwood and the basket.

But as the cameras clicked and the videocams whirred and the reporters scribbled in their notepads that cold October day in Chicago, Michael Jordan announced that he had had it. He had had it with life in a fishbowl and with the intrusiveness of the press. He felt he had nothing more to prove in the NBA. As he put it, "The desire just isn't there." In other words, the *passion* wasn't there anymore. The *joy* had been bled out of the game for him. And without the passion and joy, why play?

Michael had just been through an ordeal that would have shattered many lesser souls. He was very close to his father,

James Jordan, and it was only two months earlier that the senior Jordan's body was found in a North Carolina creek, the victim of a brutal murder. Michael had been understandably despondent over the tragedy, which was intensified by some very insensitive, outrageous, and intrusive media coverage. Sure, he told the press, "I would've made the same decision [to retire from basketball] even if my father was around." But it's not hard to imagine that the prospect of bouncing a ball up and down a court and throwing it at a hoop would seem a lot less satisfying after the incredible pain and loss he had just suffered. I'm convinced that the death of his father was a major factor in the loss of M.J.'s passion for the game.

Michael Jordan showed amazing maturity, wisdom, and good sense to leave the game of basketball when he did. And what did he do? He took a couple of years and tried to build a new career in baseball. A lot of players would have stuck with what was familiar, what was easy, what they already excelled in, even after the passion was gone. Not Air Jordan. Instead, he took a big gamble with his life, and threw himself in an entirely new direction. As we saw at the end of the previous chapter, he threw himself into this new sport with commitment and intensity. He worked hard to ignite the same passion and desire he had once felt for basketball.

After a couple of years of trying, he finally concluded that he didn't have what it takes to be a major league baseball player. The game of baseball came to the same conclusion about Michael. But by that time, something had changed inside Michael Jordan: He was ready to return to basketball. When he came back to the game, he was really back. You could see it. The old passion, the old desire, the old joy was there. The fire in the belly, the light in the eyes, the love in his heart for the game of roun'ball was all on display with every shot, every leap, every dunk, stuff, and rebound. The man was back—to the dismay of Pat Williams and the Orlando Magic and every other team in the NBA, of course—but he was really back.

Michael Jordan had the passion to lead the Bulls to new heights, new championships. I truly believe that interest plus values equals passion. True passion plus natural talent equals excellence. And passion shows. Passion wins. Nothing gets done without passion.

LOVE WHAT YOU DO; DO WHAT YOU LOVE

Peter Gammons, the baseball writer and ESPN broadcaster, tells a story about one of my boyhood idols, Ted Williams. "When Birdie Tebbetts played for the Red Sox in the late 1940s and early '50s," says Gammons, "he befriended a Harvard University psychologist who believed no one could excel at his job without loving it. The professor was fascinated by Ted Williams and pumped Tebbetts for insights. After meeting Williams, the professor told Tebbetts, 'Despite all the problems he has dealing with things outside the game and how unhappy he gets about the press and the fans, the reason he succeeds and will always succeed is that he loves to play. That is the essence of greatness.'"

That is true of every sport—and probably of every human endeavor. You've gotta love what you do and do what you love. I vividly remember an interview that Janet Evans gave as she approached the '96 Olympics, even though she was no longer the dominating swimmer she once was. Asked why she went, she replied with that big, bright, exuberant smile of hers, "I *love* swimming!"

I also have a vivid recollection of the 1992 Winter Olympics in which Bonnie Blair won her fifth gold medal in the speed skating event. What I remember most about her were her TV interviews, because her mantra, repeated over and over in interview after interview, was, "I *love* to skate!"

And how about Arnold Palmer? The man's incredible. In his late sixties, he still wows the crowd on the golf course. Asked how a man his age can still compete with the younger generation, he replies, "I *love* the game!"

And then there's Magic Johnson, who has retired from and returned to the game of basketball three times. On his latest comeback in the 1995-96 season, he was asked why he came back. With that trademark Magic smile, he said, "I *love* to play basketball!"

Doug Collins, coach of the Detroit Pistons, is an old friend. Not long ago, he told me that one night, when he was working for WTBS in Atlanta, he ran into Larry King at the CNN studios in Atlanta. Doug said to him, "Larry, I've always wanted to ask you a question. You've interviewed every famous person on earth for the last thirty-five years—kings, presidents, prime ministers, movie stars, athletes. Is there one common thread that all your guests over the years possess?"

Without an instant's hesitation, Larry said, "Yes! They all have passion. They all love what they do!"

When my friend Jim White, assistant athletic director at North Carolina State University, looked over the outline for this book, he pointed out a crucial truth about passion. "Passion," he said, "comes from a proper job fit. If you connect an individual's natural talents, interests, and values to a team slot that matches all those elements, you get an individual who is passionate about playing in that slot. Passion equals motivation. A passionate player is a motivated player. You can't force, wedge, or hype someone into a mold. The player and the slot have to match each other in order for that player to be passionate and motivated."

God has wired each of us differently, and some of us can be passionate without necessarily being dynamic personalities—that is, without being highly verbal, and outwardly excited and enthusiastic. Some of your most inwardly passionate players are outwardly quiet—but they are motivated and productive nonetheless. Most teams need a balance of the loudly passionate and the quietly passionate personality types.

Before becoming a world-renowned artist, Andy Warhol was a young man who didn't know what to do with his life. He asked dozens of people for suggestions. Finally, a woman he knew asked him a question: "What do you love most?"

"Well," he said, "I guess what I love most is painting."

"Then why don't you paint?" she asked.

"I didn't think I could make a living at it," he replied. He kept thinking about it and finally decided to give it a try—and he discovered he was not only able to make a living at it, he became rich, famous, and celebrated because of it. I think Harvey Mackay said it best: "Find something you love to do and you'll never have to work a day in your life."

PASSION IS MEMORABLE

What is it about being passionate about what you do that makes you successful in both individual and team efforts? Here's how it works: Passion connects you with other people. Passion gets noticed. People are attracted by passion and enthusiasm. Some examples:

I spoke at a dinner in Pittsburgh a while back, and I was sitting at the table with Bill Roemer, a banker and a Princeton graduate, and I said to him, "Bill, who is the most memorable professor you had at Princeton?"

He said, "Oh, that's easy. A chemistry professor who put on a pyrotechnical show every lecture. People would line up to get into his classes. They were attracted by his energy, his excitement, and his enthusiasm about his subject. I almost flunked the course, but I'll never forget that professor."

Not long thereafter, I was at a convention, sitting next to another company CEO named Andy Sharkey, who went to Yale. I asked him the same question. "Who was the most memorable professor you had at Yale?"

His instant reply: "Vince Scully, the art professor at Yale. I knew nothing about art, had no interest in the subject. But on the campus at the time, you just had to take his art course, because he was so passionate about it and so enthusiastic about art that everyone wanted to take the course."

If someone asked me the same question, the answer would be easy: James Walton at Wake Forest, my speech professor. I took two courses under him—Introduction to Speech and Oral Interpretation of Literature. These two courses changed my life more than anything. When I went into those courses, I was scared of my own shadow, but Jim Walton made those two courses so powerful I couldn't help getting excited about public speaking. Walton was a wild man—an energetic, kinetic, off-the-wall, irreverent, human firecracker. He just lit up Broadway, and as a result, I was fired up with an enormous passion in public speaking that has carried me throughout my life. Thank you, James Walton! It all started with you!

George Burns said, "I'd rather be a success at something I'm in love with than a failure at something I hate. Fortunately, I'm doing well in a business I love. I've always been in love with show business, and I still am. I love it today as much as I did for the twenty years I flopped in it."

PASSION ON THE TEAM

So passion is a crucial element of any successful endeavor. You've got to love what you do, be excited about what you do—and you've got to spread that infectious passion to the rest of the team. Emotion is contagious. The passion and enthusiasm of one player can lift the spirits of an entire team and inspire that team to victory.

Reggie White, defensive end of the Super Bowl XXXI Champion Green Bay Packers, was once asked why the players often yell and shout to their teammates when they line up for the snap. "Yelling and encouraging each other, pumping each other up is part of the game, the intensity, and the passion we have. Sometimes people think we're on each other, that we're mad at each other. The fact is, all of us love the game so much that we get real intense. We want to win, and it can make you start pushing one another around, screaming at one another, but that's just the passion we have for the game. It doesn't bother me at all, not at all. That's the kind of passion I want to carry in my spiritual life, in every aspect of my life. Passion. Love for the game. Encouraging one another. Driving each other on to be the best. That's what teamwork is all about."

That's the way it is in every team sport. Passion lifts all the players to a new level of engagement. Passion wins. Branch Rickey, the great baseball executive, was asked who was the greatest baseball player of all time, and he said, "The great players of all time are the ones with zest." While this book was being written, I heard Dick Vitale speak at a Boys and Girls Club banquet in Orlando, and in his inimitable fashion, he told those kids, "The number one quality for success is passion for life, excitement about life, enthusiasm and spirit for life."

Bob Leonard is the broadcaster for the Indiana Pacers, as well as a longtime NBA player and coach. He told me a story that took place in 1963, when he was the coach of the then-Baltimore Bullets. During that time, Bobby got to know Don Shula, who was then the rookie coach of the Colts. Also during that time, Bob Leonard became acquainted with Packers coach Vince Lombardi when the Packers came to town to play the Colts. So Bobby knew Shula and had a meal with Vince Lombardi, and he told me, "Both of those guys, Shula and Lombardi, told me the same thing about building teams. They said, 'Give me some players who are excited about playing, who love the game, who will pay the price, who are committed—and we'll win championships.'"

Passion has to be nurtured. It has to be fed. Whenever you see it begin to fade and go cold, the spark of passion has to be fanned back into a flame. You have to make sure your own passion is burning, and sometimes you have to stoke up the passion in your teammates. Once the passion is gone, it's hard to get it back. As Pete Rose said, "The first thing to go isn't the arm or legs. It's enthusiasm, it's passion. When that is gone, the player is through."

DISLODGE YOUR NECKTIE—AND MORE

You expect a pitcher to throw his arm out now and then. You expect a quarterback to be sidelined from time to time with a sprained tendon or a bad elbow. You expect players in basketball or just about any sport to be out of action now and then with a jammed finger or a hamstring injury or a groin pull. But of all the physically demanding and even dangerous endeavors that people engage in, the role of symphony conductor would probably be pretty far down the list. I mean, how can a guy in a tux with a baton in one hand get himself hurt? But it happened to

Eugene Ormandy. The man actually got a dislocated shoulder while conducting the Philadelphia Orchestra.

Writer Maurice Boyd says Ormandy hurt himself during a performance of a particular Brahms symphony. In the margin of that symphony, Brahms writes, "As loud as possible!" Then, just a few bars later, Brahms writes, "Louder still!" In the passion of trying to carry out Brahms's instructions and summon forth every decibel of symphonic energy from his players, Ormandy threw his shoulder out of joint. Boyd concludes, "I know some people who have reached middle age and have never had an enthusiasm great enough to dislodge a necktie, let alone their shoulder."

What about you? Have you ever loved what you do, and what your team does, enough to dislodge your necktie, twang your collarbone, or yank your shoulder out of its socket? Do you have passion? Do you spread your passion like an exuberant, joyful, wonderful, infectious disease? Do people around you see your passion on your face and in everything you do? Does your team draw energy and inspiration from your love for what you do?

Orville and Wilbur Wright formed a passionate team in the early 1900s. After they launched their first flight at Kitty Hawk, North Carolina, the Wright brothers wrote this note in their diary, and on many occasions later: "We could hardly wait to get up in the morning."

Years ago, Fred Shero was the coach of the Philadelphia Flyers when I was with the Sixers. He used to tell his players, "Success is not the result of spontaneous combustion. You must first set yourself on fire."

This has been a short chapter—but a passionate one. Why? Because my advice to you is quite simple: I want to see the joy on your face! I want to feel the searing, passionate heat of your excitement! I want to see you charging at your task with the intensity and passion worthy of a Super Bowl performance!

Inspire your team! Be a champion!

Be *passionate*!

Principle 5

Think "Team"!

I believe the great philosophies of our age are found on T-shirts. If there's anything you want to know about life, just go to a mall, a sports stadium, an amusement park, anyplace where T-shirts proliferate, and you will probably find the truth you seek.

My son Bobby is a student at Rollins College and a catcher on the baseball team. After Bobby's first fall practice as a freshman, his coach, Bob Rikeman, gave each of the players who made the team a T-shirt with a picture of a bunch of guys clinging to a rope for dear life and the words, "24 Guys Hanging On the Same Rope." Bobby wears that T-shirt with a lot of pride. It perfectly expresses what a *team attitude* is all about. To paraphrase Ben Franklin, teams have gotta hang together or else they'll hang separately.

Not long ago, I had a speaking engagement in Newport News, Virginia, the naval base area. After my speech, I was approached by a young man in a Navy uniform. He put his hand out, grinned broadly, and said, "Mr. Williams, I'm in business with Rich DeVos. We're teammates." I knew exactly what he meant. This young man was in the Amway business, and he was out there hustling in the boondocks, selling the product line of Rich DeVos's multilevel marketing company. Rich DeVos may not have recognized this young man if he bumped into him, but

I know Rich would have agreed and would have embraced him as a teammate.

The next time I saw Rich DeVos, I shared this story with him and his reaction was, "Wow! I guess that's the story of the Amway business!" Yes, this young man and Rich DeVos *are* teammates—Rich with his multibillion-dollar net worth, and this young guy selling Amway in his spare time—because Amway is a company that practices a *team attitude.* Everyone who is involved in the Amway world is in business with Rich DeVos, part of the Amway team. It's not a slogan. It's *reality.*

TEAM ATTITUDE: THE KEY TO ALIGNMENT

Simply stated, a team attitude is a "we" and "our" attitude instead of a "me" and "my" attitude. When you become part of a team, you're not giving up your individual goals, you're not sacrificing your personal success. You are setting your sights on an even *higher* goal so that you can *magnify* your success. Whatever an individual can achieve, a team can do bigger, faster, more effectively, and more gloriously. As someone once said, a hundred organized teammates, working in sync, can always defeat a thousand disorganized individuals.

You know what? Human beings are 97 percent water—the rest is all attitude! What is your attitude? Do you have a "we" attitude—or a "me" attitude? Some people are afraid that by taking a "we" attitude instead of a "me" attitude, they will end up losing their identity, crucifying their own interests. But that's not the way it works. When you adopt a "we" attitude, a team attitude, the shared vision and goals of the team become an extension of your own personal vision and goals. You add your efforts to the team effort, thereby empowering the team to reach its goals. At the same time, the team effort magnifies and intensifies your efforts, empowering you to reach levels of achievement you could never have imagined on your own.

The team leadership/ownership has a lot to do with building team attitude and motivating people to adopt a "we" attitude. Jim White, assistant athletic director at North Carolina State

University, observes that a healthy team attitude begins with people feeling they are fairly treated by the team leadership. "When the organization or team's goals are consistent with a player's professional goals," he says, "that player is a lot more likely to be a team player. People have to feel they are being fairly compensated and recognized for their contribution to the team—or their motivation dies."

At the beginning of this book, I quoted the legendary Celtics center Bill Russell as he described the sublime experience of "alignment" or "synergy," that magical moment when everything seems to click into place, when everything just seems to work.

Ah, the elusive mystery of "alignment" or "synergy," that moment when the entire team is synchronized, flowing together like the blended notes of a symphony! I believe one of the absolute requirements for experiencing this kind of magical alignment is that every player on the team must have a team attitude. Every player must "Think Team," not "Think Me." Writing in *Peak Performance,* Charles Garfield puts it this way: "An alignment occurs when individuals perceive that contributing to an organization or team produces direct contributions to their personal mission. The individual wants the team to succeed because it provides the context for his or her own personal achievement."

And Peter Senge, senior MIT lecturer and consultant and author of *The Fifth Discipline,* offers this observation on the relationship between team attitude and the magic of alignment: "When a team becomes more aligned, a commonality of direction emerges, and individual energies harmonize. There is less wasted energy. In fact, a resonance or synergy develops like the coherent light of a laser rather than the incoherent and scattered light of a light bulb. There is a commonality of purpose, a shared vision, an understanding of how to complement one another's efforts."

Maintaining a team attitude can be difficult in such endeavors as professional sports, where egos often become so inflated they could lift a fleet of *Hindenburg*s. But without team attitude, the team effort is doomed. With it, the sky's the limit. Baseball great Pete Rose put this attitude succinctly when he said, "What comes first is the team."

But what is a team attitude? How, in practical terms, do we reach a point where we truly "Think Team"? Actually, I believe team attitude is not one attitude but a subtle mix of many attitudes. In the rest of this chapter, we will examine the components of team attitude and see what it really means to "Think Team."

Team Attitude Requirement No. I: Be Unselfish

You gotta have *wa*.

Dodgers pitcher Hideo Nomo finished his 1995 Rookie-of-the-Year season with a record of 13 wins and 6 losses, a 2.54 ERA, and 236 strikeouts in 28 starts. Near the end of the 1996 season, he made big headlines by pitching a 9-0 no-hitter against the Colorado Rockies in Denver's Coors Field. That win moved the Dodgers within bunting distance of the play-offs. After the game, Nomo expressed through an interpreter that it was the team effort and the team standing, not his individual effort or stats, that really mattered to him. "I am more happy we got the win," he said, "than I am about pitching a no-hitter."

The Dodgers' general manager, Fred Claire, knew that Nomo meant what he said. "He has a sense of team," said Claire. "He never talks about individual accomplishments. He always says he wants to be a part of a winning team. He means it." In the story of Nomo's incredible feat published in *USA Today* sportswriter Rod Beaton added,

> Japanese baseball players use the term *wa*, an expression meaning a player sublimates personality and personal goals to the success of the team. The philosophy was detailed to Westerners in Robert Whiting's book, *You Gotta Have Wa*. Nomo has lots of *wa*.[1]

You gotta have *wa* to win in the NBA. Successful basketball teams run on *wa*. That's why my friend Bill Russell was so successful, collecting eleven NBA championship rings and five league MVP titles in his career. Bill Russell just had lots and lots of *wa*. Though the Celtics star center was one of the greatest players ever to lace up a sneaker, his focus was always on propelling the team, not enlarging his own ego. He once said, "The most important measure of how good a game I played was how much better I made my teammates play."

Pete Carril just retired after twenty-nine years coaching basketball at Princeton, and he's now on the coaching staff with the Sacramento Kings. While he was with Princeton, he would always have one question for recruiters about any high school prospect: "Can he see?" No, he wasn't asking about the kid's eyesight. He was asking whether the kid was selfish or not: Can he see others around him to pass the ball to—or does he selfishly demand every touch, every dribble, every shot? Can he give the ball up, or does he hog all the glory?

"I like players who pass the ball," Petey said. "They can see everything. A pass is not a pass when it is made after you've tried to do everything else. If your teammate does not pass the ball to you when you're open, and he doesn't say anything, then he didn't see you. If he says, 'I'm sorry,' he saw you and didn't want to throw you the ball. I love coaching players who can see." The Lakers' Magic Johnson understood the need for *wa* in the game of basketball. He once observed, "In the NBA today, you have a lot of guys looking for theirs and no one really thinking about the team. There's more to it than just doing some spectacular individual thing or putting yourself above your team. Losers don't get anything, and individuals don't win—only teams win."

One of the sights I miss on the court now that Shaq has gone to the Lakers is the beautifully unselfish interplay between the big guy and Anfernee Hardaway. Penny is *wa* personified, unselfish to a fault. Unquestionably one of the greatest all-around performers ever to play the game, Penny Hardaway does everything flawlessly, and he has the confidence that goes with greatness. Yet there have been countless times he has passed up a scoring opportunity for a teammate to score, sacrificing his stats in order to bring other players into the game, build another player's confidence, pump up the crowd, or spread the glory around. I've seen him take the ball downcourt, wide open for an easy layup, then pass it off to Shaq for a big crowd-pleasing, rim-hanging, two-handed Shaq-attaq. Sometimes his coaches have to tell him, "Penny, be a little more selfish out there!" Anfernee Hardaway has a champion's attitude, a winning attitude. He's got lots of *wa*.

I once heard Seattle Sonics coach George Karl talking about Sonics guard Hersey Hawkins. "It's a pleasure to coach a guy who's so unselfish," he said. I knew exactly what he meant.

NBA coach Pat Riley has written a book on teamwork called *The Winner Within.* In that book, he wrote, "You've got to totally get out of yourself and into the unity of the team. The spirit of unity does not guarantee you anything. But without it, you can't be successful. . . . Teamwork is the only way to reach our ultimate moments, to create the breakthroughs that define our career, to fulfill our lives with a sense of lasting significance." Out of yourself, and into the unity of the team: that's what *wa* is all about.

I recently came across a vignette in *Life* magazine (Aug. 1996) that means a lot to me since my first taste of mountain-climbing on Mt. Ranier:

> In 1953 Sir Edmund Hillary and his Sherpa guide Tenzing Norgay were the first humans to climb Mount Everest. In 1996, Hillary at age 77 said, "There has been an erosion of mountaineering values. It used to be a team effort. Nowadays, it's much too everybody-for-himself. Tenzing and I got to the top together; it wasn't first one and then the other. Now it's every man for himself. Not much you can do about it. That's just the way people are these days."

Sir Edmund Hillary knows. It takes a lot of *wa* to climb a mountain. Nobody gets to the top of the world by himself.

Unfortunately, as Sir Edmund sadly observed, *wa* is in perilously short supply in our world today. Most of our institutions seem to run on the law of the jungle, not the law of *wa*. It's survival of the fittest and the meanest, and those who are ambitious for individual success seem to leave a trail of bodies behind them—victims of political intrigue, manipulation, character assassination, backstabbing, rumor-mongering, and other forms of selfish, team-destroying behavior. Teamwork is not about who can scramble fastest to the top of the heap. It's about bringing everybody along to the mountaintop. It's about making everyone a champion.

With a goal of raising money to alleviate hunger in Africa, Lionel Richie wrote and produced a song called "We Are the World." He invited some of the most famous performers in the popular music business to come into the studio and sing—not as individuals, but as a team. It was probably the wealthiest, most recognizable, most high-powered choir ever assembled. On the day of the recording session, Richie posted a sign at the entrance to the studio that read: CHECK YOUR EGO AT THE DOOR. He understood that in order for this recording to be a success, they all had to merge their talents as a team, humbly and unselfishly. They had to have *wa*.

My friend Gil McGregor, who is an announcer for the Charlotte Hornets, has a great analogy for *wa*. He calls it "The Dirty Shoulders Principle," and he says that you can spot a player with a genuine team attitude by looking at his shoulders. A player who truly understands teamwork has "dirty shoulders," because he's always lifting up his teammates, letting them stand tall on his shoulders, supporting them and backing them up, not caring who gets the glory and recognition, but caring only that the team gets the win. A "dirty shoulders" player thinks "we," not "me." A player with "dirty shoulders" is a player with a lotta *wa*.

Imagine what would happen if we ran our political institutions in America on a model of *wa* and "dirty shoulders" instead of political attack, counterattack, lies, and hidden agendas. Imagine if we ran our offices and workplaces on a model of *wa* and "dirty shoulders" instead of office politics and game playing. Imagine how our families would be transformed if parents and kids would live together in a harmonious atmosphere of *wa* and "dirty shoulders" instead of a battle-haze of bickering and rivalry. Imagine if we ran our churches on a basis of the biblical version of *wa* and "dirty shoulders"—what the Bible calls humility, servanthood, mutual submission, forgiveness, acceptance, and love for one another.

Did you know that there are fifty-nine "one another" commands in the New Testament? Here's a partial list of the *wa* passages in the Bible:

- "Have peace with one another" (Mark 9:50).
- "Love one another" (John 13:34, and twenty other verses throughout the New Testament).
- "Be kindly affectionate to one another with brotherly love, in honor giving preference to one another" (Romans 12:10).
- "Let us not judge one another" (Romans 14:13).
- "Receive one another, just as Christ also received us, to the glory of God" (Romans 15:7).
- "Have the same care for one another" (1 Corinthians 12:25).
- "Through love serve one another" (Galatians 5:13).
- "Let us not become conceited, provoking one another, envying one another" (Galatians 5:26).
- "Bear one another's burdens" (Galatians 6:2).
- "With longsuffering, [bear] with one another in love" (Ephesians 4:2).
- "[Forgive] one another" (Ephesians 4:32).
- "[Submit] to one another in the fear of God" (Ephesians 5:21).
- "[Admonish] one another" (Colossians 3:16).
- "Increase and abound in love to one another" (1 Thessalonians 3:12).
- "Comfort each other and edify one another" (1 Thessalonians 5:11).
- "Exhort one another daily" (Hebrews 3:13).
- "Do not grumble against one another" (James 5:9).
- "Confess your trespasses to one another" (James 5:16).
- "Pray for one another" (James 5:16).
- "Be of one mind, having compassion for one another" (1 Peter 3:8).
- "Be submissive to one another, and be clothed with humility" (1 Peter 5:5).

Bruce Bickel played football at the U.S. Naval Academy (he succeeded Roger Staubach as Navy's quarterback), and he now lives in Pittsburgh. He's been active in Fellowship of Christian Athletes for years, and he's a good friend. He knows what team attitude is all about. He's got lots of *wa*. Bruce tells a story of his days in Vietnam, just before the '68 Tet offensive. After some nine thousand civilians were slaughtered by the enemy at Hue, American forces recaptured the city and set up orphanages. One of these orphanages was shelled by the Vietcong, and an eight-year-old boy was severely wounded.

Bruce rushed the boy by Jeep to a medical center, where the doctors determined that he needed a blood transfusion. Unfortunately, there was no one at the medical center who had the right type of blood, not even Bruce himself. So Bruce jumped in the Jeep and raced back to the orphanage. Running inside, he explained to the children that the injured child needed a transfusion and asked for a volunteer to donate blood.

Nine-year-old Hai raised his hand. "Me," he said, "I give."

"Good boy!" Bruce said, ushering the boy back out to the Jeep. Together, they raced over the bumpy, rutted road to the medical center. The doctors put the boy on a gurney and began extracting blood. Hai began to cry.

"Does it hurt?" Bruce asked.

The boy shook his head.

"Are you scared?"

Hai nodded—then he asked, "Sir, how long will it take me to die?"

This little boy didn't understand blood transfusions. He thought he was giving *all* of his blood so that his friend could live. It made him scared, it made him cry—but he was willing to do this for his friend. That little boy had lots of *wa*. He reached the heights and plumbed the depths of unselfishness. To paraphrase Jesus, greater *wa* has no man than this.

Team Attitude Requirement No. 2: Find a Role and Fill It

"In baseball, the individual is highlighted," said NBC sportscaster Bob Costas, "but in the end, his performance means nothing outside the team." This is true, of course, in every team sport, and this truth includes the game of baseball. You see it epitomized in that rare baseball phenomenon called "the perfect game"—a game in which a pitcher allows no runs, no hits, no walks, no base runners. To a baseball outsider, that sounds like a boring game. To the true fan, it's a thing of beauty rarely beheld.

In May of 1981, while I was with the 76ers, I went to Cleveland to interview a guard at Cleveland State. The NBA draft was coming up, and we were interested in Franklin Edwards (we eventually drafted him, by the way). I was also there in my official capacity to watch a baseball game; the Toronto Blue Jays were in town to play the Cleveland Indians. The second baseman for the Blue Jays was Danny Ainge, who had just finished an illustrious basketball career at Brigham Young and had also proved himself to be such a capable baseball player that he had made it to the big leagues. We were interested in possibly wooing Ainge out of baseball and into the NBA (he ended up being drafted by the Celtics).

So I was at the big old ballpark in Cleveland, Municipal Stadium, watching the game on a very raw, cold night. I bought a program and decided to keep score that night; I don't usually do so, but I wanted to keep track of Danny Ainge as a baseball player. As the game unfolded, Len Barker, the Cleveland pitcher kept retiring Toronto batters. By the third inning, I noticed he had retired nine straight hitters. Fourth inning, twelve hitters. Fifth inning, fifteen hitters. As I kept score on my program, I thought, *This is starting to get eerie.*

Barker was getting a lot of strikeouts, of course, but he was also getting a lot of help. I don't remember all the details, but I do recall noting that the Cleveland catcher was right in sync with every hot fastball and every floating change-up Barker threw. There was also some great fielding going on that night—outfielders snatching fly balls and line drives out of the air like a Dustbuster sucks up a fuzzbunny. I particularly remember one heroic, side-skinning, diving catch by an outfielder late in the game.

By the top of the ninth inning, Barker had retired twenty-four straight batters, and a hush descended over the entire ballpark. The crowd sensed that history was being made that night. The tension in the air was as thick as tapioca. Everyone felt it. I don't think anyone in that ballpark drew a single breath while Barker faced those last three batters. He put them away, one after the other—and by chance, I had managed to be present at that rare experience in baseball, a perfect game. I got into the locker room that night and had Barker sign and date the program for me, and it's one of my favorite baseball keepsakes.

That perfect game was a remarkable individual achievement for Len Barker, but it also represented a flawless team performance that night by the entire '81 Cleveland Indians. It takes a whole team, putting out a brilliantly synchronized and harmonized effort, to enable the guy on the mound to get the credit for a perfect game. Everybody's got to have a role, and everybody's got to fill that role with passion, dedication, and excellence.

After the record-setting, seventy-two-win 1995-96 season of the Chicago Bulls, head coach Phil Jackson described what it takes to win. "Creating a successful team," he explained, "whether it's an NBA champion or a record-setting sales force, is essentially a spiritual act. It requires the individual involved to surrender his self-interest for the greater good so that the whole adds up to more than the sum of its parts . . . I knew that the only way to win consistently was to give everybody—from the stars to the last player on the bench—a vital role on the team, and inspire them to be acutely aware of what was happening, even when the spotlight was on somebody else. More than anything, I wanted to build a team that would blend individual talent with heightened group consciousness—a team that could win big without becoming small in the process."

"Unless the whole organization is working together for one common purpose, the club doesn't win, and the manager gets fired," said former baseball manager Whitey Herzog. Every player, every leader, every coach must know his or her role and must fill that role like a hand fills a glove. Each must carry out assigned duties and responsibilities, meshing his or her efforts with those of the other teammates, so that the goals can be achieved, the vision can become a reality. There is no room on any team for separate agendas. Everyone is there to do a job—his or her unique and special job—so the team can fulfill its mission.

A strong team attitude, an atmosphere in which everybody plays his or her role to the max, can often overcome a lack of star-level, record-busting talent. When everybody carries out his or her assigned role, a team of good, well-balanced, synchronized players can knock off a team of megatalents who are just out to pump up their stats. Average players can beat the superstars. Example: The Boston Celtics have won sixteen NBA championships and every one of those teams boasted a lot of talent—let's not minimize that aspect. But you know what? Never in all those championship years did the Celtics have the individual league-leading scorer on the team. What they had was a *team,* with a team attitude, each player filling his role to the max and the entire team thinking, working, and winning as one.

It's not only true in basketball. It's true in baseball. As Brooks Robinson said, "To make a ball club a champion, the effort has to start with the bat boy and move right up to the owner." It's also true in football. NFL coach Bill Parcells put it this way: "In my line of work, teamwork is all-important. Every player, from the starting quarterback, to the special teams rookie, is interdependent. We have this sign up in our locker room: INDIVIDUALS PLAY THE GAME, BUT TEAMS WIN CHAMPIONSHIPS." It's also true in life, in any arena of endeavor we engage in.

At a young age, the man who would one day be Ronald Reagan's surgeon general, C. Everett Koop, understood the need for teamwork and role-filling. He tells the story of when he was a senior at Dartmouth, applying to the College of Physicians and Surgeons at Columbia. At his interview, the admissions panel asked him, "Do you ever expect to make any major discoveries in medicine?" His reply was a beautiful statement of his commitment to the concept of teamwork.

"I believe," he responded, "that those who make discoveries in the field of medicine are building upon the efforts of many who preceded them, but did not do that final thing which achieved success and fame. I would like to be the one who makes a major discovery, but I will be content to contribute to the process."

That answer disappointed the panel. The interview, which had been going well up to that point, suddenly foundered. "That's not the attitude we wish to encourage here," they said to him. "We want to train people who are ambitious to make major discoveries which will reflect credit on this institution."

The school's response was terribly shortsighted. The panel should have listened to the young C. Everett Koop—and learned. Because he was right. The most effective progress is made not by individuals, working in isolation to make names for themselves, but by teams, sharing their knowledge, skills, and experience, and magnifying their efforts and achievements in the process.

It's good to have players on your team with drive and ambition, but every player has to be willing and able to fill a role, to carry out a supporting function, to allow his or her contribution to make stars of others. Fact is, if you don't have role fillers and hod carriers on your team, *no one* gets to be a star.

Team Attitude Requirement No. 3: Be a Team of Cheerleaders

I recently went to Hickory, North Carolina, for a speaking engagement. While I was in town, I got to see Jim Raugh, a friend of mine from many years ago. He reminisced about his days as a pitcher for the Haverford School on the Philadelphia Mainline. He especially remembered the game against Friends Central—a sixteen-inning game that Haverford won, 1-0. "I pitched a perfect game for ten innings," Jim recalled. "But in the eleventh, I walked my first hitter. After the game, my dad came up to me and you know what he said? 'Why did you walk that hitter in the eleventh?' Ten perfect innings, plus the win, and all he could think about was that one walk in the eleventh. I'm fifty-nine years old today, but I can still hear his words in my mind like it was yesterday. Isn't that funny? That's what I remember most about that game: 'Why did you walk that hitter in the eleventh?'"

Jimmy went on to the University of North Carolina, where he became an all-American pitcher and, during his senior year, student body president. After becoming student body president, his dad asked, "Why weren't you president in your junior year, too?" Jimmy's dad was a critic. Jimmy didn't need a critic when he was growing up. He needed a cheerleader. He didn't need to have someone on his back. He needed to have someone on his side.

We all need that. We all need cheers and encouragement. Encouragement promotes growth. Praise enhances morale. Commendations increase cooperation. Carping and criticism kill your fighting spirit. On a team, it kills your team spirit.

I clipped and saved a story by Manny Topol from a January 1995 edition of *Newsday*. It is the story of quarterback Otto Graham, who played for the Cleveland Browns many years ago. Graham told *Newsday* that his most memorable game was the title game against the Rams at Municipal Stadium in Cleveland in 1950—the Browns' first year as an NFL franchise. "We were one point behind," he recalled. "We were moving down the field, in the last two minutes, and all we needed was a field goal to win. I ran a quarterback draw and picked up about 10 yards—and then I was blindsided and I fumbled."

The Browns were within field goal range when Otto Graham fumbled. The Rams recovered the ball. "I got cancer about seventeen years ago," he recalled, "and I wasn't anywhere as devastated when I had that cancer as I was when I dropped that football. It was our first year in the league, and we had a chance to win this thing, and I blew it."

Coming off the field, Graham saw coach Paul Brown coming toward him. Expecting to get blasted by the coach for the fumble, he felt like turning right around and walking to the opposite sidelines. But Brown didn't blast him. Instead, he put his hand on Graham's shoulder and said, "Don't worry, Otts. We're still gonna get 'em."

"I can't tell you how much that meant to me," Otto Graham recalled.

The situation was desperate. The Rams had them, 28-27, and the clock was running out. Somehow, the Browns defense managed to keep the Rams from getting a first down. The Rams punted, and Otto Graham came back onto the field, cheered up and charged up by coach Brown's words of encouragement. Deep in his own territory, with only a minute and a half on the clock, Graham took charge of the ball and steadily began moving it downfield. Incredibly, after only a minute-ten, he had moved the Browns 80 yards closer to the goal. With just twenty seconds left, Browns kicker Lou Groza booted a field goal, and the new Cleveland Browns franchise had taken the title with a 30-28 heart-stopping victory.

"Paul Brown knew when to kick you in the pants," said Graham, "and he knew when to pat you on the shoulder. If he had let me have it, if he had broken my spirit at that moment, we would have lost the game. Instead, he inspired me with confidence, and I passed on that confidence to my teammates in the huddle. We went right down that field and got three points."

Otto Graham proved it: Cheerleading wins games. Everybody needs a cheerleader. Every team needs to be made of cheerleaders and led by cheerleaders. Encouraging one another and building each other up is an indispensable part of a winning team attitude.

Team Attitude Requirement No. 4: Have Fun!

There's a movie that embodies all the truths we're discussing in this chapter: Team attitude, unselfishness and *wa*, find a role and fill it, encourage each other, and above all, "Have fun!" That movie is Disney's *The Mighty Ducks*, about a youth-league hockey team that rises from the bottom of the barrel to the league championship. The movie contrasts two coaching styles. One coach uses pressure and fear to motivate his team: "If you miss this shot, you'll let me down and you'll let your team down!"

By contrast, the coach of the Ducks, Gordon Bombay, learns how to build a healthy team attitude into his hockey team: In order to fly on the ice, you've gotta have *fun*! You see the contrast between these two coaching styles in the climactic moments of the film. The old intimidating coach sends his players onto the ice with growls of "Pressure! Pressure!" Gordon sends his Ducks onto the ice with a grin and a shout, "Let's have *fun* out there!" The Ducks use every impossible, fun gimmick in the book, from ballet-style pirouettes to a wedgelike flying vee. With every goal, the Ducks chant to each other, "More fun! More fun!" And the Ducks win the game.

You may think, *That's Hollywood! That's a sports fantasy. That doesn't happen in real life.* Oh, yes it does! I've seen it happen again and again in the world of sports, and in the world of business, and in every aspect of life: If you want to be a winner, have fun out there! As former Philadelphia Flyers coach Fred Shero said, "Hockey is a children's game played by men, and since it is a child's game, they ought to have fun." NHL center Wayne Gretzky agrees. "I love playing the game," he said. "It's no different than little kids who go out and play for the fun of it. We're just big kids playing a game."

It's the same in every team activity. Terry Bradshaw knows. After a Super Bowl win, the great NFL quarterback said, "I made up my mind that I was gonna have some fun in this Super Bowl. I was gonna play my game, win or lose. I didn't give a hoot. I was going to do it my way and the one thing I didn't want to do was change what got me here." Baseball, same story. The great hitter Rod Carew: "I just want to go out there and have some fun, and let baseball be the little boy's game it's supposed to be. I enjoy playing. It's fun."

For the last few seasons, Bill Veeck's son, Mike Veeck, has operated a very successful minor-league baseball team in St. Paul, Minnesota. In typical Veeckian fashion, Mike has promoted up a storm, pulled off one outlandish stunt after another, and made every visit to that little ballpark a fan's delight. Mike's philosophy—so much like his dad's—is succinctly stated in signs he has hung all around his ballpark. All the signs say one thing: FUN IS GOOD! I love it!

Every competitive situation has its pressures and stresses. Pressure is a given in any endeavor, from sports to business to ministry to government. Pressure tightens you up and keeps you from doing your best work. It can create tension and friction between you and your teammates, straining the bond, the focus, and the team attitude of the players. So you've gotta have *fun* out there. Fun lubricates your mind and your spirit and keeps the team attitude intact. Fun keeps you loose, keeps you from freezing up in the clutch situations.

So stay loose, Babe. Whatever game you're playing—whether you play it on an athletic field, in an office, on the road, or in a church—enjoy the heck out of that game. Have a blast! Have *fun* out there. As Erma Bombeck put it, "Remember all those women on the *Titanic* who waved off the dessert cart."

Team Attitude Requirement No. 5: Follow the Leader

In April 1994, then Knicks head coach Pat Riley suspended Anthony Mason, causing the star forward to miss a game against the Philadelphia 76ers. Why? Because Mason had openly criticized coach Riley for sitting him in the previous game, in which the Knicks were defeated by Atlanta. "The core objective of the New York Knicks has been, is, and always will be team first and team last," explained Riley. "The greatest challenge for a player who is part of a team is to voluntarily get out of himself and get with the program. To do that, sometimes you have to do things you don't want to in order to achieve what the team wants." Coach Riley was right. In any team endeavor, you've got to have players who are willing to follow the leader.

The leadership of the team has to exercise authority, and the team has to respect and follow the leader. This doesn't mean the leader must be a tyrant or that players must be obsequious little toadies. Leaders and players are *partners,* with clearly defined roles. But when players defy, ignore, or undermine the team's leadership, then the team attitude quickly disintegrates. You've gotta follow the leader—or the team will fly apart by centrifugal force.

Leaders and their style of leadership have a lot to do with encouraging healthy followership. Those who lead by including the players, by making them all feel important, by valuing and encouraging the players and drawing them into the overall team effort, tend to encourage enthusiastic followership throughout the team. Walt Disney was that kind of leader, and he built a team that responded enthusiastically to his leadership.

In the early days of the Disney studio, he created an inclusive team environment—so much so that he actually paid for additional art instruction for many of his animators and personally drove them to their classes and back. During the animation of his first feature film, *Snow White and the Seven Dwarfs,* he held "gag conferences" in which raw penciled animation was screened and the entire team was allowed to view the footage and express opinions on how to make the movie better. Walt led the freewheeling discussions in a very democratic style, and no opinion was ever censured or criticized. Individual gag ideas that made it into the film were rewarded with cash. Only after this process was completed and the film was pushed to be the best it could be was it finally sent for inking and painting.

People loved working for Walt, following his leadership, and being a player on his team because they knew that they were valued and respected. The same is true of any team. As Pete Rose has said, "The winning 'we' attitude starts at the top of the organization."

Team Attitude Requirement No. 6: Be Flexible

The United States Marines have two mottoes—one official, one unofficial. The official motto is *Semper fidelis,* or "Always faithful." The unofficial motto is *Semper gumby,* which means (tongue in cheek) "Always flexible." In other words, the Marines are like Gumby, that flexible, stretchable clay animation character in the children's TV show. They bend any way they have to in order to get the job done. So should you. So should I. A person who is flexible is:

- Adaptable;
- Creative;
- Coachable;
- Eager to try new ideas and new approaches;
- Not rigid or stuck in a rut.

A *semper gumby* attitude is an attitude of greatness. Take football. Most NFL quarterbacks with a decent offensive line can be productive firing off passes from the pocket, behind a wall of beefy offensive linemen. The better quarterbacks can complete passes on a rollout. But the truly *great* quarterbacks—the Joe

Montanas, the John Elways, the Dan Marinos, the Brett Favres of the game—are the *semper gumby* quarterbacks. When they don't see a hole, they make one—or they run right over the top of guys. They read defensive coverage and make adjustments on the fly. They are nimble in a broken field, and they break up tackles on the run. When a play gets busted, they make up a new play as they go along. They sense the flow of the situation, and they jink, juke, bob, and weave in order to get to the goal. That's greatness. That's flexibility. That's *semper gumby.*

And it's all part of a team attitude.

Tim Hansel tells the story about Jimmy Durante, one of the great entertainers of the last generation. Durante was once asked to do a performance for World War II veterans. He told the organizers of the show that he could do the show, but he had a packed schedule and could only afford a few minutes—just enough for a song and a short monologue. The organizers were just pleased to get Jimmy for any time at all.

So Jimmy went out on the stage and started the show. He did his song, and he did his short monologue. But then he did a couple of more songs and some more jokes. He stayed and he stayed, and the longer he performed, the louder the applause became. The organizers of the show were amazed. By the time Jimmy Durante took his last bow, he had been performing for almost an hour—much longer than the few minutes he had promised.

Backstage, the director said to him, "That was great what you did for the guys out there, staying longer than you planned. But why? You said you had to go."

"I do have to go!" said Jimmy, throwing on his coat, talking quickly as he rushed to leave. "I'm late right now to my next performance. But if you want to know why I stayed, take a look at those two guys in the front row. One of 'em lost his right arm, the other lost his left. But you shoulda seen those two guys, each putting his one good hand against the other guy's good hand, clapping their hearts out for me. How could I let those guys down when they were applauding like that for me?"

Those two soldiers in the front row knew the meaning of team attitude and *semper gumby.* Working alone, neither could applaud. Working together, flexibly adapting to the situation, they were able to hold a busy performer onstage for encore after encore.

An item I clipped out of the *Wall Street Journal* compared today's business teams and organizations to a doubles tennis team. "Doubles partners play certain roles. When one person serves, the other is at the net. But those roles are interchangeable. Each person must be prepared to do anything. If an opponent lobs the ball over my partner's head, I better hustle back there, to return it. If I take a me-first approach—'That's not my job'— you can bet we won't make it to Wimbledon." Flexibility and adaptability are absolute requisites for any successful team, whether on a tennis court or in the business world.

Let's say you're a sailor on a ship, and suddenly the cry goes up, "The ship is sinking!" What do you do? Some people would shrug and say, "So what? It's not my ship." Others would say, "What am I supposed to do about it? Your end of the boat is sinking, not mine!" Others would leap over the side, shouting, "Every man for himself!" The captain might strut around on the poop deck, growling, "I'm a captain! I don't man a bilge pump, I give orders!" And the first mate? He could say, "Hey, I'm the first mate! I've got the best stats in the fleet! So what if the ship sinks? As long as the fans on the shore keep cheering me, as long as the owners keep signing my checks, I'm just gonna keep doing what I'm doing." And if that's the way everyone on the ship responds, they're all going to end up on the bottom of the deep blue sea, wondering where their next breath is coming from.

But if everyone on that ship has a *semper gumby* attitude, you'll have every hand, from the swab who cleans the head right up to the admiral himself, pitching in, manning the pumps, dogging the bulkhead hatches, bailing by the bucketful, sending out Maydays, doing whatever needs to be done to save the ship and the crew. You've gotta be flexible. You've got to accept change. You've got to adapt to every new situation, condition, and contingency. Sure, we've all got to fill our own roles—but when circumstances change, we've got to change, too.

Semper gumby!

Team Attitude Requirement No. 7: Think in Sync

Team members have to learn to think in sync, to read each other's movements and gestures, head nods and eye flickers, to know instinctively where the ball is going to go, where the next shot or pass is coming from, where to be in order to grab the rebound. It sounds as mystical as ESP—but there's nothing psychic or extrasensory about it. Synchronized thinking is the result of all the other components of team attitude working together. When an entire team is unselfish and full of *wa,* when there is mutual encouragement and fun going on, when every player is filling his role and following the leader, when everyone plays flexibly, creatively, and with maximum adaptability, then the team is able to coalesce into a unit. The players are able to think in sync—and move in sync.

When I say you've gotta think in sync, I'm not saying you have to be a bunch of robots, that you have to have all the same opinions, that everybody has to be "politically correct." Exactly the opposite. You maintain your unity while celebrating the diversity and uniqueness of the individual players. You synchronize and harmonize best as a team when there is respect for the differences and individual beliefs of the players. You don't want everyone thinking alike, you want them thinking in sync, in harmony. There's a big difference between being the same and being in sync. It's the difference between four guys humming the same note and a barbershop quartet.

"When your team is united," said New York Jets coach Bill Parcells, "it can ward off any flak from negative perceptions. It won't make any difference what outsiders think. When your team is working together, your competition will have fewer weaknesses to exploit. But a team divided against itself can break down at any moment. The least bit of pressure or adversity will crack it apart."

The great teams are those in which the leader and players spend a great deal of time together, training and practicing together, communicating together, getting to know each other's style and moves. In the process, they become so bonded, and know each other so well, that they can read what will happen before it happens. When basketball players think in sync, they know when a teammate is making a pump fake, and when he's taking a shot—and they know where to be in case the ball needs rebounding or just a little putback to get the job done. When a pitcher and catcher are in sync, they know when the other team is stealing the signs and it's time to go to a new set of signs.

It's no different in the business world. In the restaurant business, for example, it means that the food service staff responds to an unexpected influx of customers by stepping up the pace, covering for each other when needed, and getting all the tasks done without the manager having to tell each player, "Now, you do this and you do that." Ray Kroc, founder of the McDonald's franchise corporation, put it this way: "A well-run restaurant is like a winning baseball team. It makes the most of every crew-member's talent, and takes advantage of every split-second opportunity to speed up service."

Every player has to be on the same page. One player whose thinking is out of sync can destroy what the entire team is working for. John Capossi, president of JMC Industries, says, "I realize that this is one of the oldest maxims in the known universe, but it bears repeating: the environment of business and corporate life depends so much on teamwork. When I ran training seminars for new employees at American Airlines, I kept returning to this truth. I'd explain to the agents in my group that thousands of employees worked incredibly hard every day to ensure a passenger's loyalty to American Airlines. If just one reservation was wrong, or a ticket was written incorrectly, or the flight got out late, or the crew wasn't friendly, or the bag was missing, it didn't matter to the passenger that everything else was perfect. One mistake by one employee means that the work of thousands, from the corporate office to the maintenance hangars to the cockpit crew, has gone for nought."

We need more team attitude in every human endeavor, in every arena, at every level of our society, from the sandlot to the senate, from the basketball court to the halls of the United Nations, from my family and your family to the family of Man. Mario Cuomo, former governor of New York, put it this way: "The idea of community, the idea of coming together—we're still no good at that in this country. We talk about it a lot. Some politicians call it 'family.' In moments of crisis, we're magnificent at it. At those moments we understand community, helping one another. In baseball, you do that all that time. You can't win it alone. You may be the best pitcher in baseball, but somebody has to get you a run to win the game. You need all nine people helping one another. I love bunt plays. I love the idea of the bunt. I love the idea of the sacrifice. Even the word is good: Giving yourself up for the good of the whole. There are thousands of years of wisdom in that idea."

The best explanation of this concept that I've ever heard came from Dr. Jack Ramsay, the Hall of Fame coach, who wrote, "I wanted players to play hard; play together; play the team game. Coaching requires so many qualities. It's like conducting an orchestra, getting all the parts to play in harmony so that what comes out of all these instruments is a pleasing sound—a positive, beautiful sound."

Former Princeton basketball coach Pete Carril stated the same thing. "I wanted my players to look out for each other; to have pluck, discipline, and love for one another. What gives me the most satisfaction as a coach is bringing together people who have divergent backgrounds and getting them to achieve a goal by sacrificing and integrating their skills. Of course, I like to win! It brings everybody together."

Indiana Pacers President Donnie Walsh said this about Larry Bird when he hired Bird in 1997 to coach the Pacers. "Larry Bird pulls people together. When he talks, you come into his world. That's what a coach has to do. I know coaches do things a lot of different ways, but the great ones always get all the people on the team doing the things they should be doing as a team."

So think in sync. Maintain a total team attitude. When everybody's on the same page, resonating to the same vibration from the same tuning fork, you've got something that is beautiful to watch—and very hard to defeat.

You've got a *team*.

Principle 6

Empower Individuals

Who could ever forget Mom Burgher?

By the fall of '62, I had graduated from Wake Forest and played a summer of pro baseball in Florida. I went to Indiana University in Bloomington for two years to get my master's in physical education. While I was there, I got two big life-changing breaks. One was that I got involved in sports broadcasting with the Indiana Football and Basketball Network, where I worked with John Gordon (now the radio voice of the Minnesota Twins) and succeeded another young doctoral student named Dick Enberg (maybe you've heard of him?). The other big break I got in Indiana was meeting Mom Burgher.

Her real name was Mid, but everyone called her Mom. She and her husband, Bob, ran Burgher's Grill on Walnut Street in the middle of Bloomington. It was exactly like all those center-of-town eateries you've seen in every Jimmy Stewart movie ever made. People gathered there for the conversation more than the food—and everybody who was anybody in Bloomington could be seen there, from the town fathers to the local chamber of commerce and Rotary Club types to the students and coaches from the university. Mom Burgher was always there, serving up the cholesterol-soaked fare and talking to the patrons about their hopes, their dreams, their successes, their disappointments.

Mom Burgher had no children of her own—but she had lots and lots of sons. Her kids were all the athletes and coaches who ever went to Indiana University. She called them "my boys," and she meant it. In my memory, I can still see her at the games, decked out totally in red, cheering her lungs out for her boys from her usual perch right behind the Indiana football or basketball bench. Whenever the team left town for a game, she was there to see the bus or the plane off—and win or lose, she was there late at night to greet the team when it returned. She was a friend and a counselor, and everyone knew they could come by her house for encouragement, advice, and a bite to eat, anytime of the day or night. She had that kind of influence for decades in that town.

I was in Mom Burgher's house many times during my years in Bloomington, and the one thing I remember so clearly was the pictures. She had pictures up everywhere, all over the walls, the end tables, the piano, all over the house. Years after leaving Bloomington, "her boys" would keep in touch, sending letters and pictures—lots and lots of pictures of themselves, their girlfriends and their wives, their kids and their parents.

Bob Burgher died along the way, but Mom just kept right on going, until she passed away in her eighties, leaving a legacy of half a century of influencing and empowering Indiana athletes. I know. I was one of them. She adopted me as a twenty-two-year-old kid away from home. She got to know me, to know all about my family, and she sent notes and cards over the years long after I left Indiana, throughout my baseball days, and all through my NBA days. It was always great to hear from Mom Burgher, and whenever I was back in Bloomington for any reason, I always went to see Mom, first thing.

She was an encourager, an empowerer. She was genuinely interested in me, in the dreams I had, in the problems I struggled with. She helped me put my struggles into perspective, enabled me to see overwhelming problems as solvable, told me she believed in me, and empowered me to believe in myself. If I ever felt powerless in a situation, one talk with Mom was all I needed to feel powerful, invincible, ready to tackle anything.

Empowerment means to provide strength, energy, and motivation—and that's exactly what Mom Burgher did for me and so many Indiana athletes. There was a time when I thought there must be a Mom Burgher in every college town, influencing and empowering lives like she did. But as the years have passed, I have come to realize that people like Mom are actually very rare. They probably come along about as often as a major talent like Michael Jordan or Tiger Woods. In every team environment, we need empowerers—these rare human gems who invest themselves in other people, distributing strength, energy, and confidence to the rest of the team, enabling them to accomplish more than they ever dreamed possible. You are truly touched by a miracle if one or two empowerers come into your life. I guess I've been touched by a multiple miracle, because I can name several people who have empowered me to become what I am today.

FROM INDIANA U. TO LITTLEJOHN TECH

Another empowerer in my life was a man named Bill Durney, whom I met as a professional baseball player in Miami. Bill had been athletic director at St. Louis University, then became traveling secretary for the St. Louis Browns under Bill Veeck, then moved to Miami as general manager of Veeck's Miami Marlins class AAA team. I got to know Bill Durney very well during my two years as a player and my third year as a young front office neophyte. I put myself under the guidance of this older, wiser, battle-seasoned man, and I told him, "I need an education in pro baseball, and you're the guy who can do it. I want you to be my mentor, if you'll take me under your wing."

Bill Durney could have said, "Get away, Kid! You bother me!" But he didn't do that. Instead, he adopted me. Over the next few months, I all but lived with Bill's family in his home. He was my teacher and my encourager, and I eagerly scooped up every scrap of wisdom and coaching he could give me. Throughout those years, until he died in 1968, Bill Durney was a great friend to me. Everything I learned about the business of professional baseball came from Bill Durney. He probably never heard the term "empowerment," but he was a great empowerer in my life, and I'd be a much poorer human being and sports executive today if I hadn't met Bill when I did. He had an enormous impact on my life—and one of the ways he impacted my life was that he introduced me to the great Bill Veeck.

I was twenty-two years old when I first met Bill Veeck in 1962. Three years later, I completed my first year as general manager of the Philadelphia Phillies farm club in Spartanburg, South Carolina, under Bill Veeck's mentorship. I particularly remember the way Bill encouraged me when I was feeling like a failure after the team's losing season. I was so focused on the team's lackluster showing that it scarcely mattered to me that, by other measurements, it had actually been a very good season. We had drawn 114,000 people to the games—a big year for that level of baseball. I had invested six or seven months of my life, working sixteen-hour days, my first season as a general manager was done, and I felt I was a failure, a loser.

When I poured out all my discouragement to Bill Veeck over the phone, he listened quietly. Then, when I was finished, he said, "Pat, just how many people did you draw to the ballpark this season?" I told him 114,000. "How many of those people were entertained and had a good time?" he asked. I responded that I thought they all had a good time. "Well, tell me one other thing you could have done this summer that would have provided this much fun, enjoyment, and entertainment to that many people?" I couldn't think of anything. "Listen, Pat," he said, "you never, ever have to apologize for showing people a fun time."

That advice transformed my outlook. Okay, I thought, we had a losing season—but we had still accomplished something. We had entertained people, and profitably so. Over the years that I have been in sports management, through winning seasons and not-so-winning ones, I have thought of that conversation often.

Another great empowerer in my life at this time was Mr. R. E. Littlejohn. I arrived in Spartanburg, South Carolina, in February 1965 to take over as general manager of the Spartanburg Phillies. I was twenty-four years old, and I was told to report to Mr. R. E. Littlejohn. He wasn't at home when I arrived, but I met his wife, whose nickname was Sam. She said to me, "Even if you spend the rest of your life in the sports world, you'll never meet another man like Mr. R.E." That's what Sam called him, and what everyone called him: "Mr. R.E." I look back today, over thirty years later, and I see that she was right: Mr. R.E. was definitely one of a kind.

As I got to know him, I found him to be a godly man with incredible wisdom. He had two daughters but no son of his own, so for some reason he adopted me as a son. I kid about it, but it's really true: I went to Wake Forest for my undergraduate degree, to Indiana U. for my master's, and to Littlejohn Tech for my doctorate. I couldn't have gotten a better education anywhere than the education I got from Mr. R. E. Littlejohn. He made such a profound impact on me that our firstborn son is named James Littlejohn Williams.

From Mr. R.E. I learned what I call "R. E. Littlejohn's Sixteen Rules of Success," and I plan to write a book on those sixteen rules someday. Mr. R.E. was also the key influence in leading me to a faith in Jesus Christ. He was simply the most *exemplary* human being I ever knew—and I wanted to be like him. During the four fascinating years I worked with him, he was my teacher, my encourager, my empowerer. I drew so much inspiration and strength from him that to this day—though he is no longer with us—he is one of the guiding influences of my life. Again and again, when I'm faced with an issue or a tough choice, I ask myself, "What would Mr. R.E. do in this situation?"

Another great empowerer came into my life when I went to Chicago to be the general manager of the Bulls. His name was Phil Frye, and he was a feisty, animated little guy, an attorney, and one of the eight co-owners of the team. His father had been an investor in Bill Veeck's baseball teams over the years, and Phil himself had been a good friend of Bill Veeck's. Like the other empowerers in my life, Phil Frye practically adopted me, and in my four years with the Bulls he always sought me out to be a friend and encourager to me. Once a month, he insisted I have lunch with him at the Chicago Club for food, fellowship, advice, and encouragement. I was twenty-nine years old, my first time in such a huge city, feeling overwhelmed by my job. Remember, this was not the sizzling, world-class Chicago Bulls of today, but a bottom-of-the-league team with poor attendance and no respect—basketball at its lowest ebb. Had it not been for Phil Frye and his desire to invest in my life, I never would have made it.

Throughout my twenties, I had these encouragers and empowerers in my life—and that is miracle enough for one lifetime. Incredibly, I still have some great empowerers in my life today. One is Jim Hewitt, Orlando businessman and great friend. He was one of the men who first envisioned an NBA franchise in Orlando—and he is one of the world's greatest empowerers. From the time he first brought me down to Orlando, he has done nothing but build me up and make me believe that I'm one of the greatest sports executives in the world! Throughout the time we were trying to make the Orlando Magic dream a reality, he kept saying, "We're gonna get this team in Orlando because we've got Pat Williams! No one can say no to us now!" Jimmy is a relentless cheerleader and uplifter. I believe I have been able to perform far beyond my capabilities as a sports executive because of the incredible empowerment of Jimmy Hewitt.

Another great empowerer in my life is Rich DeVos— cofounder of Amway and one of the owners of the Orlando Magic. Rich has a true love for people, and I think that's what makes him such an empowering, encouraging individual. He'll tell you of his role with Amway or with the Orlando Magic, "I'm the head cheerleader!" And boy, is he ever! He has an amazing touch when it comes to encouraging, inspiring, and motivating people.

Whenever Rich comes to Orlando, he always seeks out his staff, comes into their offices, closes the door, hugs us, and talks to us. I don't mean the usual surface chatter that most of us use in our social contacts—"Hiya, howzit goin'?" I mean, he gets right down to reality and wants to know about us, our families, our work. He asks questions and offers sincere encouragement: "Is there anything you need? Any way I can support you and pray for you? Anything I can do for you? You're doing a great job. This never would have happened without you. Thanks for getting us involved." When you part from him, you literally feel you can do anything.

What drives Rich DeVos to be such a great empowerer of other people? In part, it's the fact that when he empowers others, he actually charges up his own batteries! In an article on the success of the Orlando Magic, Rich said, "I get a tremendous boost from the people around me. When I motivate someone else, it actually does as much for me as it does for the other person. I'm motivated by a sense of being appreciated, loved—it tells me I'm important, that I make a difference in this world. The ability to have a positive impact on someone else's life is a tremendous gift to your own life."[1] Empowerment is incredible stuff: When you give it away to others, you get even more back in return!

Another great empowerer in my life is Norm Sonju, the general manager of the Dallas Mavericks for sixteen years before he retired in 1996. Norm was a businessman in Chicago when I first met him, and ever since then, he's been my volunteer big brother, my spiritual mentor, my career counselor, and a wonderful encourager. He has remained that way all these years. Perhaps the most important of all the great memories I have of Norm's friendship is that, in times of adversity, he would always apply the Scripture verse Proverbs 21:1: "The king's heart is in the hand of the Lord, / Like the rivers of water; / He turns it wherever He wishes." After citing that verse, he would always counsel me, "You know, Pat, that agent or owner or player—whatever the problem he's giving you—his heart is in the hand of the Lord. He's in control of the situation."

Still another great encourager in my life is Watson Spoelstra, the retired sportswriter from Detroit. Now in his mid-eighties, Waddy has spent the better part of his life empowering people. In fact, I have to say that in the past twenty-five years, there has not been a single month go by that Waddy hasn't called me or dropped me a note with a Scripture verse, a word of encouragement, or advice, wanting to know how I'm doing. He lives in a retirement village in Florida and his handwriting is a lot shakier now than it used to be, but Watson Spoelstra is an encourager of unbelievable strength and vitality.

Do you have any empowerers like that in your own life? If not, seek one out. They're rare, but they're out there. You might find that special person in your church, at the office, in your neighborhood, at your university, or right on your team. We all need that kind of person in our lives—and on our teams. And what about you? Are you an empowerer and an encourager to someone else? If not, why not? Every team needs them. Every player hungers for an empowerer in his own life, even if he's not aware of that need. So why not fill that role on the team you lead or play on?

Here are some thoughts that may help you become a more effective empowerer to your team.

No "Benchwarmers"

You've heard the term before: "benchwarmer." A guy who suits up for the game but never sees any action. He just sits on the sidelines—technically a member of the team, but in reality just a glorified spectator. "Benchwarmer" is such an ugly term. There should never be any "benchwarmers" on any team. On a *real* team, *every* individual has value. Every individual plays. Every individual makes a contribution. This is true no matter what team enterprise you are engaged in, no matter what goal you are reaching for.

What can one individual accomplish? Let me tell you. Not long ago, I had the opportunity to meet a young man named David Ring who lives in Orlando with his family. David was born with cerebral palsy and orphaned at an early age. He spent his formative years in foster homes and institutional care. If ever anyone would seem to have a right to give up on himself or on life, it would be David Ring. After all, with all these strikes against him, how could he ever succeed at anything in life?

David was able to accept his physical limitations—but he refused to be defeated by them. Despite the fact that cerebral palsy distorts his speech, he has become a nationally known motivational speaker, sharing his story with audiences around the country and through numerous television appearances. When you meet him, you are struck by the power of his confidence and enthusiasm about life. His challenge to people who feel limited by their circumstances is "I have cerebral palsy. What's your problem?"

We all have problems, limitations, weaknesses, painful circumstances, and disadvantages. Our task as team players and team leaders is to encourage and empower each other to transcend those limitations and reach the full magnitude of our individual potential, so that we can contribute and multiply our individual powers within the team environment.

Larry Wilson, CEO of Rohm and Haas, compares teamwork in the corporate environment to the teamwork in the sport of crew (rowing). "Crew," he says, "is the ultimate team sport. A member of a crew has a definite individual job to do. But the crew wins or loses as a team. A winning boat has every rower pulling together, and it doesn't carry anybody who is just along for the ride." Whether you are a leader or a player on your team, you must take the attitude that every player is a vital part of the team effort. That means every member must be in on the plans and goals of the team, every member must share the vision and the mission of the team. Every player must feel valued and needed, free to express views and ideas.

I love the perspective of pastor-author Charles Swindoll, who once wrote, "How important are you? More than you think! A rooster, minus the hen, equals no baby chicks. Kelloggs, minus a farmer, equals no corn flakes. If the nail factory closes, what good is the hammer factory? Paderewski's genius would not have amounted to much if the piano tuner had not shown up. A cracker maker will do better if there is a cheese maker. The most skillful surgeon needs the ambulance driver who delivers the patients. Just as Rodgers needed Hammerstein, you need someone, and someone needs you." Everyone belongs. Everyone's opinions matter. There are no "benchwarmers" on this team.

The Amway corporation believes in empowering people. Part of their mission statement says, "We are builders, not destroyers. We look forward, not backward. We are encouragers, not critics. Our focus is on continuous improvement, progress, and growth. We build businesses, but we build people most importantly."

You've got to communicate these truths continually, one-on-one and to the entire team. How do you do that? How do you create an atmosphere in which every player—from the marquee star who gets all the cheers to the guy who only gets a minute and a half on the court per game—feels like a fully participating member of the team? I believe the leader of the team sets the tone of inclusiveness. If you, as the leader, are open with your players, if you share your successes, dreams, goals, hopes, disappointments, and hurts with the team, they will think, "Wow! Coach shares everything with us! I'm really part of Coach's world!"

Vulnerable sharing and openness erases barriers and distinctions within the team, so that there is no perception of an "inner circle" or an "outer circle." Nobody's "in," nobody's "out," everybody's together. If people feel they are in the "outer circle," that they are "benchwarmers," they soon begin feeling expendable and powerless—and you lose their valuable contribution to the team effort.

Another way to make people feel included and valuable to the team is to recognize and reward individual contributions. Thank and praise people for extra effort, even in the small things. The words "Great job!" and "Great effort!" can go a long way in empowering individuals. A person who feels recognized and rewarded does not develop a "benchwarmer" mentality.

Remember, everybody plays, everybody contributes, everybody counts! There are no "benchwarmers" on this team!

Pull and Cheer for Each Other

If I had to distill good team chemistry to one single, simple factor, it would be *players pulling for each other*. Take a team of divided, contentious, rivalrous superstars and pit them against a team of modestly talented players who truly pull and cheer for each other—which team would you bet on? I'd bet on the team where players pull for each other. More than likely, that's the team with the winning chemistry.

Once, when I was in Puerto Rico to speak at an insurance convention, I was introduced to a couple from Hilton Head, South Carolina, Tommy and Cindi Bell. When Tommy said his name, I recognized it. "Tommy Bell," I said. "You played football for the University of South Carolina, didn't you?"

"I sure did," he said, "I was a placekicker."

He told me he really appreciated what I had said in my talk about empowering individual team members, and he shared with me a story from his own experience. "We were playing North Carolina State," he said, "and just eleven seconds before the end of the first half, I was called in to kick a field goal. It was a tough one, a fifty-two yarder, and no one expected me to pull it off. Well, I booted it and that ball sailed right between the uprights. It was the greatest feeling in the world. I charged off the field like I had just won the game. In the locker room at halftime, the coach was standing next to me. 'Well, Tommy,' he said, 'you got lucky today, didn't you?' Instantly, all that great emotion went out of me. I was devastated. I had expected him to say I had done a great job. But he just thought I was 'lucky.' I spent the rest of my career trying to show Coach I wasn't just lucky. I was never the same kicker after that."

You want to empower a player? Then lift him up, don't put him down. Be an encourager. Encouragement empowers. Discouragement destroys. As Billy Martin, longtime Yankee infielder and manager, once said, "There's nothing greater in the world than when someone on the team does something good, and everybody gathers around to pat him on the back."

I've recently become friends with Peggy Noonan, the former speechwriter for Presidents Reagan and Bush. In January 1996, I was in New York for a speaking engagement and I asked Peggy if she could come to the event and critique my speech. That afternoon, as I was getting up to speak, the back door opened and in came Peggy Noonan. She took a seat in the back, and I gave my talk. Afterwards, she came up to me, put out her hand, and the first words out of her mouth were, "I wouldn't change a thing! That was an A-plus presentation." Whew! Coming from the speechwriter for the Gipper, that was high praise—and did I feel empowered!

Sandy Koufax, the great Dodger Hall of Famer, is a big basketball fan. In 1995, when the Magic were in the finals, Sandy called me—I had never met him before—and said he knew tickets were scarce, but he would like to buy some tickets for a play-off game. I said, "Sandy, I think we can figure out a way to get you in." So he and his wife came, and we spent an hour together in my office before the game. I was thrilled. It was awesome.

I found out later that Sandy and his wife are marathoners, so just prior to entering my first marathon—the Disney Marathon in January 1996—I called Sandy and asked him for any advice he could give me. "I have four pointers for you," he replied. "Number 1: Enjoy it. Number 2: Go slow. Number 3: Drink water at every stop. Number 4: When you go out to eat that night, don't go to a restaurant with steps." The day of the race came, I ran, and I finished. That afternoon, the first call on my answering machine was from the great Sandy Koufax wanting to know how I did, letting me know he was thinking of me. It blew me away. But more—it empowered me to continue marathon running.

In September 1996 Disney World in Orlando celebrated its twenty-fifth anniversary, and I got to attend the big party at Disney-MGM studios, which included a celebrity parade down Main Street—movie stars, sports stars, a big parade in old-time automobiles. In the lead car was Bob Hope, ninety-four years old, his wife beside him. They led the parade, and the crowd just loved them—applauding, cheering, waving. You could see that Bob Hope is an old man, but he looked very robust, especially as he responded to the applause of the people. As I watched him, I couldn't help thinking of a story I had recently heard about him. Asked why he didn't retire and go fishing, he replied, "Fish can't applaud." It was really true: As his car went by, as he waved back and smiled to the people, I could see his eyes light up as he drank in the applause he had earned over some seventy-odd years in show business.

Every now and then, we all need a little applause. We need to know that we are affirmed and appreciated. We need a little praise for a job well-done. Understand, I'm not suggesting you lavish a bunch of empty, phony praise on people. Praise should always be honest and specific, never hollow and insincere. In fact, the most effective praise is often that which is restrained and understated.

Late in Babe Ruth's career, the Yankees had a bench coach named Cy Perkins. Whenever Babe hit a home run and sat next to Perkins when he came back to the dugout, Cy would say, "Nice hitting, Babe." Babe would reply, "Cy, can the Baby hit them?" Even as the biggest star in baseball, Babe Ruth was like a little boy who just loved to be praised.

Dr. Edwin Wilson of my alma mater, Wake Forest University, was also once a student there, and he remembers a word of praise that once meant a lot to him. "My religion professor, Olin T. Binkley, gave me the first compliment I ever received as a Wake Forest student," he recalls. "On the first paper he returned to me, he wrote, 'Your work pleases me,' followed by his initials, O.T.B. Those words of praise were restrained and cautious, but I treasure them beyond other words because they came from a man of uprightness and honesty such as I have seldom known." Carefully measured doses of praise, strategically administered by people whose word can be trusted, mean a lot more than lavish bouquets of empty phrases.

Former major league catcher Jim Hegan knew how to use carefully selected words of encouragement to keep his pitchers empowered to hang in there and get the job done. "A catcher," he reflects, "has to be a sort of amateur psychologist to get the most out of his pitchers. He has to know which ones need to be jollied and which ones have to be needled, which ones have to be slowed down and which ones tend to get lazy and careless. It is a good general rule that pitchers like to be encouraged. All the great catchers made a point of cheering up their pitchers after some hitter got a big hit off on them. They would tell the pitcher, 'That hitter was a lucky stiff! He closed his eyes and swung! Just keep that good pitch coming and the next guy's gonna pop up!'"

Australian tennis coach Harry Hopman was a genius at encouraging and empowering individuals to be their best—and that's why he's been able to produce so many incredible Aussie tennis stars. He did it primarily by means of encouragement and believing in people. One player he coached had a lot of great upper body strength and skills but was slow-footed and couldn't stay with the ball. Harry nicknamed him "Rocket" and told him he could be the fastest player on the court if he wanted to. And

Rod "Rocket" Laver became one of the best—and one of the fastest—tennis players of all time. Harry took another kid who was thin and didn't have much power in his serve or his backhand, and he nicknamed him "Muscles." He told this kid he believed in him, and together they would build unbeatable power into his game. And Ken "Muscles" Rosewall became yet another of Harry's world-class success stories.

When someone believes in you, it makes you believe in yourself. And when you believe in yourself, you are empowered to do things you never could have dreamed possible.

Empowering Through Failure

One of the most important acts an empowerer does is to pick people up when they've failed, then send them back into the game. Failure is a great teacher, and it's a big mistake to give up on people who are capable of learning the lessons of failure. Obviously, there are some people who never learn and eventually have to be cut from the team—but they're *way* in the minority. Most people emerge from failure wiser and better equipped to succeed. If you show a player you believe in him and you are pulling for him, especially after he's fallen flat on his face, you will empower him to succeed mightily in the future.

One of the biggest games of the 1996 NFL season was the rough-and-tumble grudge match between the San Francisco 49ers and the Green Bay Packers on *ABC Monday Night Football,* October 14, 1996. Green Bay's historic Lambeau Field was filled to overflowing—a record 60,716 roaring Wisconsin "Cheeseheads." The 'Niners, meanwhile, had trekked to the fabled Frozen Tundra to make a point: They weren't about to be manhandled by the Packers again as when they were knocked out of the play-offs the previous January. It was a wild, seesaw game that ended with an incredible 53-yard Packers field goal in overtime, giving the Rambos of Lambeau a sensational 23-20 victory.

There were a lot of memorable moments in that game, but one that stands out to me is a moment I suspect most viewers of that game have forgotten. After the Packers star receiver Robert Brooks took a season-ending knee injury in the very first play of the game, quarterback Brett Favre needed to find new sets of chest numbers to aim at. Several receivers stepped up to the job, including Don Beebe, Desmond Howard, rookie Derrick Mayes, and veteran Antonio Freeman. For some reason, Freeman really struggled in that game. By the middle of the third quarter, he had dropped three passes, including one short pass right into the cradle of his arms while he was wide open. After dropping what should have been an easy catch, one of the ABC booth announcers said, "Well, that's it for Freeman. Three dropped passes. His confidence is gone." And other announcer chimed in, "Yep, Favre won't be throwing anything his way again."

On the very next play, Favre backpedaled to the 45 and launched a cruise missile to the left sidelines at the 20—right into the hands of (you guessed it!) Antonio Freeman. The 'Niners were as surprised as the ABC announcers: they only had Freeman single covered, and Favre not only caught the 'Niners napping, he gave the once-struggling Antonio Freeman a much-needed dose of confidence. He went to the man who had failed three times and put him back in the game. That's empowerment of the individual—big-time!

It reminds me of the way Jesus restored and empowered a failure named Peter after he had "dropped the ball" three times, each time denying and rejecting Jesus. In John 21, Jesus goes to Peter and three times asks him, "Do you love me?" In effect, Jesus asks him this question one time for each time Peter had denied and failed Him. Each time Jesus asks the question, Peter's head sinks lower with the realization of the threefold failure he has committed against his Lord. But then Jesus reinstates Peter. "Feed my sheep," He says, placing Peter, the former failure, in charge of His entire church. In essence, He is saying to Peter, "You've blown it three times, but that's in the past. Don't worry about it. Next play, the ball's coming to you. So relax, Pete. You're the man. You're gonna do fine. Get out there and gain some yards!" That's Jesus, rescuing a player on His team from failure, restoring him to the game, empowering the individual.

Tom Watson, the founder of IBM, understood this principle. One of his top junior executives once spent $12 million of the company's money on a project that failed miserably. The young exec trudged into Watson's office and plunked a resignation letter on the boss's desk.

"What's this?" asked Watson.

"My resignation," said the demoralized young man. "I thought I'd save you the trouble of firing me."

"I don't want your resignation," Watson snorted gruffly—but grinning all the same. "I just invested $12 million in your education! Why would I want to get rid of you now? Get back to work!"

Use failure as a learning experience, a launching pad for success. Instead of kicking a player when he's down—or worse, firing him—find ways to empower him and get him back into the game.

Empowering Through Teamwork

One of the most important ways you empower your players is by making sure they feel a part of the overall effort. Everyone is pulling in harness, no one is doing it all alone. Knowing we're all in it together empowers players to work harder and longer, in a more focused way, in order to achieve the team's vision.

I love the story of a guy who was driving out in the country. In the road ahead of him, a fox scampered across the road. To avoid hitting the animal, the motorist swerved into a shallow ditch. He got out, surveyed the damage, saw that he was hopelessly stuck, and walked to the nearest farmhouse for help. There he found a farmer who had nothing but an old, blind mule named Dusty. The motorist, the farmer, and Dusty went back to the car, where the farmer hitched the blind mule to the car.

Then the farmer snapped his whip and yelled, "Pull, Jasper, pull!" Dusty didn't move. The farmer hollered, "Pull, Brownie, pull!" Dusty remained motionless. "Pull, Jenny, pull!" Still nothing. Finally, the farmer yelled, "Pull, Dusty, pull!" The mule jerked forward, strained mightily, and rescued the car from the ditch.

The motorist thanked the farmer, then asked him why he had called the mule by three wrong names. "Well, Dusty's blind," the farmer said, "but if he thought he had to do the work all by himself, he wouldn't even try."

Ernie Banks, the great infielder and power hitter for the Chicago Cubs of yesteryear, didn't become a professional baseball player by himself. He never could have made it, he recalls, without the help of a father who worked and sacrificed so that he could have a chance to play the game. His father left for work before dawn and came home after dark—working so many hours that he hardly ever saw the sunlight. When Banks signed his first contract with the Cubs, he sent a three-word telegram to his dad: "We did it!"

Knowing we are not alone helps us to feel empowered. We can do anything when we are all pulling together, when we know we are truly a team.

Pass It On!

At the beginning of this chapter I listed the empowerers who have had such a powerful impact on my life, from Mom Burgher to Rich DeVos—and I talked about the need to bring empowerment full circle, to reinvest in others what someone has invested in you. Well, it's amazing what happens when you're writing a book. During the very week that this chapter was being written, a young man named Adam Lippard came into my office and wrote the ending for this chapter—the ending you are about to read.

Adam is a full-time employee with the Orlando Magic. He started as an intern, worked in our marketing department for two years, and is now our strategic planning manager—a brilliant young sports executive. He went to high school in the Pittsburgh area, got his undergraduate degree at Syracuse, and got his master's degree in sports administration at Ohio University. He's a very impressive young man—and I suspect you'll be hearing about him in the years to come.

Adam Lippard came to me and said, "Pat, what will it take to become the president of a major-league sports team by the time I'm thirty?" (He's twenty-six now.) "Will you help me? I've read your books, and I know you've had people who helped you over the years, people like Bill Veeck and R. E. Littlejohn. Would you do that for me?"

I grinned and said, "Adam, I'd love to."

He said, "When can we start?"

"Right now," I replied. "I will make a commitment to you that I will invest everything I can in your life that has been invested in mine, so that you can become everything you have the potential to be."

It will be interesting to see how this relationship plays out. He's an ambitious young man and it wouldn't surprise me if Adam was running his own ball club by the time he is in his thirties.

That's my goal—to somehow pass along a measure of the encouragement, insight, confidence, inspiration, and strength that has been given to me by Mom Burgher, Bill Durney, R. E. Littlejohn, Bill Veeck, Phil Frye, Rich DeVos, and others. So much has been invested in Pat Williams over the years; how can I do any less than pass it on to the next generation, to people like Adam Lippard, to my own sons and daughters, to the athletes and young staff members in our Magic organization, to the young people in my church, in the groups I speak to, to the readers of this and other books I have written? I *have* to live that way. We *all* have to live that way, or the empowerment we have received from the Mom Burghers and R. E. Littlejohns in our lives will have come to nothing.

I took my oldest son, Jimmy, to the 1995 All-Star Weekend in Phoenix. Jimmy—then a twenty-year-old junior in college—had a fabulous, memorable time. We went to all the events, and Jimmy got to meet many of the legendary players in the game of basketball. Friday night, we went to the Kenny Rogers barbecue, heard Kenny perform, and got to meet him and his beautiful bride-to-be, Wanda, backstage afterwards. Saturday night, we went to Bill Cosby's comedy show. Sunday morning, we went to the chapel where Dave Dravecky spoke and Glenn Campbell did the special music.

After coming out of chapel, we were crossing the hotel lobby when we happened to bump into Isiah Thomas, the great Piston player and newly installed general manager of the Toronto Raptors expansion team. I wished Isiah well in his new position and introduced him to Jimmy. Isiah's eyes lit up as he shook Jimmy's hand. "I know you!" he said. "I know all about you!

I've read about you, I've seen you on television shows with your brothers and sisters. Oh, I know who you are—Jimmy Williams!"

Well, I could tell Jimmy was absolutely staggered. We chatted a while with Isiah, then went to the game that afternoon. That night, as we were flying home to Orlando, I asked Jimmy, "Ten years from now, what will you remember most about this weekend? Meeting Kenny Rogers? Seeing Bill Cosby perform in person? Meeting the players? Seeing the game?"

"Oh, no," he said. "What I'm gonna remember most is that Isiah Thomas told me he knew who I was." That's not just a nice memory for my son Jimmy. That's *empowerment.*

I've known Robin Roberts, a Hall of Fame pitcher for the Phillies, since his rookie year in 1948 (I was eight years old and living in Wilmington, Delaware). Recently, he wrote a great story about empowerment in his life. "Late in the 1948 season, I was invited to a party in honor of Connie Mack who was still managing the Philadelphia Athletics at eighty-six years of age. I went to the gathering with Cy Perkins, who had been an A's catcher under Mr. Mack for fifteen years beginning back in 1915. It was a thrill for me just to be there, and I went up to the honoree and said, 'Mr. Mack, I'm Robin Roberts. I pitch for the Phillies.'

"He looked me straight in the eye and said, 'You don't have to introduce yourself to me, Mr. Roberts. I've seen you pitch.' I was greatly flattered and have always wished that I could think of things to say like that."

Teams are all about empowerment. A team where the leaders and players fail to empower each other, encourage each other, and motivate each other is not even a team. It's just a collection of talented egos. But a team that practices mutual empowerment is a unified force, an environment where miracles come to pass, where championships happen, where the full, powerful potential of our humanity is unleashed!

Principle 7

Build Trust and Respect

In my previous book, *Go for the Magic*, I told a story from the life of nationally syndicated radio answer man Bruce Williams, host of the longest-running call-in show on radio and author of such books as *In Business for Yourself* and *House Smart*. Someone brought my book to Mr. Williams's attention, and he was kind enough to read a passage from *Go for the Magic* on the air. Let me tell you, Bruce Williams is such a wise and insightful fella (with a name like Williams, how could he *not* be!) that I just had to tell another Bruce Williams story in this book.

While this book was being written, Bruce received a call on his show from an entrepreneur with a problem: The poor guy was a control freak—he absolutely *had* to be at the shop all the time, looking over his employees' shoulders, putting his fingerprints on every single aspect of the operation. He couldn't leave for a minute. He couldn't delegate anything. Though the guy's business was making very good money, he could never take a vacation because he just knew his enterprise would go to heck in a handbasket without his constant micromanagement of every detail.

"In that case," Bruce told the caller, "you're a failure."

The caller was stunned to hear this. "I just told you," the caller protested, "I run a very successful business!"

"Maybe the *business* is successful," said Bruce, "but *you* are a failure. If you can't trust the people who work with you to keep your business profitable and shipshape while you take a break for a week or two, you've failed as a businessman."

And Bruce proceeded to tell his own story. He lives on the west coast of Florida, but he also owns businesses in several other states. "Do you think while I'm here doing this radio show that I'm worrying about how my businesses are being run in all those other parts of the country? No way! I've hired good people, I keep in touch with them, I visit my businesses on a regular basis—but I *trust* the people I've hired to do their job and to keep making money for me. You see, I don't like to think of them as working *for* me. They work *with* me. It's all a matter of respect and trust. They respect me, I trust them, we're a *team*."

He went on to recall an incident that happened some years earlier—an incident that nearly cost him his life. "On December 5, 1982, at 3:32 in the afternoon," he explained, "I hit a tree going flat out in a Cessna 182. I was the pilot of that airplane, and it was pilot error, as simple as that. So during that month of December, I had very little on my mind—and the few random thoughts I did have were confined to staying alive. With severe internal injuries, a smashed-up leg, and major contusions to my head and face, the very last thing on my mind was how my businesses were doing.

"But you know what? The following quarter, while I was out of action, was our best quarter on record! Clearly, one of two things was true: Either (1) I was totally superfluous and expendable to my own business enterprises, or (2) I had surrounded myself with good people, and they simply carried on, did their jobs, and kept my business enterprises running well in my absence. I prefer to believe the second is true. I had hired a great team, and I had also raised some great kids (my kids were all adults, some in college, and they all pitched in while I was laid up), and I could trust them with my various businesses.

"On my radio show and in my various speaking engagements, I tell this story to make a point: In order to be successful, you have to be able to delegate. And in order to delegate, you have to be able to trust your people. Accept the fact that they may make mistakes (and will probably learn from them) and they may do things differently than you—and that's okay. If you've trained them well and shown them the ropes, they won't bring your business to its knees while you take a week or two off. Your team will still function and your business will go on and prosper."

What Bruce is talking about are two interlocking, irreplaceable, absolutely essential ingredients of teamwork: *respect* and *trust*. A team that operates in an atmosphere of respect and trust can accomplish unimaginable feats and reach unbelievable heights. But any team—no matter how talented—that lacks respect and trust between leaders and players, or among the players, is a team that is ripe for disintegration and humiliating defeat.

Rely on Each Other

Trust starts with respect. You can't trust someone you don't respect. Players have to respect themselves, their teammates, their leaders, and their opponents. When you respect and trust your teammates, when you know you can rely on them and they'll come through, you have confidence as an individual player and as a team—and confidence wins. Former Dodgers manager Tommy Lasorda said, "I've learned that the only way to get respect from people is to give them respect. And that's my way of doing it."

Not long ago, a young man from Oregon, Steve Hanamura, called my office to make an appointment with me. He was going to be in Orlando and wanted a few minutes to meet me and talk. It wasn't until he entered my office that I realized he was blind.

We sat down and talked, and he said something very surprising: "One of my hobbies is running marathons."

"What?" I said. "How do you do that?"

"I have a friend," said Steve. "Her name is Kit Sundling-Hunt, and we run marathons together. She hooks a bungee cord between us, and we have worked out a system of signals. By tugging on the cord, she can signal me that a turn is coming, or a hill, or an obstacle. It works great—and let me tell you something: Running at the end of that bungee cord has taught me an awful lot about teamwork and trust!"

I thought, *Wow! That's really a powerful illustration of what teamwork is all about—trusting each other, relying on each other. Amazing!* The great Cal Ripken of the Orioles—unquestionably one of the best all-around players in the history of the American League—once said, "My father taught me about teamwork. It's important to rely on teammates to make winning happen. It's important for me to be counted on by my teammates." That's trust. That's the ability to rely on each other.

Tom Haggai tells a story that illustrates the importance of being able to rely on each other in the team environment: During a hike in the woods, a troop of Boy Scouts came across an abandoned section of railroad track. Each boy took a turn attempting to walk the length of the rail—but each in turn lost his balance and tumbled off. As the other boys tried and failed to balance themselves on the rails, two of the boys held a whispering conference a few yards away. Coming out of the huddle, they challenged their friends, "We'll make you guys a bet that we can walk that whole piece of track without falling off."

"Both of you?" sneered the other boys. "None of us could do it. What makes you think the two of you can do it?"

"Well, if you're too chicken to bet us—"

"You're on!" yelled the others.

The two boys jumped up on the track, each on one of the parallel rails. They each extended a hand to balance the other, and together, hand in hand, they walked the entire section of track with no difficulty whatsoever. That's reliance on one another. That's teamwork. That's trust. Trust is the glue that holds a team together. Trust wins games and championships.

Another story illustrates the power of a team where players truly trust and respect each other. A farmer became concerned because his five sons constantly quarreled with each other. There was no brotherly trust, no brotherly respect—only fighting, arguing, rivalry, and name-calling. Finally, the farmer called his sons together in a circle around him. In the middle of the circle, he threw down a bundle of sticks that had been securely tied together by two stout strings. Then he held up a shiny coin. "This twenty-dollar gold piece," he said, "goes to the one of you who can break this bundle of sticks in half."

Going around the circle, each of the five sons tried to break the bundle of sticks. They tried crashing it over their knees, stomping on it, throwing it to the ground, but to no avail. "It can't be done," they complained.

"Yes, it can," said the farmer, pocketing the gold piece. He bent down and pulled the first string, and it fell undone. Then he pulled the second string—and the sticks collapsed in a heap. The farmer reached down, lifted the first stick, easily snapped it in two, and handed it to his first son. Then he broke another, handed it to the second son, and so on, to the fifth son. Then he picked up the two strings that had formerly bound the sticks together.

"This string is called *respect*," he said. "And this one is called *trust*. With these two forces binding you together, no enemy can ever break you or defeat you. But if you quarrel and contend with each other, you will defeat yourselves."

LOVE AND CARING

I remember 1969 not only as the year I arrived in Chicago to take over as general manager of the Bulls but also as the year the Chicago Cubs made their great pennant run. The '69 Cubbies were one of the most fascinating, exciting sports teams in Chicago history, capturing the heart of the Windy City. I got to know some of the future Hall of Famers on that team. There was Ernie Banks, "Mr. Cub," one of the team's first black players, a nine-time all-star who spent his entire nineteen-year career in Chicago, and who hit his 500th homer in Wrigley Field. And there were names like Billy Williams, Ron Santo, Randy Hundley, Don Kessinger. And there was the great Cubs pitcher, Ferguson Jenkins, whom I used to catch in the minor leagues, and who led the league in strikeouts in '69. The legendary Leo Durocher was the manager of that team.

They eventually lost the National League pennant (if you are old enough to remember, you know that 1969 was the year the "Miracle Mets" rose to win the Series). But they had an incredible ride, and Chicagoans will never forget that amazing season. Years later, the '69 Cubs' backup catcher, Gene Oliver, reflected on what made that team so special. He said,

> We were a team! On the Cubs, it was, "I for you, we're all in this together, win, lose, or draw." There was a sense of camaraderie. We were brothers. We cared about each other.
>
> Over the last 25 years, we have stayed close to each other. If I was ever in need or they were ever in need, or had a problem, they would pick up the phone, and I would be there in a minute and vice versa. The whole team was that way. We have overwhelming concern and respect for one another. We stay in touch. We love each other. We're concerned for each other and we're always there for each other.
>
> When our great pitcher, Ferguson Jenkins, lost his first wife, and later his second wife, a little bit of all of us died with him. And I guarantee you Fergie would say, "I'd have never gotten through this ordeal without my 1969 teammates."

The legendary Packers coach Vince Lombardi put it this way: "If you're going to play together as a team, you've got to care for one another. You've got to love each other. Each player has to be thinking about the next guy and saying to himself: 'If I don't block that man, my teammate's going to get his legs broken. I have to do my job well so that my teammates can do theirs.' The difference between mediocrity and greatness is the feeling these guys have for each other."

Now let's face it: Sometimes, we get on a team with players or coaches we don't hit it off with. The chemistry just doesn't come together. There are personality mismatches. There are people we just don't like or who don't like us—yet we're thrown together on a team. What do we do? How do you respect a player or coach you just don't like?

The Hall of Fame Cincinnati Reds second baseman, Joe Morgan, had the answer: "You don't have to like someone to get along with them or work together as a team." How do you do that? Simple: You love them.

"What?!! I don't *like* a teammate, so I'm supposed to *love* this person?!! Williams, you are *really* losing it!"

No, I'm not. But I should define my terms a bit. Fact is, we use that word "love" very loosely, to mean a lot of different things. There's romantic love: "Oh, Marsha! I love you! Be my love!" There's "love" that is really only a craving: "I love pizza!" There's love (sometimes spelled ♥) that is a fondness for places or things: "I ♥ NY" or "I ♥ my dog." All of these "loves" are feelings, emotions, sentiments. I'm not talking about any of that stuff.

When I say that love can enable you to build respect and trust on a team, even when you don't like one or more of your teammates, I'm talking about a love that is not an emotion. This kind of love is a choice. It's a decision. It's not something you *feel*, it's something you *do*.

If you go to the New Testament and start reading, you'll come across the word "love" many times. In the Greek language in which the New Testament was originally written, there are actually three words for "love"—*eros*, meaning romantic or aesthetic love, an emotional attraction to people or ideas or things; *phileo*, meaning family or brotherly love, the love of mankind, the love that Philadelphia, "the City of Brotherly Love" was named for; and *agape* (pronounced uh-GAH-pay), meaning a deliberate decision to love, even when the object of that love is unlovable.

It's human nature to focus on the negative, on the irritating, frustrating, or annoying aspects of another person. *Agape*-love says, "I'm going to look past the irritations in our relationship. I'm going to focus on what's best for the team and on what's best for you. I'm going to make a decision to accept you, respect you, and work with you—and when I do that, you'll be able to trust me, and we'll be a *team*."

If you want to see how it works in practice, just read through the gospels of Matthew, Mark, Luke, and John. Take a good look at the team Coach Jesus had put together. It was very short on chemistry and very long on rivalry. In places like Mark 9, Luke 9, and Luke 22, we see the team of Jesus torn by rivalries and arguments, all centered on ego, on who is the greatest player on the team. What is the answer of Jesus to this problem? Love—unconditional, in-the-will, not-in-the-emotions *agape*-love. In John 17, as He was preparing to go to the cross, Jesus prayed for His team these words (which I have paraphrased slightly from the New King James Version):

> I pray that they all may be one, completely united in trust and respect for each other, as You and I are united, Father—You in Me and I in You—so that they also may be one, united in Us. I pray that through the unity of this team, Our team vision may be achieved, which is that the whole world would discover and believe that You sent Me. . . . I pray that the *agape*-love with which You loved Me may be in them, so that they would *agape*-love each other, proving to the world that I live *in* them and *through* them.

That's from verses 21 and 26—and though I have freely paraphrased the text, I believe it's absolutely faithful to the meaning of the passage. Take out your Bible and check me out on this. That's the kind of love I'm talking about—a caring for each other that transcends personality differences and petty clashes, enabling us to respect and trust one another so that we can get the team job done. A team that truly *agape*-loves is a team that can hang together and hold together through any stress, any opposition, any problem, internal or external. A team that truly *agape*-loves has a big advantage over a team that is rife with personality clashes, rivalries, and disunity. *Agape*-love is a winning quality.

Pastor-author Charles Swindoll put it this way: "Nothing, absolutely nothing pulls a team closer together or strengthens the lines of loyalty more than love. It breaks down internal competition. It silences gossip. It builds morale. It promotes feelings that say, 'I belong,' and, 'Who cares who gets the credit?,' and, 'I must do my very best,' and, 'You can trust me because I trust you.'"

"WE ARE FAMILY"

I believe trust and respect starts at the top. The leaders of the team—the owners, managers, coaches, executives, officers, pastors, parents—set the tone of genuine caring and *agape*-love for the team. Caring is the first job of leadership. A team leader, such as a coach or a military drill instructor, often has to take on the role of tough guy, taskmaster, and tormentor—and a player will never be able to take the pain, the exhaustion, the yelling, the confrontation of being coached and disciplined unless he believes that the leader is doing it all for the good of the player and the good of the team. If the player doesn't sense the caring, if he thinks, "Man, Coach is just a sadistic old so-and-so, I can't stand to be around him anymore," he'll quit. But if a player says, "Man, this is hard, but Coach is being tough on me for my own good, because he really cares about me and wants me to be the best I can be," he'll work his heart out, he'll become a champion.

In the 1996 NBA draft, we selected Brian Evans of Indiana University. Brian played under coach Bobby Knight, as tough a taskmaster as there is. Brian made an interesting statement to me: "Much of the time I really hated being under Coach Knight. It was so difficult, and I thought I'd never get through it. But now that I'm out of school and in the pros, I can see that Coach knew what he was doing with us and did what was best for us."

The great Michigan football coach Bo Schembechler was a tough guy, a screamer, a rager—and most of his players loved him and respected him. Ever wonder why? Why would a bunch of college kids put up with being verbally whipped and pummelled on a daily basis for the sake of a game? Why are the toughest, loudest, tail-kickingest coaches often the most beloved by their teams? Because those teams know their coach really cares. The Michigan teams always knew that Bo Schembechler cared. He once said, "Deep down, your players must know you care about them. This is the most important thing. I could never get away with what I do if the players felt I didn't care. They play for me and put up with me because, in the long run, they know I'm in their corner."

In his autobiography, *An American Journey,* Colin Powell tells a great story about caring in a team environment. Powell loves to talk about the troops that fought in Operation Desert Storm—especially a young black private who was interviewed by ABC correspondent Sam Donaldson on the eve of the ground war. "How do you think the battle will go?" asked Donaldson. "Are you afraid?"

"We'll do okay," the G.I. replied. "We're well trained, and I'm not afraid." He gestured toward his buddies, who were gathered around him. "I'm not afraid because I'm with my family."

The other soldiers shouted, "Tell him again! He didn't hear you!"

"This is my family," the soldier repeated, "and we'll take care of each other."

The genuine respect and trust of teamwork creates a sense of belonging, a sense of community and shared purpose that goes even deeper than mere esprit de corps. It is a sense of mutual commitment and intense bonding that is so strong it can withstand any storm of external opposition, any eruption of internal conflict and misunderstanding. The team can survive and prevail because "this is our family, and we'll take care of each other."

This deep level of caring not only takes you through games and campaigns and championships. It lasts a lifetime. It's the greatest feeling in the world.

NO ROOM FOR PREJUDICE

I grew up in Wilmington, Delaware, in the 1940s and '50s. It was a segregated community—not in a vicious or hateful sense, but certainly in a de facto sense. I went to Tower Hill School in Wilmington, and we simply had no nonwhite students there— none. Later, I went to Wake Forest University, and there again, I was in an all-white environment—not because of a policy of discrimination but because that's just the way it was at Wake Forest in those days, 1958 to 1962.

The first time I really had any contact with nonwhite people was in 1956, following my sophomore year in high school. My dad, Jim Williams, and Bob Carpenter, the longtime owner of the Phillies, worked together to start the first high school all-star football game for the state of Delaware. The game, which would benefit mentally retarded children, was a passion for both of them. It was a North-against-the-South game, and it so happened that two of the better football players in the North were a pair of African-American young men from Howard High School in Wilmington.

For two weeks, all the players from high schools in the North trained at a prep school outside of Wilmington. The only problem was that the headmaster of the prep school was nervous because there were southern students on the campus at the prep school, and the assumption was that southern students were likely to be prejudiced against blacks. The headmaster was worried that there would be unrest if black athletes were housed on the campus. The only way the prep school would allow the practice facilities to be used was if the two black players would practice during the day, but stay off-campus at night.

My father and mother thought it was a stupid condition but accepted it. "If they have to stay off-campus," they said, "then let them stay at our house." I had just gotten my driver's license at the time, so for two weeks, I got up early and drove Joe Peters and Alvin Hall out to the prep school every morning for practice. At the end of each day, I picked them up and brought them home, and they stayed in our guest room. I was profoundly affected by this experience. I could see that here were a couple of guys who were just like everybody else in every way except the color of their skin, and I thought, *This is nuts! Why should Joe and Alvin be treated so differently from white kids? What is wrong with people that they think that segregation is normal or moral? This is crazy!* This experience had a big impact on me.

In 1962, I left Wake Forest and signed with the Phillies organization. I was sent to Miami, a Florida State League farm club in the Phillies minor league system. I was twenty-two years old, and for the first time in my life, I was on a team with black athletes—quite a number of them, in fact. One was an eighteen-year-old pitcher named Ferguson Jenkins, who would go on to become a major leaguer and a Hall of Famer. Also on that team was Alex Johnson, a future American League batting champion.

The state of Florida was highly segregated in those days, and whenever we would go on the road, we would have to stop the bus at a hotel or boardinghouse in the black section of town and leave off the black players. In the morning, we'd take the bus to their place, pick them up, and go to the ballpark together for the game. Whenever we'd stop to eat on the road, the black players all had to stay on the bus, and we would get their order, take their food out to them, and they would eat on the bus while all the white players ate inside. We did this on all our road trips, all summer long.

It reminded me of what we went through with Joe and Alvin back in '56, and it struck me as totally out of whack. Why couldn't these guys go into the restaurant, sit down, and have a meal, the same as me? How did they feel, having to sit in that stuffy old bus, eating a sandwich on a bench seat instead of sitting comfortably in a restaurant? After all, these guys were my teammates, my brothers—yet we had to practice segregation on our team in order to avoid offending the narrow-minded people of our society.

One of the black players on that team was Fred Mason, a player from my hometown. He was older than I was, a legendary athlete in Wilmington, and I had known him for years. The Phillies had signed him as a first baseman, and he was playing in their minor league system. I had a car and Fred didn't, so when the '62 season ended, he asked if I would drive him home. "Sure," I said. So, right after our last game in Ft. Lauderdale, we jumped in the car and headed north.

Around one o'clock in the morning, in the dead of night, we stopped at a service station in Jacksonville to get gas. Fred got out of the car to use the men's room. I was out at the car, finishing up with the pump, when I heard a commotion. I looked up to see the station proprietor chasing Fred Mason out of the men's room with a monkey wrench in his hand. The man's face was twisted in hate, and a stream of curses and racial epithets ran from his mouth like raw sewage.

Fred and I both jumped in the car. I floored it and we peeled out of there. For a long time, Fred didn't say a word, he just shook. So did I. We just kept driving north, and we didn't stop and Fred didn't get out of the car until we were north of the Mason-Dixon line.

As I think back on these incidents and the history of racial conflict in this country, I can't help wondering where America would be and what we could have accomplished if we, as a society, had not been so blinded by prejudice and racism. I can't help wondering what might have been possible in this country if we could have operated on teamwork principles of respect, trust, and *agape*-love, instead of attitudes of separatism, division, and hate.

Lou Tepper is no longer the football coach at the University of Illinois, but since 1992, he led a unique racial integration program on his team that tackled prejudice. Lou said, "When a young man comes into our program, he must pledge to work with, live with, and love all races. That means sitting next to players of another race at meetings and rooming with them on the road. Prejudice is a great time-saver; it allows one to form an opinion without bothering to gather the facts."

Successful teams *must* be places of genuine love and acceptance. Players must learn to accept each other regardless of race, color, creed, or religion. As all sports become more internationalized, as athletes from all over the world come to play on these teams, as corporations and economies become global, there is no room for racism, sexism, or any other -ism that separates people from people. This is true at every level—high school, college, and pro. For the good of the team, for the survival of our society and our world, we *must* learn to accept people who are different than we are. We must learn to celebrate each other's differences, not separate from each other because of them.

WHEN YOU LOVE, YOU LEVEL

One of the most important ways we build respect and trust on a team is by being uncompromisingly truthful with each other. Truth is inextricably bound up with love, and the essence of being truly committed to each other is (as Ephesians 4:15 tells us) "speaking the truth in love." When you love, you level. You tell the truth. As author James Baldwin once said, "The moment we break faith with one another, the sea engulfs us and the light goes out."

How many of us really want to face the truth about ourselves? The truth can be tough. But we have to face the truth in order to be the best we can be, in order to take the team as far as it can go. We have to respect and love each other enough to speak the truth to each other. We have to trust and love each other enough to receive the truth from each other.

Sometimes you have to confront a teammate for his or her own good and for the good of the team. That's hard, and most of us shrink from confrontation. All too often, people try to soften confrontation with a lot of praise before getting to the tough stuff: "Bob, you're a great ball handler. Your dribbling? First class. Your shooting and rebounding? Couldn't be better. And you always keep your uniform so neat and tidy, your hair's always combed, and you've got that winning smile. Everywhere I go, I hear people saying, 'Bob is really well-groomed.' But having said all that, I really have to tell you, Bob, that spitting on the ref is really not an appropriate thing to do . . ."

C'mon! Don't sugarcoat—level! You don't have to be mean—just be honest. Do you know what all that sugarcoating and praise does? It makes the other person feel he or she is being "set up." The whole time you're oozing flattery about what a great guy this person is, what a great job this person is doing, he's in suspense, waiting for the other shoe to drop. His suspense mounts, his anxiety percolates, his defenses go up, he steels himself for the inevitable criticism—and he's not listening to a thing you're saying.

Someone once said, "Always sandwich criticism between two slices of praise." Bad advice. Sounds good, but it doesn't work. Buttering people up before confronting them is just a weasel way out of being straight—it may make you feel better, but it doesn't do the other guy any good. Do you want the confrontation to heal instead of hurt? Then when you go to that person, underscore *relationship*, not praise. When you level, say, "I'm committed to you, I love you, I want the best for you. After all we've been through together, you know that. I'm leveling with you for your good, not because I want to hurt you." Keep it short, focus on caring and relationship, and get to the point.

That's speaking the truth in love. It means respecting the other person enough to tell the truth, straight from the shoulder. And it means trusting the other person to take it like a true team player.

IF YOU TRUST, YOU WIN

One of the people who was kind enough to review the outline of this book for me was Duke University's basketball coach Mike Krzyzewski. Coach K wrote a very thoughtful letter back, and one of the things he said really hit me in the area of trust:

"People must be able to understand," he said, "that if they identify with the team goal, their individual goals will be achieved. Most people who are involved with teams try to achieve individual goals and say that they will lead to team success. My belief is that you must throw yourself completely into the team, and then your individual goals will be accomplished. In fact, it may be at an even higher level. It is amazing what can be accomplished when all individuals involved trust one another. The best way to turn a crisis into a success is to have a group of people who trust one another."

Christian speaker and writer John Croyle tells the true story of a father who once took his two grade-school-age children for a river ride on a pontoon boat. The father's attention was focused downriver when suddenly the motor chugged to a stop. Turning about, he realized to his horror that his daughter was not in the boat. Looking down in the water, he saw his daughter's red sweater tangled in the propeller—the reason the motor had stalled. His boy began screaming: "Sherry's in the water, Dad! Look! She's down there!"

Leaning over the side, the father saw his daughter's face, about six inches beneath the water, her eyes open and pleading, looking straight into his. Her cheeks were puffed out as she held her breath. Caught in her sweater, she couldn't get to the surface.

The father went over the side and tried to shove the motor up, but it wouldn't budge. He could see the look of helplessness on his daughter's face. She was waiting for him to do something. So he filled his lungs with air, went under the water, pressed his lips to hers, and blew air into her lungs. He did this three times while straining to free her—all to no avail. Then an idea came to him. He broke the surface and shouted up to the boat, "Son! Get me the knife! The one we clean the fish with!"

Several seconds passed, a seeming eternity, and then the boy appeared with the knife. The father took it from the boy's trembling fingers, then slipped under the water and slashed at the red sweater, cutting the girl free. As he lifted her up into the boat, he saw that she had serious cuts and bruises from the propeller— but she was alive!

At the hospital, where the doctors determined that she would be all right after her long underwater ordeal, someone asked the girl, "You must have been so scared. How did you keep from panicking?"

"Daddy always taught me that if you panic, you lose," she replied. "I didn't want to lose. Besides, I knew Daddy would figure out a way to get me out of the water."

That's trust. That's respect. That's love. That's the core ingredient of all teamwork. If you panic, you lose. If you trust, you win.

Principle 8

Build and Model Character

In May of 1996, I received a letter that made me very proud of our Orlando Magic team. It read, in part:

Dear Mr. Williams,

I am writing this letter to say "Thank you" for the manner in which the Magic organization and players treated my sons the last two times the team was in Philadelphia. The players may remember them—they are twin boys, and one of the twins has cerebral palsy. The first time the team came into town, our son with CP was in a wheelchair following an operation (he is now back to walking with canes). He absolutely *loves* the Magic. He also collects 8x10 pictures of the players and tries to get them signed at the hotel when the team arrives in town.

For the past three years, we have gone to every Magic game when they come to town. The players were always great. Shaquille O'Neal and Nick Anderson both went out of their way to come over to the children, talk with them a bit, and sign their pictures. Anfernee Hardaway signed two pictures for them. Dennis Scott said he would mail a photo back to my son, and both coach Brian Hill and Shaq posed for a picture with the children.

I'm sure the players get pressured in every city they go to, but it was nice of them to take some time, because it does mean a lot to the kids. I hope we were not a bother; we try not to be. I can understand and respect the players' need for privacy, but on the other hand, the boys love to meet and collect pictures of the players. In the case of my son with cerebral palsy, I try to do as much as I can for him. Most of his life, he's been told he cannot do certain things. Meeting his heroes and getting an autograph really builds his self-confidence. The kids will probably want to go down to the hotel next year to see the team arrive—but if we are in the way, just let us know.

Good luck in the play-offs and if you can, please thank the players from some fans who really appreciate their kindness and generosity.

Sincerely,
Joseph Flannery
Downingtown, Pennsylvania

Where do you file a letter like that? You file it under C for character. Let me tell you, when I get letters like that (and I get many such letters), I thank God for our Orlando Magic team, a team of unique people. As the legendary UCLA basketball coach John Wooden often said, "Ability may get you to the top, but it takes character to keep you there."

One of the team-building experts I asked to read the outline for this book was sports marketing consultant Jon Spoelstra, author of a new book called *Ice to the Eskimos*. After examining my outline, he responded with the insight that there are four ingredients he looks for when putting together a team for any task, in any arena, whether in sports or in business. And the first ingredient he looks for, above all else, is *character*. If a prospective player has character, then Jon looks further to see if that player has three additional ingredients—talent, work ethic, and competitiveness. "But if a person doesn't have character," he adds, "then that person doesn't qualify, period. I refuse to let big talent fool me into forgiving bad character."

Another sports leader who critiqued the outline of this book for me was Geoff Petrie, vice president of basketball operations for the Sacramento Kings. Geoff wrote me and said,

> You cannot win consistently or be successful unless you have a character factor on your team. When I say "character," I don't mean only a *competitive* character—that is, the desire to win and to make the sacrifices necessary to winning. By character, I mean you also need to have a *moral* center of some substance on your team. That's the kind of character to carry you through difficult times and the periods of struggle that all teams face at some point during almost every season.
>
> You see it all the time in our league: If your best player, or your best two players, are not your most competitive people and your best people in terms of the types of character previously discussed, your team has very little chance for success. You need to have solid people who are emotionally stable, who are competitive, and who have a sense of being part of something that takes on a magnitude that is much greater than anything they can achieve on their own.

What is character? I would define character as the sum of all the positive traits and strengths that enable a player to compete effectively and cleanly, in a way that moves the team closer to its goals and sets a positive example to fellow teammates and spectators.

Talent and competitiveness should never be confused with character. A basketball player who has nothing but awesome talent or intense competitiveness may be able to compete effectively, but he is incapable of competing cleanly. He may get the team some wins and even some championships, but in the process he makes his team the object of condemnation among the fans and penalties on the court, and he ultimately hurts the team's morale and unity. It just isn't worth it. He would destroy our team. He would destroy our reputation. He would violate the vision and the values of our sports organization. We always put character first.

So what are some of the traits that make up good player character? In the next few pages, we'll explore a few of those traits. You could probably think of some additional character traits, but these are the ones I will focus on in this chapter. I believe that a team that seeks to recruit people of character must seek out:

- People of faith;
- People of honesty and integrity;
- People with a strong work ethic;
- People of maturity;
- People of responsibility;
- People who start, persevere, and finish;
- People of courage;
- People of humility;
- People who use their influence wisely.

So come with me. Let's look at each of these traits and compare ourselves against these measuring sticks.

PEOPLE OF FAITH

To build a team of character, you have to have people of faith.

I have so many memories of being part of the 100th running of the Boston Marathon in April 1996. I've already shared several memories of that marathon elsewhere in this book. Another of those memories is from Hopkinton, Massachusetts, where the whole thing starts. It is there that forty thousand runners and all the assembled media gather before the start of the race. For hours before the marathon begins, there is a tremendous, supercharged atmosphere of excitement, anticipation, and tension. It's fun—but it also churns your gut.

So it's truly a gift of God's grace that, right across the street from the starting line, there is a little community church with a grassy front yard. Every year, about an hour before the race, the church offers an outdoor service for the runners, with music, speakers, and prayer. One of the speakers at the 100th Boston Marathon was Cosmas Ndeti from Kenya, one of the top marathoners in the world, and a winner of the Boston Marathon a couple of years in a row. Cosmas is an absolutely radiant

Christian—a very positive, enthusiastic, spiritual man. He stood up and spent about ten minutes addressing the runners who had gathered there. His theme was "running the race of faith," and he based his talk on Philippians 4:13—"I can do all things through Christ who strengthens me." What a powerful send-off for a five-hour run!

Many times, as I was chugging up a hill, as I felt my lungs straining and my leg muscles cramping, as I wondered when my second (or third or fourth) wind was about to arrive, I thought back to that beautiful, confident smile on the face of Cosmas Ndeti as he repeated those powerful words of the apostle Paul, and I repeated to myself, *I can do all things—even run the next mile, and the mile after that and the mile after that—through Christ who strengthens me!* I actually felt that this great African marathoner was on my team, urging me onward, mile after mile.

That's what it's like to have people of character, people of faith on your team. They provide the spiritual lift that translates into greater endurance and higher performance. People of faith have the depth of soul and the spiritual power to elevate a team toward its vision and its goals.

I believe that people of faith tend to get more enjoyment out of the game and tend to compete out of healthy motivations. I've known many players over the years who had a drivenness, an unhappy intensity in the way they competed. They played in order to prove something to themselves or others, or in order to win the applause of others and fill some emotional or spiritual hole inside, or in order to become rich and famous. Players who have a rich spiritual life seem to play the game for other reasons. They play to serve and glorify their God. While they are aggressive and competitive, they are also centered and at peace with themselves.

Orel Hersheiser is one of the dominant pitchers in the game of baseball, with both the '88 World Series-winning Dodgers and the Cleveland Indians. He attributes his ability to perform well in the game, to enjoy his achievements, and to handle his disappointments to his faith in God. "My faith has been a balancing agent in my life," he once said. "Christ thrills me with who I am in Him, and reminds me gently who I'm not. When I suffer, I know I am still loved. When I'm on top, I remember my accomplishments mean nothing in light of eternity.

"My biggest surprise was to discover that Christ is real. He's not some nebulous concept, some idea, system, approach, or philosophy. He's a Person, Someone I can know. And He knows me. How do I know? Because He changed me from a sinner to a forgiven sinner.

"He also realigned my motives. I still had the same character and personality, but my mind was renewed. Now I wanted to do what He wanted. I wanted to be the best baseball player I could be. Now my motives were right. I was free to enjoy my pursuit, not to be frustrated by it. I became more dedicated to paying the price, to working out, to listening and learning."

Former baseball star Andre Thornton believes his faith made him a better player. "Too many people think you can't be a good man and a success, too," he says. "Or they think you can't be a moral man and aggressive. You can't be a hard-nosed player and pray, too. I may not have had the macho attitude some people think winners must have, but I wanted to win badly. I ran the bases well, I slid hard, I was aggressive on the field."

A. C. Green of the Phoenix Suns puts it this way: "True champions measure themselves by a higher standard. Nobody's perfect. If we try to become champions by competing against imperfect people or measuring up to someone else's imperfect victories, we measure ourselves against imperfection. The more we become like Christ, the more goals we'll reach. He wants us to win, so He leads us into championship living. We win inwardly when we measure up, to the best of our ability, to the standard He sets for us. It may take years for others to see our championship qualities and acknowledge them, but eventually the inner peace, character, strength, obedience, and other championship qualities God places within us will show up."

One of the most important advantages of having people of faith on your team is that faith conquers fear. The apostle Paul put it this way: "For God has not given us a spirit of fear, but of power and of love and of a sound mind."[1] Oswald Chambers, a great man of faith, explains how it works: "The remarkable thing about fearing God," he said, "is that, when you fear God, you fear nothing else; whereas if you do not fear God, you fear everything else."

While this book was being written, the Indiana Pacers came to Orlando for the first exhibition game of the 1996-97 season. Just before the game, I ran into Roger Brown, who was a great Pacers player some years ago, when the Pacers were an ABA team. Roger, a legend in the ABA, is now in his fifties. He made this trip to Orlando with the team not in any official capacity but just as a guy who had a lot of great history with the team. I hadn't seen Roger in a while, so when I saw him just ten minutes before tip-off, I said, "Hey, Roger! How are you doing?"

He shook my hand and said, "Pat, I've got cancer."

Well, that's a pretty direct response! And I have to tell you, I was stunned. I've never had anyone say that to me before in response to a greeting. I said, "Roger, I'm so sorry. Tell me what happened."

"I began getting stomach pains this past spring," he said, "and I was concerned, so I went in to get it checked. They opened me up, and the cancer had spread through my large and small intestines and a few other places, so they just sewed me back up and told me I've got six months to live."

In response, I said something to Roger that is not normally in my nature to say—not in such a blunt fashion, anyway. But Roger had been frank with me, so I was equally frank with him. "Roger," I said, "do you know where you're gonna go when you die? We're all gonna die. But if you know Jesus Christ in a personal way, you're assured of eternal life." My heart really went out to this guy, and I wanted to make sure he had the matter of his relationship with God settled.

"I know Jesus," he responded simply, "and I know I'm going to be well taken care of when the time comes." He seemed very calm and at peace—even upbeat. "Well, Pat, it's great to see you again. Should be a great game."

And with that we took our leave of each other. It was a strange mixture of feelings I experienced as I walked away—a feeling of sorrow that this once great player had such limited time left on earth, a feeling of rejoicing that he had settled the issue of eternity, a feeling of gratefulness that I had been bold enough to ask him, and a profound sense of inspiration over the fact that I had spent a few minutes with a man of quiet faith and courage. When Roger Brown died in the spring of 1997, my immediate thought was that moving conversation we had the previous fall.

I've seen that faith is the wellspring of so many other positive character qualities. Out of faith comes courage, as well as honesty, integrity, maturity, perseverance, humility, and a strong work ethic. All of these are important qualities, but it all starts with faith.

PEOPLE OF HONESTY AND INTEGRITY

To build a team of character, you have to have people of honesty and integrity. Here's another situation that happened to me while this book was being written. I went to a sports memorabilia show at a mall in Orlando, and the major attraction was the great Hall of Fame pitcher Jim "Catfish" Hunter. I'm a big collector of autographs, photos, signed balls, and so forth, so I had a lot of fun meeting one of the great legends of baseball. As we chatted, I said, "You know, Catfish, we had a mutual friend by the name of Clyde Kluttz."

His eyes lit up and he said, "You knew Clyde?" Clyde Kluttz was a longtime major league catcher who later scouted for teams in the Carolinas, around the 1960s and '70s. He has since passed away. "You know," said Catfish, "Clyde Kluttz signed me twice. The first time, he signed me right out of high school for the A's. The second time, he signed me for the Yankees. The reason I signed with him twice was that I really trusted him. Clyde was the most honest man I ever knew, and whatever he told you, you could take it right to the bank."

I thought, *Wow, Clyde Kluttz has been gone more than fifteen years, and yet the mere mention of his name, and Catfish Hunter responded immediately with a beautiful word picture of a man with absolutely sterling character. In his mind, Clyde Kluttz equals honesty, integrity, your word is your bond. That says a lot. That says it all.*

I see honesty and integrity as two sides of the same coin. To be an honest person means to be totally, uncompromisingly committed to the truth. To be a person of integrity means to be whole and unfeigned, always to have your walk match your talk. The public you and the private you are one and the same. You don't project an image to the world; you show the world who you *really* are. A person of integrity doesn't just resist temptation; he or she steers far away from temptation.

Honesty and integrity are not matters of degree; you're either committed to being truthful and real—or you're not. If you're "fairly honest," then let's face it: What you're really admitting is that you are *dis*honest. As Tom Peters said, "There is no such thing as a minor lapse of integrity." I'm not saying it's possible to be perfect, but an honest person sets a conscious goal of perfect truthfulness. And when you fail to keep that goal? Hey, just be honest about it!

Coach Mike Krzyzewski of Duke University considers honesty and integrity to be essential components of teamwork and team character. "I have a policy on my team," he says, "that when we talk to each other, we must have eye-to-eye contact. I tell our players we can always deal with the truth. Don't lie or cheat yourself or others. Being straightforward gets everyone on the same page quickly. Honesty helps develop a strong sense of integrity and wholeness in our individual and team character."

I'm trying hard to teach the importance of absolute honesty and integrity to my eighteen children—and I think it's paying off. Not long ago, I received the following letter from one of my adopted sons:

Dear Dad:

I'm sorry for what I did. I stole the money and I don't feel good about it. 'Specially now that I thought about it. That money is what keeps me alive. I took it although I knew it was wrong. I took it because I felt I needed it for the weekend. But now I realize that you need it more.

I just wanted to apologize and tell you that I'm ashamed of myself for stealing from someone I love. Dad, thank you for letting me live in your house. From now on, I'll respect you more than I've done. I won't promise that I won't steal again because I know I will. And when I do it again, I'll feel more ashamed because I broke a promise to my father.

Dad, I can't tell you in writing how much I love you, but I can tell you I'm very proud of my father. You've taught me enough about what's right and wrong. It was my choice to choose wrong and that's why I'm ashamed. Also, because I probably broke my father's heart.

Sometimes I don't realize how much you do for me, but I need to. Dad, I'm writing this letter from my heart. You don't have to believe it, but it really is.

Love, [My Son's Name]

He's learning. He's man enough to admit what he did and to make amends. And he's honest enough to admit that he's got a problem with temptation. He's dealing honestly with his dishonesty—and that's all you can ask. He's developing character—and I think he's going to grow to be a man of honesty and integrity someday. I think he'll make a great team player.

PEOPLE WITH A STRONG WORK ETHIC

To build a team of character, you have to have people with a strong work ethic. I have some good friends, twin brothers named Boyd and Blaine Cornwall. They have an unusual and fascinating lifestyle: They are caddies on the PGA tour—and they have combined their love for the game of golf with a singing and speaking ministry that takes them around the country. They travel from tourney to tourney in their van, caddying and lining up singing and speaking engagements in the locales where they caddy. Whenever they're in central Florida, they use our house as a stopover.

Not long ago, Boyd and Blaine were in Orlando for the Disney Tournament, and while we were having dinner together, they both told me about the great golfing phenom who emerged during the 1996 PGA season. "You're just not gonna believe Tiger Woods," they said (I don't mean they spoke in unison, but when you have a conversation with twins, it's hard to remember who said what). "We've been caddying a long time, and we've *never* seen a golfer like this guy. Tiger is six-foot-one and weighs 155 pounds, and he's the hardest-working golfer we've ever seen in our lives!"

"Hardworking?" I wondered. "How does a guy work hard at golf?"

"Hey, Tiger Woods *trains* for golf," they said, "like guys in the NFL train for football. He lifts weights—big-time. He even outlifted a lot of guys on the Stanford football team! And last week, before the San Antonio tournament, Tiger was out on the links early in the morning, practicing his driving. We had to leave for a while, and we came back at six o'clock that evening and he was still out there, working on his chipping and short game. He outdrives every golfer we've ever seen, and he does it with machinelike accuracy. You know, he's been playing since he was three years old. There's never been a golfer to come along like Tiger Woods. He has a work ethic that just won't quit!"

"Gee," I said, "he was working on his game from early morning till six o'clock in the evening. You think he took a lunch break in there?"

"Boy," they said. "Sure hope so."

That work ethic paid off for him immensely in 1997 when he became the youngest golfer and the first African-American to win the Masters Tournament.

One of the worst and most costly character defects in the world today is laziness—and we all pay for it. It is our individual and collective productivity that creates wealth, creates opportunity, and grows the economy. People who have a weak work ethic are a drag on the entire team. If I decide to dog it for a while, somebody else on the team has to take up the slack. The whole team effort suffers.

At singer Tiny Tim's funeral in 1996, his widow, Susan Khaury, said, "He always wanted to exceed the expectations. If he was supposed to do one song, he did three. If he was supposed to do two or three, he did five. No matter how he felt, the show must go on."

A while back I spoke at a convention in Seattle. The night before I went to the health club in the hotel and saw some of the

Utah Jazz players working out. They were in town to play the Sonics the next night. Karl Malone was there and pushed himself through a punishing one-hour workout. I asked him why he was working so hard the day before a game. He said, "It's the best way to stay ready. As I get older I have to work harder. I want to play until I'm forty, so I've got to be ready for the young guys. Besides, I've got to go up against Shawn Kemp tomorrow night."

Willie Davis is a CEO and a member of a number of corporate boards today, but three decades ago, he was an all-star defensive end for the Green Bay Packers. He recalls a game against the Philadelphia Eagles that taught him a life lesson in the importance of a strong work ethic. Late in the third quarter of that game, a runner started down the far side of the field. Willie's first impulse was to cross the field and try to intercept him. But he'd been playing hard, he was a bit winded, and he thought, "Why overextend myself? I've got teammates who are closer, and who should be able to handle him."

But Willie's teammates didn't get to the runner, who scored a touchdown. By the end of the game, the Packers had lost—by less than a touchdown. That loss has haunted Willie Davis for the rest of his life. To this day, he regrets not making that extra effort to get to the runner. Leaving the field after that loss, Willie promised himself never again to leave the field with a sense of regret, a sense of "if only." He determined to give every game, every task, every challenge in his life 100 percent of his energy and his effort—whether in sports or in the business world. "Every day," he says today, "I tell myself not to let an opportunity slide by that I could have taken advantage of."

Former Miami Dolphins head coach Don Shula has a similar explanation for his success. "There's no secret to being a successful football coach. You need talented athletes, and you have to know how to teach them. In fact, a coach is first and foremost a teacher. Then it all depends on how hard you work. The harder you work, the greater the dividends. I'm no genius."

People who go through life only putting out half an effort, or even 80 or 90 percent, are rarely happy with the life they make for themselves. The words of the brilliant former prime minister of Great Britain Lady Margaret Thatcher are so true: "Look at a day when you were supremely satisfied at its end. It's not a day when you lounged around doing nothing. It's when you've had everything to do *and you've done it.*"

NBA commentator Hubie Brown tells a wonderful story of the work ethic of Kareem Abdul-Jabbar. When Brown was hired as an assistant coach by the Bucks in 1972, he wanted to be the first person at the gym, so he reported four hours early only to see Abdul-Jabbar alone practicing the sky hook. Abdul-Jabbar had been MVP the two previous seasons and led the league in scoring both times.

He often was put down by critics who said he was a player kissed by the gods—great height *and* great athletic ability. But what should be remembered is that he also worked harder than most. Brown adds this to his story: "Before the other players arrived, Abdul-Jabbar left the court. He didn't want them to know he practiced three hours before the scheduled team practice because it implied that they should have done the same. He did it all season."

A lot of people don't know it, but Michael Jordan wasn't always a superstar. In fact, if you look at his high school career, you find that the guy the world now knows as Air Jordan was cut from the varsity team his sophomore year! "When I got cut from the varsity team," he recalls, "I learned something. I knew I never wanted to feel that bad again. I never wanted to have that taste in my mouth, that hole in my stomach. So I set a goal of becoming a starter on the varsity." As a result, Jordan worked hard and trained hard to become the best basketball player he could possibly be. And it paid off: By his senior year, Jordan was a starter on the varsity team.

Now that he's a superstar, you might think that Michael Jordan would ease off. He doesn't need to work out, practice, and train like he used to, right? Wrong! "I approach practices the same way I approach games," he says. "You can't turn it on and off like a faucet. I can't dog it during practice and then, when I need that extra push late in the game, expect it to be there. But that's how a lot of people approach things. And that's why a lot of people fail. They sound like they're committed to being the best they can be. They say all the right things, make all the proper appearances. But when it comes right down to it, they're looking for reasons instead of answers. If you're trying to achieve, there will be roadblocks. I've had them, everybody has had them. But obstacles don't have to stop you. If you run into a wall, don't turn around and give up. Figure out how to climb it, go through it, or work around it. Hard work is the answer."

The Champ, Muhammad Ali, put it this way: "The fight is won or lost far away from witnesses. It is won behind the lines, in the gym, and out there on the road, long before I dance under those lights."

PEOPLE OF MATURITY

To build a team of character, you also have to have people of maturity. When I say *maturity*, I don't mean chronological advancement. We all know young people who are mature beyond their years—and old people who are immature. I don't believe that maturity comes from how long we have lived or the things we have experienced. I believe maturity is the product of our *choices*. We choose, moment by moment and day by day, whether we will grow in character or retreat from character.

Whenever we encounter an obstacle, a challenge, a frustration, a temptation, or an injustice, we have a choice to make. We have an attitude choice and we have a behavior choice. It's completely up to us whether we will respond in a way that leads to growth—or if we will simply take the easy path or the path of momentary gratification. The easy path may be to blow up in frustration, to shrink back from challenges, to give up, to wallow in self-pity, to make excuses for ourselves, to moan about how unfair life is, to demand that someone else rescue us, to yield to temptation—all choices that keep us mired in immaturity. People who are committed to growth and increasing maturity will choose to accept personal responsibility, to tackle the challenge, to persevere, to take life on despite its inequities, to stand on their own two feet, to resist temptation and avoid the easy path.

Abigail Van Buren, the widely read "Dear Abby" columnist, once defined maturity as:

- the ability to stick with a job until it's finished;
- the ability to do a job without being supervised;
- the ability to carry money without spending it;
- the ability to bear an injustice without wanting to get even.

I believe another important aspect of maturity is emotional stability, self-control, the ability to master one's own feelings. "As a kid, I often threw temper tantrums when I lost," recalls Bulls head coach Phil Jackson. "Losing made me feel humiliated and worthless. My obsession with winning was often my undoing. I would push so hard to succeed when things weren't going my way that it hurt my performance. There's a line between playing hard and playing angry."

People of maturity exhibit poise under pressure. When everything is riding on the next pitch, they don't get rattled. They keep their eye on the ball. A reporter once asked Babe Ruth, "How do you always come through in the clutch? I've seen you in the bottom of the ninth in a big game, with the score tied, a full count, thousands of screaming fans, incredible pressure—and you come through with the game-winning hit. You look as cool as the center seed of a cucumber. How do you do it?"

"I don't know how it happens," replied the Sultan of Swat. "I just keep my eye on the ball and I get the hit."

People of maturity don't bring their personal problems into the game. Everybody's got personal problems: difficulties with the spouse or kids, business worries, a loved one with cancer, secret areas of hurt. Some people go around wearing their problems on their sleeve, wearing expressions of gloom and misery, hoping someone will notice and say, "There, there. How you must be suffering!" People of maturity don't crave attention and sympathy, and they don't let their problems bring the rest of the team down.

There is a time and place for dealing with personal problems—in a counselor's office, in a support group or recovery group, in a small group Bible study, or over coffee with a trusted friend. But you don't take your personal problems into the huddle, into the locker room, or into the game, where it saps the team's energy. When you're a team player, your job is to lift and energize the team, not weigh it down.

PEOPLE OF RESPONSIBILITY

Every successful team is made up of people who take responsibility for their own actions. They don't shift blame. They don't make excuses for themselves. They own up to mistakes and failures, and they face the consequences squarely. Joe McCarthy, Yankees manager from 1931 to 1946, used a baseball analogy that applies to every aspect of team competition and life itself. "Never alibi yourself just because a ball takes a bad hop," he said. "Anybody can field the easy ones."

People of responsibility understand and live out the words of the former "Chaplain of Bourbon Street," Bob Harrington, who said, "I am in charge of me." Every player and every leader must take full ownership—and if necessary, full blame—for all of his or her own decisions, actions, and words. We are not helpless victims, we are players in the game. You don't have a mature team until everyone says, "It's my responsibility."

Bobby Bowden, head football coach for Florida State University, knows that, fairly or not, a coach is held responsible for his players' conduct every minute. When confronted with a problem, Bowden deals with the situation *his* way. "Long ago, I made up my mind not to make decisions based on public opinion. I never wanted anybody telling me how to discipline my players. I try to treat these players as I would my own children. People write to me saying how a kid 'is a disgrace to the team' and that I ought to kick him off. I write back and ask, 'What if he were your son? What would you want me to do then?' Usually I don't get a letter back."

In 1986, we won the draft lottery and had the first pick in the draft—my last draft as G.M. of the Philadelphia 76ers. The best player in the NCAA was Brad Daugherty, a terrific seven-foot center who played for coach Dean Smith at North Carolina. We brought Daugherty in for an interview, and one of us asked him, "What is the unique relationship every North Carolina player has with Dean Smith? We've met a lot of players from that program and it seems that over the past thirty years, there's been a special relationship there in Chapel Hill. Everybody loves and respects Dean Smith, without exception. Why is that?"

Daugherty didn't even pause to think about it. He had a ready answer. "Coach teaches us," he said, "that we're responsible for getting up every morning by ourselves, we're responsible to get to class on time, we're responsible to get to practice every day, we're responsible to graduate and get our degree, and we're responsible to go out in society and get a job. That's what he teaches, and that's why we all love Coach Smith."

A few years later, when I was G.M. for the Orlando Magic, we brought Bobby Hurley in for an interview. Bobby was a great point guard for Duke, and though we ended up not drafting him (that was the year we won the lottery and went for Penny Hardaway instead), we had a great talk with Bobby about his career at Duke University and playing for coach Mike Krzyzewski. In the course of our interview, Bobby told a story that Coach K. used to relate to his players at Duke. He said that the most mature human being is the one who takes responsibility for all his actions and can say, "This was well-done and I did it," and, "This was done poorly and I did it." If you can take responsibility for both the good and the bad, you're ready to go on to the next level.

"My outlook comes from West Point where I was a cadet," Mike Krzyzewski reflected. "My players get tired of all my West Point stories. I tell them that when you're a plebe there, the upperclassmen yell at you a lot and you have only three answers: 'Yes, sir!,' 'No, sir!,' and, 'No excuse, sir!' So you can be walking out of a room and your shoes are supposed to be shined all the time, and you're with your roommate, who walks through a puddle of water and splashes some of it on your shoes. Two steps later, an upperclassman says, 'Halt!' He looks down at your shoes and says, 'Why are your shoes so muddy?' And you can't say, 'Hey, man, I was walking down here and my roommate splashed mud on me!' You have to take responsibility. You have to say, 'No excuses, sir!' Because the fact is, your shoes are muddy. Whose responsibility? Your responsibility. So when you're out on the court and you throw a pass, it's your responsibility. I hate players who say, 'Hey, man, you were supposed to catch that!' I say, 'Did you help that player get in the right position and the right frame of mind so he could catch it?' That's what being responsible is all about."

Every so often, there's a big hue and cry about university athletic programs using their athletes for public relations, exploiting them, and not really caring about their education. I think the best response to that kind of criticism comes from John Thompson, the very intense but highly effective coach at Georgetown. He said, "I'm sick and tired of hearing, 'You caused Johnny to flunk!' I tell them, 'Chum, the education is here, I'm going to support your effort to get an education, but it's *your job* to get the education. It's your responsibility to get it for yourself, no one else's.'"

And that's the way it is. People have to take responsibility for themselves—especially in a team environment. No buck passing. No blame shifting. No crying because society owes us this or that. Personal responsibility: That's the name of the game.

PEOPLE WHO START, PERSEVERE, AND FINISH

To build a team of character, you also must have people who start, persevere, and finish. In November 1995, I was at a bookstore doing a signing for my book, *Go For The Magic*. This was shortly after Shaq had broken his thumb in a preseason game, and he was out of action for a number of weeks. A woman and her little daughter were there, and the mother greeted me and said, "Would you see that Shaquille O'Neal gets this card?"

"I'd be glad to," I said. Naturally, curiosity got the better of me, so I looked at the card and this is what it read:

Dear Shaq,

My name is Angel Mary Abbott. I am five years old. Mom is writing this letter for me. I am learning to write. I am sorry that you got hurt and cannot play ball. It's easy for me to get hurt. I have a rare skin disorder called epidermolysis bullosa. I get blisters all over—even my mouth and down my throat. When I fall my skin falls off too. It hurts a lot.

Does your finger hurt? Do you have to wear a dressing? My mom does my dressing every day after my bath. Does it hurt for you to take a bath? Sometimes I have bad bath days. The water hurts my blisters.

When will your hand be better? Do you wish you could play? It's hard to watch other kids play. Sometimes my daddy runs for me when I can't. I hope you get better real soon.

Love, Angel

P.S. Do you still wear a new pair of shoes for every game?

Now, there's a mother and a daughter who could teach us all something about perseverance. You've got to have perseverance in order to succeed as a team or as individuals. It's a quality Walt Disney used to call "stick-to-it-ivity." It's the ability to keep going and going and going and going—just like that doggone Energizer bunny!

Perseverance is more important than brains, more important than skill, more important than talent, more important than strength, more important than luck. If you fall down a thousand times, then success means *getting up a thousand and one times*. As my friend Richard DeVos, the cofounder of Amway, often says, "Perseverance is stubbornness with a purpose."

But you know what? A lot of people never get a chance to prove whether or not they have what it takes to persevere. They never get a chance to see if they've got stick-to-it-ivity or not. Why? Because they never get started!

Bob Richards, decathlete, pole vaulter, and two-time Olympic gold medalist, offers this surprising observation: "There are many people who could be Olympic champions and all-Americans—but they never tried. I'd estimate that five million people could have beaten me in the pole vault the years I won it. *At least* five million. There were men who were stronger, bigger, and faster than I was. They could have done it, but they never picked up a pole. They never made the feeble effort to pick their legs off the ground and try to get over the bar."

In order to finish, you first gotta start. In order to persevere, you first gotta try. Unfortunately, all too many people today want some guarantee of success before they'll even try. Jim Ryun—the great former miler and now a U.S. congressman—puts his finger on the attitude that leads to sickliness and malaise in any team or individual effort: "I've had a chance to talk to high school athletes whom I thought were close to being able to break four minutes in the mile. I don't want to mention names, but what I hear them say is, 'There is no guarantee I'll have the success you had, so I don't want to make the commitment.' That pains me, because there has to be that sense of adventure, a willingness to take on the challenge. When you lose that, you've lost the essence of what middle distance running is all about."[2]

We all need to be challenged to greatness—and we need to challenge ourselves to dare great things. During the darkest days of the Civil War, President Lincoln would often slip into a Wednesday evening service at the New York Avenue Presbyterian Church in Washington, hoping to gain a bit of strength and inspiration to stay the course in that terrible war. After one fiery and dramatic sermon delivered by the church's pastor, Dr. Gurley, one of Lincoln's aides asked the president his opinion of the message.

"It was well thought out, powerfully delivered, and very eloquent," the president replied.

"Yes," said the aide, "I thought it was a great sermon, too."

"Oh, I didn't say I thought it was a *great* sermon," countered Lincoln. "In fact, I felt the message failed."

"How so?"

"It failed because Dr. Gurley did not challenge us to do something *great*."

People of great character are not afraid of tackling great challenges and facing great obstacles. They are not afraid to begin and to try. They do not expect guarantees of success. They would rather be 0 for 10 than 0 for 0. When they lose, they are resilient, they bounce back, they start over and go all out to win the next one. People of character understand that strength and growth do not come from winning easy battles but from plunging into hard-fought battles, win or lose, whatever may come.

Lou Holtz, former Notre Dame head football coach, has a great observation about hanging in there. "If you don't make a total commitment to whatever you're doing, then you start looking to bail out the first time the boat starts leaking. It's tough enough getting that boat to shore with everybody rowing, let alone when a guy stands up and starts putting his life jacket on."

The basketball department at Louisiana State University—Shaquille O'Neal's alma mater—puts out a lot of inspirational, motivational posters to encourage its players. I've probably got them all. One of them featured these words by Robert H. Schuller—words I believe are very profound and full of inspiration for any individual or team effort:

> People are unreasonable, illogical, and self-centered.
> Love them anyway.
> If you do good, people will accuse you of
> selfish ulterior motives.
> Do good anyway.
> If you are successful, you will win
> false friends and true enemies.
> Succeed anyway.
> Honesty and frankness make you vulnerable.
> Be honest and frank anyway.
> The good you do today will be forgotten tomorrow.
> Do good anyway.
> The people with the biggest ideas can be shot down by
> the smallest people with the smallest minds.
> Think big anyway.
> People favor underdogs but always follow top dogs.
> Fight for some underdogs anyway.
> What you spend years building may be destroyed overnight.
> Build anyway.
> Give the world the best you've got and
> you'll get kicked in the teeth.
> Give the world the best you've got anyway.

Success always starts with trying. Before a skyscraper is built, someone has to turn the first shovelful of dirt. There are no guarantees of success—but if you never start, I guarantee you'll never succeed. To be a player of character on a team of character, you have to be a person who starts the job, a person who perseveres through the battles and over the obstacles, and a person who finishes. Napoleon was right when he said, "Victory belongs to the most persevering." There is no other way to win.

PEOPLE OF COURAGE

To build a team of character, you also have to have people of courage. Two years ago, I was one of a number of people in the sports world invited to attend the opening of Ted Williams's Hitters Hall of Fame in Hernando, Florida—a huge thrill for me as a baseball fan. I was told to report to a certain hotel where a limousine would pick me up and take me to the country club where the reception was to be held. They told me to be ready at 5:30, and I was there at 5:30 on the dot. The limo was waiting, and as the driver let me into the car, he said, "We have another passenger, so it'll be just a few minutes before we leave." So I settled into the back of the limo. A few minutes later, the door opened, and guess who plunked down right next to me?

Joltin' Joe DiMaggio—the Yankee Clipper himself!

I had never met him before. I was speechless. In fact, I almost swallowed my teeth. He had his accountant, his lawyer, an entire entourage with him. We started the thirty-minute drive to the country club, and I took out my book of photographs of famous baseball players: I had brought it along, hoping to do a little hero-worshiping at the reception. I had an 8x10 glossy of DiMaggio in my book, so I turned to him and asked if he would sign the picture, which he did. I later learned that DiMaggio is the toughest autograph in the world to get; he just doesn't like to do autographs. Well, after I had him sign the first picture, I whipped out another glossy and handed it to him, and said, "Would you mind—?"

He frowned down at the photo, then he scowled at me. "Who are you?" he asked, obviously irritated. "Are you some sort of collector? How did you get in here?" Can you blame him?

The poor guy had gotten into this limo expecting a quiet, private ride to the reception—and he finds himself cornered by an autograph hound! Fortunately, somebody in his entourage knew who I was and introduced us, and Joe did sign the second picture.

The two-day ceremony for the opening of Ted Williams's Hitters Hall of Fame was an incredible party, populated by some of the greatest names who ever played the game of baseball. Me? I was in baseball fan heaven! I got a ball signed by everybody there, about twenty-five Hall of Famers—everybody but DiMaggio. Fact is, I was chicken! I was absolutely petrified to approach him again for another autograph. On the last day, after the final ceremony, a lot of people were milling around, saying their good-byes, and getting ready to head off to the airport. I just couldn't gather up the courage to go up to Joe and ask him to sign this ball! I saw Ralph Kiner, the great Hall of Famer, who had been very kind to me. So I said, "Ralph, would you do me a favor? Would you please take this ball to Joe DiMaggio and ask him to sign it?"

Ralph looked like I had just asked him to broadjump the Grand Canyon. He said, "Oh, no, no, uh-uh, no way, nosiree!" He was as intimidated by Joltin' Joe as I was! I said, "Ralph, I would really, really, *really* appreciate it!" He sighed, hung his head, and took the ball. Then he tiptoed over to Joe, and Joe looked at him, recognized him, and quickly signed the ball.

So that's my story. At that particular point in my life, I was a coward, and I admit it. And the point of this story is, well, *don't be such a coward!* Teams run on courage. Winning takes place because players are willing to risk pain, injury, and loss. Championships are won by big, brave hearts, filled to the brim with courage.

When I think of courage, I think of Jackie Robinson, the man who broke the color barrier in baseball. During his career, Jackie Robinson won many honors. His first year in the National League, he was awarded Rookie of the Year, and he went on to win the Most Valuable Player award and achieve a .311 lifetime batting average.

When he was signed by the Brooklyn Dodgers in 1945, Robinson made a deal with general manager Branch Rickey. He agreed that he would never fight, even if provoked. Rickey knew that there were many prejudiced ballplayers in the league and that they would not make it easy for Robinson. He wanted to make sure his new player could withstand the inevitable pressure of being the first black in the major leagues and that he wouldn't spoil his image with fistfights in the ballpark.

Robinson wasn't sure he could take that kind of pressure without blowing up. "Mr. Rickey," he asked, "are you saying you want a coward on your ballclub?"

Rickey shook his head no.

"I'm supposed to turn the other cheek? Is that it?" Robinson asked.

Rickey nodded yes.

It was tough—but Jackie Robinson kept his word to Branch Rickey. When he was verbally assaulted, when opponents tried to get him riled, when they slid into second with their spikes high, Robinson kept his temper in check. Oh, he got even in his own way—but he did it with class. He'd channel his anger into aggressive play and stuff it down his opponents' throats by bashing out a base hit or making a diving catch. That's courage. That's character. That's team attitude at its finest.

A lot of people think courage is the absence of fear. Fact is, everybody has fear. There are a lot of ways to respond to fear—we can run from it, we can be paralyzed by it, or we can manage it. Courage is the healthy management of our fears. It is the *character* response to fear, the positive response to fear. It's not cowardly to feel afraid. It's only cowardly to let fear control us. When we control our fear instead of letting fear control us, that's called courage. Ralph Waldo Emerson put it this way: "Do the thing you fear and the death of fear is certain."

Bill Walsh, the originator of the famous "West Coast offense" for the San Francisco 49ers, understands how to inspire a team to overcome fear and demonstrate winning courage, even in losing situations. In his book *Building a Champion: On Football and the Making of the 49ers*, he writes:

> When a wildebeest or zebra is finally entrapped by the lion, it submits to the inevitable. Its head drops, its eyes glaze over, and it stands motionless and accepts its fate. The posture of

defeat is also demonstrated by man—chin down, head dropped, shoulders slumped, arms hung limply. This posture is often visible as players leave the field in the later stages of the game when things are going against them. I often brought this to our players' attention using the example from nature, and we became very sensitive to it. I would remind them never to allow this to occur. I would assert, "Even in the most impossible situations, stand tall, keep our heads up, shoulders back, keep moving, running, looking up, demonstrating our pride, dignity, and defiance."

In other words, use your physical bearing and your mental attitude to punch through the haze of defeat. Carry yourself like a champion, throw your fierce pride and courage right back in your opponent's teeth, and keep advancing toward your goal.

In the spring of 1997 I visited the Anaheim Angels training camp in Arizona and met Rod Carew for the first time. I've admired him for years as a seven-time American League batting champion and now a hitting coach with the Angels. Today, I—like so many people around the country—also admire Rod Carew as a human being of great courage. And most of all, I admire the spirit of his beautiful eighteen-year-old daughter, Michelle, who died of cardiac respiratory failure in April 1996, after a long, difficult battle with leukemia.

About a month before Michelle died, Rod Carew wrote a letter describing the "astounding improvements" in her condition. In fact, she was able to come home from the hospital for a while. For months prior to that brief improvement, she had dealt with incredible bouts of pain, soaring fevers, septic shock, infections, swelling, and several surgeries. Through it all, Rod and Marilynn Carew, with their daughters Stephanie and Charryse, stood by helplessly, watching her suffer.

When the story of Michelle's illness hit the national media, the Carew family was hopeful that a bone marrow donor might be found who could save her life. Unfortunately, Michelle needed a rare match for her genetic mix—a combination of African-American, Panamanian, and Caucasian. No such donor became available.

By April, as Michelle became unable to speak, the Carew family held her and said their good-byes. The evening Michelle died, Rod went to the ballpark and visited with the Angels in the clubhouse before game time. He drew strength from them; his teammates and colleagues in the baseball community had always been a second family to him. But he also imparted strength to them. "That was the toughest time for me," Angels outfielder Jim Edmonds said of that night, "but it was a little pick-me-up to see him." That's the way Michelle wanted it. "Daddy, go to work," she often said. "The guys need you."

Though Michelle herself received no miracle of healing, the story of her courageous battle inspired a miracle of a different kind. Within a few days after the news went out that Michelle needed a marrow donor, more than seventy thousand people across the country registered with the National Marrow Donor Program, and there is no way of knowing how many lives will eventually be saved as a result.

"When she was diagnosed," said Carew, shortly after Michelle died, "she wanted me to do something not only for her but for the other kids with leukemia. She wasn't concerned about herself. She'd be happy to hear she was able to save some lives." The words of a courageous father, describing his courageous daughter.[3]

Any team, involved in any game in any arena—whether in a ballpark, on a hardwood court, in an office, in a church, or on a battlefield—needs the character quality of courage. People of courage inspire a team to dare great things, to go farther than any other team has gone before. On any team, you've gotta have the courage to face your fears, your obstacles, and your opponents—and to beat them.

PEOPLE OF HUMILITY

To build a team of character, you also have to have people of humility.

Because I do a lot of public speaking around the country, I spend a fair amount of time in airports, hotels, and limousines—

so I get to meet a lot of limo drivers and collect a lot of limo stories! Whenever I get in a limo, I always ask the driver, "Who are some of the most memorable people you've ever driven?" The answers are always fascinating and usually focus on one character trait: *humility*.

My driver in San Diego was a guy named Jerry who had been a limo driver for nearly ten years. His most memorable passengers: "Dustin Hoffman and Joan Rivers," he replied without hesitation. I asked him what made them so memorable. "They were so down-to-earth and pleasant to be around. Just regular, real people." Thomas, who drove me back to the Atlanta airport from Stone Mountain, Georgia, answered my question the same way: "My most memorable passengers? That's easy. Richard Simmons and Nell Carter—they're real people, real down-to-earth. The way they are in public is exactly the way they were in my limo. Genuine, humble. Those are the two I remember."

On another occasion, my limo driver for the eighty-minute drive from O'Hare Airport to Lake Geneva, Wisconsin, was Joe Curtis. In response to my standard limo questions, he told me about his six trips with Henry Kissinger, plus trips with other well-known passengers such as Colin Powell, Maureen O'Hara, Joe Namath, John Havlicek, Bob Cousy, and Debbie Reynolds— all people he spoke of with great admiration. I asked him if there was one common trait they all possessed, and he said, "Absolutely. No matter how big they are in the public eye, here in my limo, they were just regular people. They were genuinely humble—no airs about them. They didn't act like big shots or make unreasonable demands or expect special treatment. They were just nice people. I remember Dr. Kissinger actually insisted on sitting up in the front seat with me."

On a trip to Pebble Beach, California, I flew to Monterey, where I was met by my limo driver, Dugan. He told me his most memorable passenger was Leonard Firestone, son of the founder of the Firestone Tire Company and a former ambassador to Great Britain. He was going to visit a family to pick up a yellow labrador puppy. All the way over, he worried whether the family would like him, whether they would trust him to provide a good home for their puppy. Here was a guy worth millions, yet he was concerned if people would like him! Wonderful humility!

I think my favorite limo story of all comes from a trip I took to northern Idaho in July 1996. I had a forty-five-minute drive to the Spokane airport with a driver named Kenny, who spent twelve years escorting guests for the Johnny Carson *Tonight Show*. His most memorable guest: "No question," he replied. "Vincent Price—the guy in all those horror movies. In person, he was a very nice, humble man. He never made any demands on people, treated everyone with respect, a very down-to-earth guy. One night, I drove him home and parked the limo in his drive. He said, 'Have you had dinner?' I said, 'I'm going to pick up something on my way back.' He said, 'Well, why don't you come in for a while?' I said, 'Well, I'm really supposed to get right back.' He said, 'Call your company and tell them you have a bad flat tire.' I said, 'But I don't have a flat.' Price said, 'Yes, you do.' I was puzzled at first, but then he added, 'If you don't stick around for a while, I'll never get the two hours I need to cook dinner for you. You'll never get to eat my Chateaubriand with Bearnaise sauce and steamed mushrooms.' Can you believe he did that? So I stayed and had dinner with Vincent Price. It was a dinner I'll never forget."

Humility is one of the rarest character traits in the world today. It is also one of the winningest. In this era of big egos, greed, glitz, and self-promotion, humility is not a trait that is much in demand or high esteem. It is interesting to note, however, that in the game of basketball it is usually the biggest stars who demonstrate the greatest humility. Penny Hardaway, Michael Jordan, Hakeem Olajuwon, David Robinson, Moses Malone, Julius Erving, John Havlicek—these and so many great names in the game of basketball are truly the humblest, most gracious, most selfless people it has ever been my privilege to know.

Why is humility so little prized in our society today? Perhaps because people don't understand what true humility is. Humility doesn't mean a sense of humiliation, of I'm-not-worthy. It's okay to like yourself. It's okay to be confident. It's okay to have a healthy sense of self-esteem. You can have all these things and still be humble. A person of humility is simply a person who doesn't have to go around proving to everybody else how good he is. A humble person lives in the security that he or she has nothing to prove. A humble person can feed the ball to another player who's in a better position to make the shot, secure in the fact that he is moving the team toward the goal, even if he shines a little less.

I remember visiting the office of Jerry Colangelo, president and CEO of the Phoenix Suns, at the team's beautiful $90 million facility. Three objects in his office attracted my attention:

- A photo of the house in Chicago Heights where Jerry grew up. It was an inelegant structure, partially constructed from the wood siding from a couple of boxcars.
- An amphora from Italy, dated at around 100 B.C. and used to store olive oil. This object reminded Jerry of his Italian roots.
- An old accordion that Jerry's grandfather taught him to play.

I asked him what the significance of these objects was in his life, and Jerry replied, "These three objects help keep things in perspective for me. They remind me of where I came from and how far I've come. Above all, they teach me the importance of humility. Everything I have is a gift that could vanish"—he snapped his fingers—"like *that*."

Humility is the great lubricant of teams. It reduces friction, smoothes out the performance of a rough-running team, and enables the various parts of a team to function well together. The finest collection of highly paid, highly talented, self-centered egos in the world will never be a true team. Ego is the antithesis of teamwork. The nature of teamwork is servanthood and selflessness; the virtue of teamwork is humility.

PEOPLE WHO USE THEIR INFLUENCE WISELY

To build a team of character, you also have to have people who use their influence wisely. There were about twenty of us in the conference room at the Magic facility as Al Lucia did a "Walk the Talk" seminar for the executives of our organization. In the middle of his presentation with an overhead projector, Al flashed this quote on the screen. He had a piece of cardboard over the bottom of it, so you couldn't see the name of the person who originated the quote. Here is what it said:

> I'll show you some of the amazing wonders that have come about because people dared to dream their dreams—and then had the courage, ingenuity, and perseverance to hammer those dreams into reality!

I thought, *Great quote!* Being a collector of quotations, I just loved it. I had my notebook open and I was just writing it down as fast as I could write. Then Al removed the cardboard, and revealed the source of the quote:

> Pat Williams,
> in *Go for the Magic*

And the room just exploded in laughter, because everyone saw me diligently writing down my own quotation!

It just goes to show, you never know what kind of influence your life is having on others. Sometimes your words and your deeds go out into the world, ricochet around a bit, and come right back at you! So it's important to be aware of the influence we have on others. It's important to be responsible role models—because we never know who may be watching and what words and actions of ours someone may imitate or throw back in our faces.

Barry Halper is an avid baseball collector in North Jersey and a good friend. During a recent visit to his home—which is really a shrine to the great American pastime—he showed me one of his prize possessions: a 1949 advertising poster for Chesterfield cigarettes, featuring some of the great stars of baseball happily endorsing what we now know as "coffin nails" and "cancer sticks." A few years ago, Barry was able to get this poster signed by all of the players who were featured on it, and here is what these baseball greats wrote above their autographs:

- Ted Williams: "Barry, I'm going to give the money back—$5,000."
- Stan Musial: "Gave them up many years ago."
- Joe DiMaggio: "Haven't had one in 36 years."
- Ewell Blackwell: "Quit over 10 years ago."

Aware of their positions as role models, these great players recanted their endorsement of a product that we now know has destroyed many millions of lives. It reminds me of the statement Mickey Mantle made just before his death in 1995 due to alcohol-related liver disease at age sixty-three: "You talk about a role model? This is a role model: Don't be like me. I want to get across to the kids not to drink or do drugs, everything. I think the moms and dads should be role models. God gave me the ability to play baseball and I wasted it. I was given so much, and I blew it. I'm going to spend the rest of my life trying to make it up. I want to start giving something back."

As this book was being written, I received a letter that made me very grateful that our Orlando Magic organization is made up of players who are aware of their influence—and who constantly use it for the benefit of others. Here's the letter:

Dear Mr. Williams,

When our family read in today's *Chicago Tribune* that Horace Grant had one of the highest salaries in the NBA, we cheered, and I want to tell you why.

In early June 1994, my daughter wrote to Horace begging him to just stop by for a moment and say hello to her mom, who was fighting a battle against leukemia but who never missed a Bulls game. My daughter had worked in a restaurant near the Bulls practice facility and was acquainted with most of the Bulls players.

The very next day, Horace came by and brought my wife a large bouquet of yellow roses. Not only did he sit and talk with her for more than an hour—in no hurry at all—but he gave her the jersey he wore when the Bulls defeated the Suns for the championship, signing it, "To Geri, my dear friend." I was teaching that day, but I got to see that conversation on videotape, which is now a family treasure, along with the jersey.

Well, just before Horace left for Orlando, he stopped by again for a brief chat and to say goodbye, and he promised to send my wife some of his favorite movies on videotape that they had discussed. I cannot tell you how much this meant to Geri. I cannot resist the tears when I remember the joy she had in telling me.

Geri died that November, leaving our nine children in sorrow. But when we all returned home after the first evening of the wake, there was a bouquet waiting for us, signed, "With love and prayers, Horace Grant."

The following January, my son-in-law and I got tickets to the Bulls-Magic game. We brought a huge poster with "WE LOVE YOU, HORACE!" on it, but somehow no Chicago camera caught us!

So we think there is not enough money in the world to repay this gentle, sweet person for his unforgettable kindness, and we wish him and your team the best of fortune for this season.

God bless you for having Horace!

Sincerely,
George Herman

And those kind words bring a few tears to my eyes, let me tell you! Yes indeed, we are very blessed to have Horace Grant and a lot of other great role models—and simply great human beings—in our Orlando Magic organization.

There were a lot of hurt feelings and negative press reports when Shaquille O'Neal took his leave of the Orlando Magic and headed for L.A. There's no point in sugarcoating it: We felt, and still feel, that Shaq and his agent, Leonard Armato, owed us better than the treatment they gave us. No question, Shaq left a trail of hard feelings in his wake.

But I don't want the unpleasantness of his departure to erase some of the great memories I have of the big guy. I still believe that even though Shaq has "gone Hollywood" there's still a big heart beating inside that seven-foot-plus frame. I'll always remember some of the generous, positive things he did in

Orlando, often when nobody was watching—quiet acts of kindness performed without fanfare or PR.

One example: Soon after Brian Hill joined the Magic as an assistant coach, his daughter Kim had to be hospitalized. Brian doesn't talk about Kim's situation very much, but she has an incurable condition called cystic fibrosis and periodically goes through tough bouts with the disease. While Kim was in the hospital, a beautiful arrangement of roses arrived in her room. Since she had just moved to Orlando with her family, she wondered who could have learned about her condition and sent her the roses. It turned out that Shaq had overheard someone talking about Kim's condition in the locker room, and his first response was to send flowers. The card read, "Get well soon. Your friend, Shaq."

Though I'll miss seeing the big guy doing his slammin' and jammin', his stuffs and his alley-oops here in the O-rena, I wish him well—and I hope he keeps that great big heart of his open to the needs and hurts around him in L.A. He's got a lot of influence everywhere he goes, and I hope he always uses it to help others.

In July 1996, I spoke at an Amway rally in Kansas City, Missouri. If you've never been to an Amway rally, it's one-third Mardi Gras, one-third Billy Graham crusade, and one-third Notre Dame pep rally. During a break in the festivities, one of the hosts of the rally came up to me and asked me to take a letter to our former coach, Brian Hill. I said I'd be glad to, so he wrote out a note and handed it to me. Then he added, "Go ahead and read it, Pat. I want you to know what a great guy Brian Hill is." Here (slightly edited) is what the letter said:

Brian,

You probably don't remember me, but I was a camper at the Pocono Invitational Basketball Camp, back in the summer of 1977. You were my coach in that first session. In fact, my friend, Perry Williams, and I stayed for an additional session so we could visit Lehigh University, as you suggested we should.

I had the honor to host Pat Williams at an Amway rally, and I told him about when you coached us at basketball camp.

He said he would give you this note, and I'm grateful for the opportunity to write and thank you for making a powerful impact on my life almost twenty years ago. I'll never forget the week I spent with you as my coach at that camp. We even won the camp championship!

You may not realize it, but the week I spent at that camp changed my life—especially your recruiting of me to come to Lehigh University. I've kept every letter you sent me, and have them at my home today. One of my goals is to become a basketball coach at the high school level. I hope I can do as well as you have!

Thank you for the encouragement and belief you gave me. It has played a part in the success I have had in my life. I hope we meet again soon. Good luck this season—and thank you again for the assist you gave me in 1977. It has helped me make many baskets in the game of life.

Fondly,
Greg Felder

Today we see many sports stars shirking their responsibility as role models, and trashing the elevated position and honor God has given them by reason of their talents. Some even shrug and say, "Look, I never asked to be anybody's role model." But the great stars of the game understand that with great success and fame in the game comes great responsibility—like it or not.

Karl Malone of the Utah Jazz understands this responsibility—and he accepts it and uses it to influence others in a positive way. "We don't choose to be role models," he says. "We are chosen. Our only choice is whether to be a good role model or a bad one." And my friend Julius Erving accepts this responsibility as an opportunity to serve God and others. "As a Christian layperson," he says, "I feel I have a ministry, which exists because of the platform I have been afforded. I'm blessed with the ability to be an agent of change in people's lives, through deed or inspiration or association or mentoring. I take being a role model very seriously."

Herschel Walker of the Dallas Cowboys is another athlete who takes this responsibility very seriously. I heard a touching story about Herschel in September 1996, when I flew to Atlanta for a speaking engagement in Stone Mountain. My limo driver was Bill Pharis, and of course I asked Bill to tell me about the most memorable experience he had as a driver. "Last January," he said, "Herschel Walker was in Atlanta for a big sports convention. He was due to leave on a 7 A.M. flight, but a nine-year-old boy at the convention asked Herschel if he could come to his show-and-tell at school the next morning. At first, Herschel said he couldn't—but then he reconsidered. He canceled his flight and completely changed his plans. I picked him up at 7 A.M. and drove him thirty miles to the boy's school in Marietta, Georgia. The guy spent an hour with those kids, then left on a later flight. Can you believe he did that? Man, that really made an impression on me." It made an impression on me, too—and can you imagine the lifelong impression it left on those kids?

Another person who takes his influence on young lives seriously is Michael Jordan. Once, when my son Richie was home for spring break and the Bulls were in town to play the Magic, Richie got to be the ball boy. Before the game, I introduced Richie to Michael Jordan. Richie was speechless as he looked up at Michael. A lot of stars are kind enough to shake a kid's hand or sign an autograph at such moments, but Michael went a step further. He took a few moments to share his philosophy of life with Richie. "If you want to really make it in life," he said, "there are three things you have to do, Richie. First, if you want to do something and you love doing it, then do it. Second, whatever you choose to do, work hard at it. Third, you've got to get it done in the classroom to be successful. Stay in school." How could a kid not be deeply impacted by that potent little message from the heart of Michael Jordan?

Pete Hamill wrote an insightful profile of Michael Jordan for the November 1996 *TV Guide* titled "Why He's Simply . . . The Best." Hamill described his experience of trekking over the dry, dusty hills of central Mexico and encountering a little Mexican boy herding goats. The boy wore tattered jeans, sneakers tied with twine, and a T-shirt. The sight of that shirt surprised Hamill because it was red, bore the jersey number 23 and the name JORDAN. Here was a Michael Jordan fan herding goats in the hills of Mexico, far away from the fast-paced world that Air Jordan inhabits. Hamill asked the Mexican boy why he was such a big-time Jordan fan, and the boy's answer was a tribute to the basketball star's character and commitment to excellence. Hamill writes:

> "*Porque su papá fue asesinado,*" he whispered. Because his father was murdered. And, in a small boy's voice, "*Y todavía es el campeón de todo el mundo.*" And still he is the champion of the whole world.
>
> That he is, muchacho. That he is.[4]

That's the kind of player Michael Jordan is. Whether in a one-on-one encounter with a young ball boy named Richie Williams or on a worldwide stage that reaches into the dusty hills of other countries, Michael Jordan is a powerful influence for good, a great role model, and an excellent human being. Even apart from his superhuman performance on the basketball court, all teams could use more players like Michael Jordan.

Back in 1995 I spent some time with Ernie Banks, "Mr. Cub," who was in Orlando for a promotional appearance. I asked him, "How did you get your positive approach to life, your enthusiasm and zeal for living?"

Ernie answered, "I got it from Buck O'Neil, the great baseball legend. I met him when I was a young player. He came to our house to meet my parents, and I saw his positive, upbeat personality. Then I played for him for two years with the Kansas City Monarchs, and he was the same way.

"After I spent two years in the army, I joined the Cubs in 1953. By then Buck had joined the Cubs, too. I saw the same consistency of his enthusiasm and joy for life. So Buck really influenced me, and I just adopted what I saw in his life for my own life. You live life for the moment and live it to the fullest. I've learned to set my problems aside and get on with life. Most people's lives are so mundane and overwhelmed with adversity, but I've never let that happen to me.

"I've got three children now in their thirties, and they're just like me. They've adopted the same upbeat, positive approach to life that I have. And it all started with the positive influence that

Buck O'Neil had on me forty-five years ago when I was just starting my baseball career."

I once introduced my sons Stephen, Thomas, and Alan to Cal Ripken, the legendary shortstop of the Baltimore Orioles. He told them three things they will always remember to get the most out of playing baseball:

1. Have fun and enjoy playing.
2. Play all the different positions.
3. Work hard at it.

My sons will never forget those three ideas—or the baseball great who took the time to share those ideas with them.

And I'll never forget the time another baseball legend gave to me in May 1996. The Magic had gone to Atlanta for a play-off series against the Hawks. Whenever I travel someplace, I try to take advantage of everything there is to see there and to meet all the people I can in that community, because I never know if I'll be back. In Atlanta, the one person I've always wanted to meet is "The Hammer," Hank Aaron, the man who broke Babe Ruth's all-time home-run record in 1974. I called his secretary, introduced myself, and asked, "Could I stop by while I'm in town? I'd love to get him to sign a book for me." She said, "Be here at four o'clock."

I arrived on the dot and went into his office—and there was the great Hank Aaron. He gave me a full hour of his time, and it is one of the most memorable hours I have ever spent. Hank Aaron is truly one of the nicest people I've ever met. During our chat, he said, "I've got a commemorative rug of my career right here, and I'd love to sign it and give it to Shaq."

"I'll give it to him," I said.

"And say, would you like a ball from the unplayed 1994 World Series? I'll sign it for you."

I couldn't believe my good fortune. "I'd love that," I said.

He grabbed a ball, signed it, handed it to me, and said, "And how about one of my bats? Would you like that?"

I pinched myself to see if I was dreaming, then said, "You know, I think I would!"

So he took a bat and wrote on it, "To Pat, best wishes, Hank Aaron."

As we concluded our conversation, I thought, *Boy, I'd like to take away a piece of Hank Aaron's thoughts, a bit of what it is inside him that made him such a legendary player.* So I said, "Hank, what is the greatest life lesson you ever learned?"

Without a moment's hesitation, he responded, "My mother taught me to do unto others what you'd have them do unto you. That has been the guiding principle of my life. Also, treat people with respect, particularly your elders. If you respect others, they'll respect you, and you can respect yourself. If you don't show respect to people, you'll always have trouble in life. Also, I learned from my mother to have belief in God. No matter how much success you have, you need faith in Him. That's the way I was raised, and I still try to live my life that way."

With that I parted—and I took away with me a piece of the great Hank Aaron, Role Model. He is a man who is extremely aware of his influence, and he uses it for the benefit of others.

A role model is a person who *knows* the way, *goes* the way, and *shows* the way. You can't fake positive influence. It has to be real. It has to be lived out on a daily basis. As John Maxwell put it, "People do what people see. They forget my sermons, but follow my footsteps."

CHARACTER MATTERS

Character gives teams and individuals the winning edge. Character lifts teams and individuals to their goals. Character brings the team vision within reach. How does it happen? It's not hard to understand.

People of faith on your team keep the entire team positive and motivated to achieve great things on behalf of a higher calling. People of honesty and integrity build respect and trust, which enables the team to think in sync and act in sync. People who are able to start, persevere, and finish a task provide the winning edge of commitment, drive, stamina, and extra effort to train hard and play hard. People of maturity are poised under pressure and come through in the clinches. People of courage refuse to knuckle under to opposition and superior forces; they win by confounding the naysayers, doomsayers, and gloomy oddsmakers. People of humility want to win as a team, not hog all the glory; they provide the "team" in teamwork. People with a strong work ethic are committed to training hard and playing hard; they provide the "work" in teamwork. People who live their lives as positive role models make it worth being on a team; they reflect credit on the entire organization and the entire profession.

Character counts. Character matters. Character wins.

Teamwork Is the Destination

Back in August 1995, Daniela, one of my Brazilian daughters, ran cross-country in a track meet at Lake Mary High School. As she stood in line to collect her medal, I noticed a T-shirt on the girl next to her. The lettering on the shirt read,

WHEN TEAMWORK IS THE DESTINATION,
VICTORY HAPPENS ALONG THE WAY.

I thought to myself, *By George, that's it!* Teamwork is not the means to an end, it's the end itself! Teamwork is the destination. If we achieve the true goal of teamwork, then victory will be an experience we enjoy together, again and again along our journey toward our completeness as a team.

There are layers and layers of depth to this mystical concept we call teamwork. It goes far beyond merely getting a bunch of people together to accomplish a task. At its best and deepest level, a team is a union of souls who have learned simultaneously to celebrate and transcend their differences. They have learned a level of love for one another and trust in one another so that all their actions mesh like well-engineered gears. They share a single vision and a single passion. They have come to understand one another so well that much of their communication takes place without any words at all; they communicate with their eyes, their facial expressions, their body language, their hands. They are transparent to one another. They have nothing to hide from one another. Their oneness elevates their play to a level that transcends the natural.

True teamwork is startlingly beautiful to witness. When you have gone as deep as you can go into this experience we call teamwork, you find an experience unbelievably rich, warm, deep, and nurturing. You find something called *community* or *fellowship*, something that the first-century Christians called in the Greek language *koinonia*.

If you read the book of Acts in the New Testament, you see that the early Christians were in alignment. They experienced synergy. After the risen Jesus Christ left them, the Holy Spirit invaded them and took hold of them. The Spirit welded them into a *koinonia*-team-community. They experienced that elusive, mystical bonding that enabled all their energies to pulsate in a unified, synchronized, harmonious flow toward their goal—the goal of turning the first-century world upside down with the good news of Jesus Christ.

Ultimately, at its deepest and finest, true teamwork is a spiritual experience. I hope you will not leave this book with the idea that true teamwork can be generated by a bunch of techniques or gimmicks or easy steps. Teamwork comes about only when we are absolutely committed to the principles of teamwork, to our teammates, and to our vision. And I would take it a step further and say that the deepest, richest, most meaningful, most intense form of teamwork takes place when we are also committed—body, mind, and spirit—to God.

PUTTING IT ALL TOGETHER

The experience of alignment or synergy—and the almost mystical elevation of the team's effort that accompanies it—is nothing less than a miracle. If you've ever experienced it, you know what I mean. As I said at the beginning of this book, I truly believe there are ways we can *make miracles happen* on our teams, be it a sports team, a business team, a church team, a family, or any other team endeavor. We can't turn miracles on and off like a light switch, but we can take steps to create a welcoming environment for the miracle of alignment to strike. We can tap into the miraculous synergy of teamwork so that the elusive experience of team alignment can take place on an ever-increasing basis. The way we do that is by building these eight teamwork ingredients into our teams:

1. Acquire top talent. Start with the best possible raw material—the people with the best skills, strengths, and experience for the job. Balance those skills and strengths well, and blend them with compatible personalities, and you have something wonderful on your hands: team chemistry.

2. Demonstrate and develop strong leadership. Leadership conceives and communicates the team vision, sets the team goals, models character, shows the way, and motivates the players.

3. Encourage team commitment. Build loyalty (commitment to one another), sense of mission (commitment to the vision), class (commitment to quality and excellence), competitiveness (commitment to winning), accountability (commitment to continual improvement), mental toughness (commitment to hustling and finishing), and self-discipline (commitment to self-control and self-mastery).

4. Inspire team enthusiasm and passion. Every leader and player on the team must have an intense emotional and spiritual desire to achieve the goal and turn the vision into reality.

5. Build a strong team attitude. The team must learn to sacrifice selfish wants, transcend differences, and think in sync.

6. Empower individuals. Team leaders and players must continually build each other up and enable each other to have confidence in themselves.

7. Create a team environment of mutual respect and trust. Synergy and alignment depend upon players speaking the truth to each other in love, so that they can respect each other, trust each other, and function as one.

8. Build on a foundation of team and individual character. Talent alone is not enough. Everything else that a team consists of—strong leadership, passion and commitment, respect and trust, team attitude—is built on a sturdy foundation of such character qualities as honesty, integrity, humility, courage, faith, maturity, and a strong work ethic.

These are the eight essentials of teamwork. When all of these elements are working together in an effective, balanced way, then miracles start to happen. The players fall into alignment. Their strengths are magnified by the magic of synergy. Wins and championships fall into place. The atmosphere around your team crackles with the energy of joy and success.

There's no other feeling in the world like the feeling of absolute teamwork, where everything has clicked into place, where magic and excitement become your daily diet. When you've experienced it, you know it. And you never want it to stop.

TREATING PEOPLE RIGHT

As this chapter was being written, I had the great experience of hosting on my weekly radio show former Washington Bullets center, now general manager, Wes Unseld. He was in town for the 1996-97 season opening game against the Magic, and we had a great time talking on the air about everything under the sun, from basketball to Wes's childhood. He shared with me a great story from his boyhood in Louisville, Kentucky.

His family lived next door to a family with nineteen children—seven from the mother's first marriage, seven from the father's first marriage, and five from their marriage together. The father of this family was named Charles—the same as Wes's own dad. Whenever he heard a woman yell, "Charles!" in the neighborhood, Wes could never be sure at first if it was his dad or the man next door who was being called.

On one occasion, Wes heard the lady next door call out, "Charles! *Your* children have joined up with *my* children, and they're beating up *our* children!"

Well, that's a kind of teamwork, I suppose—*his* kids and *her* kids teaming up against *their* kids. But the family as a whole was clearly not functioning as a team. Joining up with one group to defeat another group is not, in my mind, the highest expression of the teamwork concept. Two more stories illustrate what I believe is the real heart and soul of teamwork.

Just as this book was being completed, something happened in our family that illustrated for me what it means for family members to think and act as a team. We were having a Thanksgiving outing at the beach with all the kids. It was great fun. We had a big bonfire on the beach, sand games, Frisbees—just a really terrific family time. It was a trouble-free, tranquil day until nighttime when Thomas came running up to me, yelling, "Stephen got hurt!"

Thomas and Stephen are my two fifteen-year-old twins from South Korea. In a few seconds, I was able to find out what had happened. Stephen and Thomas were running around on the beach chasing one another. Stephen is supposed to wear his glasses wherever he goes, and not only was he not wearing his corrective lenses, he was actually running around at night with sunglasses on! Predictably, he ran headlong into a wooden post standing up in the sand. He had injured his head, his shoulders, his side, and his hand. I ran to where Stephen was sitting in the sand and inspected the damages; nothing too serious, but his right hand was bruised and swelling.

I grabbed Thomas and Stephen and dashed into the condo to get some ice to bring down the swelling. When I turned around, I found that Thomas had gotten a glass of milk and was handing it to his injured brother.

"What's the milk for, Thomas?" I asked.

"To heal the bone," said Thomas, pointing to his brother's swollen hand. I could see the wheels turning in the boy's head.

He was thinking, *Bones need calcium, milk has calcium, so to heal the bone, give milk to Stephen.*

"Well, Thomas," I said, "I don't think it's gonna help much unless we can find a way to mainstream that calcium right into the bones of Stephen's hand."

Thomas may have had the wrong cure, but he had the right idea. He felt responsible for his twin brother, and he wanted to do something—anything—to help him. Thomas and Stephen are teammates, and they take care of each other as teammates. That's the way families are supposed to work. In fact, that's the way the entire human family should work.

Some years ago, nine contestants took their positions at the starting line of the hundred-yard dash. The event was the Seattle Special Olympics, and each of the contestants had either a physical or mental disability. There was a loud, echoing crack from the starting pistol, and all nine contestants took off down the track. Just a few steps out of the blocks, however, one of the runners stumbled and went sprawling onto the dusty clay track. As he lay there, he began to cry. The other runners heard the fallen boy, stopped, and rushed back to him. Not just one or two of them, but *all* of them.

The first to reach the boy was a girl with Down's syndrome. She bent and kissed him on the side of his face and said, "That will make you feel better." Then the other contestants helped the fallen runner to his feet. His knee was hurt and he couldn't run on that leg, so all nine contestants linked arms and walked together to the end of the track, crossing the finish line as one.

They had come to compete against each other. They finished the race together. They linked arms so that no one would be left behind, crying in the dust. That's teamwork.

I'm not saying there's anything wrong with competition. I've competed all my life, and I think there's nothing healthier in life than competition. But when you get right down to it, teamwork is not, first and foremost, about competition. It's about coming together, joining together, and working together. It's about respecting, trusting, and loving each other. It's about caring for each other. It's about building a community together that is focused on a goal.

In my previous book, *Go For the Magic*, I talked about a trip I made to New York to accept a Well Done Award at Carnegie Hall from Dave Thomas, one of several awards he gave out in conjunction with his book, *Well Done*. It was a wonderful book, and I read it on the flight home from New York. As I read, one particular passage caught my attention. It read,

> In life it's amazing how many teams we all belong to. My life is no different from anyone else's in that way. Some people think my belief in teamwork is old-fashioned. But I know from experience that it's the key to success. Throughout my career, I've been most successful when I was part of a team, where everyone shared in the hard work, the vision, and the success. Teamwork is the starting point for treating people right. Most people think that teamwork is only important when competing against other teams. I don't. Competition is only part of the teamwork picture. In most things we do in life, people have to work together rather than against each other to get something done. So I think win-win situations and partnerships are the most important part of teamwork. The best teams in the world are the ones that help people become better and achieve more than they ever thought they could on their own. So it's no mystery that teamwork is such a big part of success.

No matter what team we find ourselves on, no matter what task we seek to complete or what goal we hope to achieve, we should always focus more on the things that bind us together than the issues that divide us or the ambitions that drive us to compete against each other. We *must* focus on loving each other and treating people right. We *must* become one as a team. We *must* become family. That is the heart and soul of teamwork.

STARTING HERE AND NOW

When I ran the Boston Marathon in April 1996, I experienced what I had long heard was one of the highlights of the race: You run past the Wellesley College campus, and all the Wellesley women are out on the street, screaming and yelling and cheering the runners on. You can hear them a half mile before you get there. All of that cheering really gives you a lift as you pound along the course of the marathon. But what I *really* wanted to do was veer off the beaten path and run through the Wellesley campus, because there's an inspiring spot right in the middle of the campus. At that location is a sundial bearing an inscription that reads,

The shadow by my finger cast
Divides the future from the past.
Behind its unreturning line
the vanished hour, no longer thine.
Before it lies the unknown hour
In darkness and beyond thine power.
One hour alone is in thine hands
The Now on which the shadow stands.

And that's my closing challenge to you in this book. Whatever arena you compete in, whether you have been called to lead a team, build a team, or play on a team, you've got to get going now. You need to get after today while it's still today. If you're not on a team, you need to get yourself on one now, so that you can begin to enlarge your vision, multiply your possibilities, and magnify your strengths and achievements in a team environment. Theodore Roosevelt put it this way: "Do what you can, with what you have, where you are." Amen, Teddy.

Not long ago, I took my kids to the First Baptist Church in Orlando. The guest speaker was Jay Strack, one of the top youth speakers in America, and a good friend of mine. He had everyone turn in their Bibles to Judges 3:31, and he proceeded to introduce everyone there to a fella named Shamgar. I'm willing to bet you've never heard of Shamgar, even if you are well-versed in the Bible. Shamgar was one of the judges of Israel—evidently a judge who didn't have a very good press agent. Shamgar only gets one verse in the Bible—that's it. Deborah, Barak, Samson, and the other famous judges of the Old Testament go on for page after page, but Shamgar just gets this one verse:

After him was Shamgar the son of Anath, who killed six hundred men of the Philistines with an ox goad; and he also delivered Israel.

Not a lot to go on, is it? Yet Jay Strack was able to extract three very powerful lessons from this verse—lessons that are very timely and practical in our own day, as we approach the beginning of a new millennium, and very applicable to the issue of teamwork. When Jay told us he had three lessons to share from this story, all of us in the church looked at each other and wondered where he was going to find three lessons in that one little verse!

The first lesson, said Jay, was this: *Start where you are.* That's what Shamgar did: He started where he was. Where was he? Well, he was on a farm. How do we know that? Because he had an ox goad. And if he had an ox goad, he had oxen. If he had oxen, he used them to work on his farm. So Shamgar started where he was.

Second lesson: *Use what you have.* That's what Shamgar did: He used what he had. What did he have? Just an ox goad—a long pole or stick with a prod on the end of it. That's all he had. If he'd had a sword or an assault rifle or a Sherman tank, I'm sure he would have used that instead. But all he had was an insignificant stick. Still, he did something very important with something very insignificant. In the hands of Shamgar, that spindly little stick became as awesome a weapon as a Tomahawk cruise missile, and he used it to defend his nation from a powerful enemy. He used what he had.

Third lesson: *Do what you can.* Shamgar did what he could. And what did he do? The Bible says he killed six hundred Philistines with an ox goad. It's hard to imagine he would take on six hundred charging Philistines at one time with an ox goad. He probably did it guerilla-warfare-style—jumping off a cliff to nail one, coming out from behind a tree to surprise another, sneaking around a rock to get another, and little by little, he killed six hundred of the enemy. He did what he could. Martha Stewart said, "If you can't do it all, do something."

And the end of the verse says that he delivered Israel. He did something extraordinarily important. Prior to saving his country, who would have given this guy a ghost of a chance? If I had been a betting man back then, I wouldn't have bet a dime on Shamgar—an ox-rancher armed only with a stick against one of the fiercest armies of the ancient world. But Shamgar demonstrated what every one of us must know—that to make anything of our lives, we've got to start where we are, use what we have, and do what we can.

Throughout this book, you've been reading about how to build a great team, how to be a great team player, and how to be a great team leader. Now it's time to put it into action. Take Shamgar as your role model. Start right where you are. If you're living in Quincy or West Overshoe or Wistful Vista, then that's where you've gotta start. You can't start in New York or Paris or London. You've got to start geographically where you are, and you have to start chronologically where you are—with today. You can't do anything about the past. You have to get after it now.

And you have to use what you have. Grab your ox goad and get the job done. What is your ox goad? What do you have to work with? You have the talents God has given you, the passion He has placed in your heart, the people He has surrounded you with, the vision He has set before you. You've got a mind, an imagination, a brain that's chock-a-block with ideas. God willing, you've got your health, and you've certainly got this very hour that you are living in. The moment you put this book down, *pick up your ox goad and get going!* Do what you can. Your dream is waiting for you. Go after it with all you've got. The best time to plant an oak tree was twenty years ago. The next best time is now.

There's a sign at NASA's Kennedy Space Center in Cape Canaveral, Florida. The sign reads: IT TAKES A TEAM TO LAUNCH A DREAM. So assemble your team and launch your dream as high and far and fast as it will go. Find some people to lock arms with, some people to win championships with, some people to experience miracles with, some people to *love*—then lift each other to greatness! Become a fellowship of winners!

Be a team!

Notes

Principle 1: Acquire Top Talent

1. Prov. 16:33.
2. Leigh Montville, "Trials of David: San Antonio Spurs' Center David Robinson," *Sports Illustrated*, April 29, 1996, pp. 90ff (electronically retrieved on CompuServe Information Service).
3. "Special Report: Workforce—How Ya Gonna Keep 'Em?" *Business Week*, June 3, 1996 (electronically retrieved from America Online).

Principle 2: Be a Great Leader

1. Reggie White, *In the Trenches* (Nashville: Thomas Nelson, 1996), p. 195.
2. Mark 10:42-45.

Principle 5: Think "Team"!

1. Sept. 19, 1996, p. 9C.

Principle 6: Empower Individuals

1. *Selling Power*, Nov.-Dec. 1996, p. 28.

Principle 8: Build and Model Character

1. 2 Tim. 1:7.
2. *USA Today*, June 21, 1996, p. 10C.
3. Louis Berney, "A Father's Grief," *USA Today Baseball Weekly*, Apr. 24-30, 1996, p. 14.
4. *TV Guide*, Nov. 2, 1996.

About the Author

Pat Williams is senior executive vice president of the Orlando Magic. He has proven the power of these principles as he helped found the Orlando Magic basketball team in 1989. As part of the Magic management team, Pat has helped guide the team from a losing expansion club to one of the top teams in the NBA in just eight seasons. Before taking the helm at the Magic, Williams was the general manager of the Philadelphia 76ers for twelve years, including their 1983 championship season. Pat was also general manager of the Atlanta Hawks and the Chicago Bulls, a post he took at the age of twenty-nine. Pat and his wife, Ruth, reside in Winter Park, Florida. They are the parents of nineteen children, including fourteen who have been adopted from four foreign countries.

Pat Williams is also one of the nation's best motivational speakers and is available to speak to teams of all kinds across the country. To find out his availability for speaking engagements, contact his office at (407) 647-3212.

Even More Praise for *The Magic of Teamwork*

Before publication, I sent manuscript copies of this book to many of my friends in the sports, business, government, entertainment, and religion fields. Knowing the busy schedules of all these people, I figured I'd be fortunate to get back a handful of endorsements for the jacket. Instead, I heard back from almost all of them! Evey time I went to the mailbox, I found another fistful of enthusiastic responses to *The Magic of Teamwork*.

I wanted to share them all with you, but my editors pulled me back to reality. "Pat," they said, "where are you going to put them? If we print all of these endorsements, there'll be no room for the book!" So we edited each comment down to just a line or two, and we've placed them at both the beginning and the end of the book. I hope you enjoy this book as much as these other great team-leaders around the country have—and may *The Magic of Teamwork* be yours!

—Pat Williams

"Pat's approach to team concept is right on the money. No one is more important than the team."

Red Auerbach
Former Head Coach, Boston Celtics

"Pat has captured the essence of teamwork and has written a wonderful book about it. A must for any coach or leader."

Jerry Tarkanian
Head Basketball Coach, Fresno State

"Pat Williams's book explains how individuals striving for the same goal can unite to obtain unbelievable success."

Pete Rose
Former Major League Baseball Star

"Anyone interested in putting together a team, on any level, in any field, will have the ideal blueprint with Pat's book."

Matt Guokas
Analyst, NBC Sports

"Pat Williams has spent a lifetime building teams. Who better to write a book on teamwork."

John Feinstein
Bestselling Author of *A Good Walk Spoiled*

"I've observed some great baseball teams over the years. Pat Williams has described all the qualities of successful teams."

Eric Gregg
National League Umpire

"An outstanding example of what Pat has learned in his very challenging and successful career."

Phyllis George
Miss America 1972 and
Former TV Sports Announcer

"Pat Williams has written a classic on the importance of teamwork. This book will impact thousands of teams."

Jerry Colangelo
President, Phoenix Suns

"Pat Williams removes the magic and mystery behind winning. He sets out the winning elements within the framework of teamwork."

Tony LaRussa
Manager, St. Louis Cardinals

"Pat's thoughts and presentation on the subject of 'team' are delightful, unique, and valuable."

Mike Schmidt
Baseball Hall of Famer

"This inspirational and exciting read is the cumulation of a great man's commitment to perfection and his joy in the accomplishments of others."

Bill Walton
Basketball Hall of Famer

"From a business perspective, I'm impressed—as a parent, I'm elated. These principals are for everybody!"

Terry Meeuwsen
Cohost, *700 Club*

"HOLY COW! What a great book. Pat Williams has captured all the key elements of great teams."

Harry Caray
Broadcaster, Chicago Cubs

"Pat Williams has hit another home run."

Bill Fitch
Head Coach, Los Angeles Clippers

"Pat Williams has spread his magic."

Mike Krzyzewski
Head Basketball Coach, Duke University

"*The Magic of Teamwork* is full of common sense—the kind of thing any organization needs to function smoothly."

Pete Carril
Former Head Basketball Coach,
Princeton University

"If there is anyone who knows about great teamwork it's Pat Williams. When Pat talks about teamwork, I listen."

Red Holzman
Former Coach, New York Knicks

"There's nobody better than Pat Williams to write about teamwork, and *The Magic of Teamwork* proves it."

Jerry Reinsdorf
Chairman, Chicago Bulls and Chicago White Sox

"In *The Magic of Teamwork*, Pat Williams has captured the nuts and bolts of how to become a winning team, be it family, business, or sports!"

Johnny Oates
Manager, Texas Rangers

"Great book! Great concepts! Another bestseller!"

Ben Kinchlow
Cohost, *700 Club*

"Put the Boston Celtics on your first print. Our team will absorb and enjoy every word."

Rick Pitino
Head Basketball Coach, Boston Celtics

"I recommend *The Magic of Teamwork* to those who are interested in what makes teams successful and also what makes businesses, families, and individuals successful."

Tom Osborne
Head Football Coach, University of Nebraska

"Encompasses all the principles and philosophies of teamwork that I hold valuable."

George Karl
Head Coach, Seattle Supersonics

"After reading *The Magic of Teamwork*, I have a much better idea of what it takes to make a team successful."

Bob Boone
Former Manager, Kansas City Royals

"A must-read for everyone—athletes, fans, and everyday people who want the most from life. You won't put it down."

Dr. Jack Ramsay
Former NBA Coach and NBA TV Analyst

"*The Magic of Teamwork* is one of the best books I've read on this intangible aspect of team sports."

Steve Spurrier
Head Football Coach University of Florida

"Pat Williams is one of the top basketball executives in the history of the game."

Chuck Daly
NBA Hall of Fame Coach

"Anyone who is running a business, coaching a team, or raising a family can profit from and enjoy this book."

John Thompson
Head Basketball Coach, Georgetown University

"Pat Williams is the best authority I know on teamwork. He's not only been an NBA general manager for years but has also adopted about three 'starting fives.'"

Bob Cousy
Former Boston Celtic Great

"Pat hits on all the key ingredients that help make a team great."

Dan Reeves
Head Coach, Atlanta Falcons

"*The Magic of Teamwork* relates that the best teams in the world are the ones that help people become better and achieve more than they ever thought they could on their own."

Bobby Richardson
Former Second Baseman, New York Yankees

"Nobody has used teamwork more effectively than Pat Williams. His book is very instructive on his successful techniques."

George Mikan
Basketball Hall of Famer

"Pat Williams has described perfectly the ingredients of great teams. I love the book."

Robin Roberts
Baseball Hall of Famer

"*The Magic of Teamwork* is a must-read for everyone. What an inspirational book. I'm ready to play again."

Brooks Robinson
Baseball Hall of Famer

"Pat Williams's research and insight into the phenomenon known simply as 'team' is recommended reading for all people placed in any type of leadership position."

Doug Collins
Head Coach, Detroit Pistons

"Pat Williams sinks another winner!"

Lamar Hunt
Owner, Kansas City Chiefs

"Pat Williams and teamwork are synonymous. This book is a must for those who are in the 'people business'—parents, pastors, coaches, teachers, and leaders."

Dr. Jerry Falwell
Founder, Liberty University

"What a 'great game plan' to build any team on or off the court. A must-read to be ready mentally, physically, and spiritually for the game of life."

Digger Phelps
Former Head Basketball Coach,
University of Notre Dame

"I never would have earned my gold medals had it not been for the support of the team I trained with every day. I very much enjoyed reading *The Magic of Teamwork*."

Bonnie Blair
U.S. Olympic Gold-Medalist, Speedskating

"Anyone who cares about improving his quality of life should read *The Magic of Teamwork*. What a valuable message Pat Williams is sending—the peace and harmony achieved by learning to interact with our families and coworkers with respect, consideration, and a team spirit."

Terry Bradshaw
NFL Analyst, FOX Sports and
Former Quarterback, Pittsburgh Steelers

"Pat Williams tells us what the essence of teamwork is and how we can continue it as a great American tradition."

Peggy Noonan
Former Political Speech Writer

"I've been putting together football teams for many years. Pat's new book says it all. I loved it."

Dick Vermeil
Head Coach, St. Louis Rams

"Pat Williams knows teamwork. He is an outstanding leader in a highly competitive field—professional sports. Most important, he has great spiritual insight. Pat has produced an interesting and valuable book that should be must reading for every manager or aspiring student. Highly recommended."

Dr. Bill Bright
Founder and President, Campus Crusade
for Christ International

"Few sports executives and leaders have experienced the success of Pat Williams. His book will provide enjoyable reading, and the fundamentals stressed are invaluable."

Bart Sarr
Hall of Fame Quarterback
and Former Coach, Green Bay Packers

"Wow! What a great book about teamwork! I wish this book was written thirty years ago when I started managing."

Sparky Anderson
Former Major League Baseball Manager

"*The Magic of Teamwork* will be a great help to anyone who is trying to build a team, whether it be in business or athletics. The personal examples are superb."

Lou Holtz
Head Football Coach,
University of Notre Dame, 1986-1996

"*The Magic of Teamwork* is Pat Williams's best book yet. I predict it will make the 'All Star Team'!"

Jay Strack
Speaker and Author of *Above and Beyond*

"Pat Williams has written a masterpiece on how to put teams together. I have known Pat for thirty years and really trust his opinions on team building."

Jerry West
NBA Hall of Famer

"Pat Williams has covered the entire gamut of team building. He doesn't miss a thing in this wonderful book."

Lute Olson,
Head Basketball Coach
University of Arizona

More formulas for success from Pat Williams, senior executive vice-president of the Orlando Magic . . .

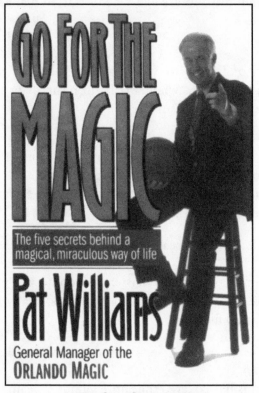

Go for the Magic

Before Pat Williams moved to Orlando to join the management team of the NBA's expansion team, he sensed there was a feeling in the air there that anything is possible and that anyone is capable of turning his or her wildest dreams into reality. Walt Disney is credited with that magical feeling of the city, and using Disney's principles for success, Williams has done that himself with the Orlando Magic, helping them become the dream team of the 90's and beyond. In *Go for the Magic*, Williams provides inspiring examples of others who have followed Disney's principles for success, with hopes that you too can transform your dreams into a success story.

0-8407-7436-2 • Hardcover • 256 pages